Value War:
Public Opinion
and the Politics of
Gay Rights

Value War:
Public Opinion
and the Politics of
Gay Rights

Paul R. Brewer

ROWMAN & LITTLEFIELD PUBLISHERS, INC.
Lanham • Boulder • New York • Toronto • Plymouth, UK

ROWMAN & LITTLEFIELD PUBLISHERS, INC.

Published in the United States of America
by Rowman & Littlefield Publishers, Inc.
A wholly owned subsidiary of The Rowman & Littlefield Publishing Group, Inc.
4501 Forbes Boulevard, Suite 200, Lanham, Maryland 20706
www.rowmanlittlefield.com

Estover Road
Plymouth PL6 7PY
United Kingdom

British Library Cataloguing in Publication Information Available

Library of Congress Cataloging-in-Publication Data

Brewer, Paul Ryan.
  Value War: Public opinion and the politics of gay rights / Paul R. Brewer.
     p. cm.
  Includes bibliographical references and index.
  ISBN-13: 978-0-7425-6210-3 (cloth : alk. paper)
  ISBN-10: 0-7425-6210-7 (cloth : alk. paper)
  ISBN-13: 978-0-7425-6211-0 (pbk. : alk. paper)
  ISBN-10: 0-7425-6211-5 (pbk. : alk. paper)
  1. Gay rights—United States—Public opinion. 2. Public opinion—United States.
I. Title.
  HQ76.8.U5B74 2008
  323.3'2640973—dc22   2007037833

Printed in the United States of America

⊗™ The paper used in this publication meets the minimum requirements of
American National Standard for Information Sciences—Permanence of Paper for
Printed Library Materials, ANSI/NISO Z39.48-1992.

To Barbara

Contents

List of Tables and Figures   ix

Acknowledgments   xi

1   Introduction   1

2   Public Opinion about Gay Rights   19

3   Whose Rights? Public Opinion about Gays, Lesbians, and Homosexuality   43

4   From the Podium and the Pulpit: Opinion Leadership and Gay Rights   67

5   Using Values to Frame Gay Rights: Traditional Morals, Equal Rights, or Special Rights?   87

6   The Foundations of Opinion about Gay Rights: Changes over Time, Differences across Contexts   109

7   The Meanings of Public Opinion about Gay Rights   129

Appendix A: The Pooled 2003–2004 Pew Research Center Surveys   149

Appendix B: The 1993 ANES Pilot Study and the 2003 October Pew Survey   150

Appendix C: Content Analysis Procedure   152

Appendix D: The 1999 Experiment   153

Appendix E: The 1992, 1996, 2000, and 2004 American
            National Election Studies   155

Bibliography   157

Index   165

About the Author   171

List of Tables and Figures

Tables

3.1. Public Opinion about Gays, Lesbians, and Homosexuality
(ANES Pilot Study, 1993)   51

3.2. Influences on Support for Employment Nondiscrimination
Law and Gays in the Military (ANES Pilot Study, 1993)   52

3.3. Public Opinion about Gays, Lesbians, and Homosexuality
(Pew Research Center, October 2003)   54

3.4. Influences on Support for Same-Sex Marriage and Civil
Unions (Pew Research Center, October 2003)   55

4.1. Influences on Support for Same-Sex Marriage and Civil
Unions (Pew Research Center, 2003–2004)   75

4.2. Influences on Support for Same-Sex Marriage, Civil Unions,
and the "Traditional Family" Frame for Same-Sex Marriage
(Pew Research Center, October 2003)   80

5.1. Use of Equality and Morality Language in Open-Ended
Responses, by Experimental Condition (1999 Experiment)   97

6.1. Support for Gay Rights Policies and Feelings toward Gay
Men and Lesbians (American National Election Studies,
1992–2004)   111

6.2. Influences on Support for Anti-Discrimination Law and
      Gays in the Military (American National Election Studies,
      1992–2004)   118

6.3. Influences on Support for Allowing Same-Sex Couples to
      Marry (American National Election Studies, 2004)   121

Figures

2.1. Public Support for Gay Rights, 1977–2006   22

2.2. Public Support for Same-Sex Marriage and Civil Unions,
      2003–2006   25

3.1. Public Opinion about Gays, Lesbians, and Homosexuality,
      1973–2006   46

3.2. Public Opinion about Gays and Lesbians, Homosexuality,
      Same-Sex Marriage, and Civil Unions by Choice of "First
      Homosexual Person That Comes to Mind" (Pew Research
      Center, October 2003)   57

4.1. Support for Same-Sex Marriage by Predispositions
      and Education   76

Acknowledgments

I began studying public opinion about gay rights in early 1996. At the time, I was a master's student in political science at the University of North Carolina-Chapel Hill. The controversy over President Bill Clinton's effort to overturn the ban on gays in the military was only three years in the past. The defeat of the Employment Nondiscrimination Act, the decision of the United States Supreme Court in *Romer v. Evans*, and the passage of the Defense of Marriage Act were months away. The first same-sex marriages in Massachusetts would not take place for another eight years.

During the decade of research that followed, I received help from many people. Pam Conover guided me in writing the master's thesis that would provide the seed of this book, and Marco Steenbergen advised me on the dissertation that followed (with the assistance of John Brehm, Stuart Macdonald, and George Rabinowitz). My subsequent research on public opinion about gay rights was improved by suggestions from numerous colleagues, including David Allen, Rory Austin, Steve Balla, Jamie Druckman, Seth Goldman, Ted Jelen, Jeffrey Koch, Ken Sherrill, Lee Sigelman, and Barry Tadlock. I owe Kim Gross and Clyde Wilcox debts of gratitude for encouraging me to write this book. I also thank everyone at Rowman & Littlefield who worked with me, including Christopher Anzalone, Michael McGandy, and Claire Rojstaczer.

The book would not have been possible without the data collected by a range of survey organizations. Access to data from the American National Election Studies and the Pew Research Center for the People and the Press was particularly invaluable. Special thanks go to Mike Dimock for helping me with the Pew data (as well as for hosting my wedding reception). I am also grateful to the students who participated in the experiment that I conducted in 1999.

Portions of Chapters 5 were previously published in *Political Communication* ("Framing, Value Words, and Citizens' Explanations of Their Issue Opinions," 19 [2002]: 303–16) and *Public Opinion Quarterly* ("Values, Political Knowledge, and Public Opinion about Gay Rights: A Framing-Based Account," 67 [2003]: 173–201). Chapter 6 is a revised, expanded, and updated version of an article published in the *Journal of Politics* ("The Shifting Foundations of Public Opinion about Gay Rights," 65 [2003]: 1208–20). These articles were published by Taylor and Francis, Oxford University Press, and Blackwell Publishing, respectively.

Most of all, I would like to thank my family for their support. My parents, Linda and Daniel, encouraged me to get a Ph.D. and become a professor, while my brother, John, blazed a trail to graduate school for me. My mother also pitched in as a second coder for my 1998 content analysis. My wife, Barbara, has been a wonderful colleague in addition to being my best friend and soul mate. Our golden retriever Molly exhibits little interest in scholarly research, but she has been a loyal companion throughout the writing of this book.

1

Introduction

We stand with [President George H. W. Bush] . . . against the amoral idea that gay and lesbian couples should have the same standing in law as married men and women.

> —Pat Buchanan, speech to the Republican National Convention,
> August 17, 1992

I don't think we should deny people rights to a civil union, a legal arrangement, if that's what a state chooses to do. . . . I view the definition of marriage [as] different from legal arrangements that enable people to have rights. And I strongly believe that marriage ought to be defined as . . . a union between a man and a woman. Now, having said that, states ought be able to have the right to pass laws that enable people to be able to have rights like others.

> —President George W. Bush, interview with Charles Gibson,
> October 24, 2004

In 1992, two contenders for the United States presidency made gay rights a theme of their campaigns.[1] On the Democratic side, eventual winner Bill Clinton pledged to lift the ban on gays and lesbians in the military. "People should have a right to serve their country," he argued.[2] In the Republican primary campaign, Pat Buchanan highlighted his opposition to gay rights as part of his conservative insurgency against the incumbent, George H. W. Bush. Though he eventually lost to Bush, Buchanan was able to parlay his primary successes into a speaking slot at the National Republican Convention. Addressing a national television audience on August 17, he denounced "homosexual rights" and proclaimed, "There is a religious war

1

going on in this country for the soul of America. It is a cultural war, as critical to the kind of nation we will one day be as was the Cold War itself. And in that struggle for the soul of America Clinton [is] on the other side, and George Bush is on our side."

That same year, voters in Colorado and Oregon decided the fates of two ballot initiatives dealing with gay rights.[3] In a 57 percent to 43 percent vote, Oregonians rejected Measure 9, which would have banned state protection or promotion of a range of sexual behaviors, including homosexuality. Meanwhile, Coloradoans approved Amendment 2, a proposal to bar "protected status based on homosexual, lesbian, or bisexual orientation" and thereby void existing gay rights laws in the cities of Denver, Boulder, and Aspen. Colorado for Family Values, the organization that drafted Amendment 2, hailed its 53 percent to 47 percent victory, whereas Equal Protection Colorado, its leading opponent, looked for ways to reverse the outcome.

The events of 1992 provided striking illustrations of the rise of gay rights on the political agenda. These same events also portended the ways in which gay rights proponents and opponents would attempt to mold public opinion over the next decade and beyond: through messages about gays, lesbians, and homosexuality (such as the one captured in the original title of Measure 9, the "Abnormal Behaviors Initiative"); through partisan, ideological, and religious cues (such as the signals sent by Clinton and Buchanan); and through efforts to frame, or define, gay rights in terms of equality (as in the very name of Equal Protection Colorado) and traditional morality (as in the very name of Colorado for Family Values).

It is not difficult to see why each side in the debate about gay rights took its case to the public. Both sides recognized that public opinion had the power to influence political outcomes. By shaping—and, in turn, responding to—what ordinary Americans thought about gay rights, politicians and political activists hoped to shape public policy and, in many cases, their own political fortunes. The events of 1992 highlighted the potential consequences of public opinion about gay rights, both in direct terms (as in the votes on Measure 9 and Amendment 2) and in indirect terms (as captured, perhaps, by the political fates of Clinton, Buchanan, and Bush).

To be sure, the clashes that took place in 1992 were by no means the first in the political contest over gay rights.[4] During the 1950s and 1960s, the Mattachine Society—the first American gay rights organization—and the Daughters of Bilitis—the first American lesbian organization—launched efforts to place gay rights on the public agenda. The Stonewall Uprising of 1969 provided gays and lesbians with a highly visible symbol of resistance to official repression. In its wake, such newly formed groups as the National Gay Task Force (later the National Gay and Lesbian Task Force) and the Lambda Legal Defense and Education Fund began to push for changes in public policy, including the passage of antidiscrimination laws and the repeal of sodomy laws. By the late 1970s, the gay rights movement had begun to achieve victories. Anita Bryant's 1977 "Save Our Children" campaign marked a new wave of resistance, however. Bryant, a popular singer and former Miss America, led a successful drive to repeal a Dade County, Florida ordinance protecting gays and lesbians from discrimination. Gay rights foes soon exported her approach to other locales.

During the 1980s, the AIDS epidemic served as a focal point for political mobilization by pro-gay organizations. Such efforts drew new attention from policymakers and the media, giving gay rights advocates greater visibility in arguing their case. A number of cities and states passed gay rights laws during this decade. Still, the movement suffered a setback with *Bowers v. Hardwick*, a 1986 United States Supreme Court decision that rejected a challenge to a Georgia law criminalizing homosexual behavior.[5] Moreover, anti–gay rights forces achieved new victories at the ballot box during the 1980s, including the passage of a 1988 anti–gay rights ballot measure in Oregon.

These events set the stage for what happened over the course of the 1990s and beyond. During the early to mid 1990s, the debate about gay rights focused primarily on employment nondiscrimination laws and military service. One crucial event came in 1993 with Clinton's post-inauguration effort to overturn the ban on military service by gays and lesbians, which sparked a political firestorm and resulted in the "don't ask, don't tell" compromise. Other key moments came in 1996, when the United States Supreme Court struck down Amendment 2 as unconstitutional and Congress narrowly voted down the Employment Non-Discrimination Act, a bill that would have protected the rights of gays and lesbians in the workplace.

Over time, however, the debate about gay rights shifted from an emphasis on employment nondiscrimination and gays in the military to a newer emphasis on legal recognition for same-sex couples. An early step in the transformation took place in 1993, when the Hawaii Supreme Court ruled in *Baehr v. Lewin* that the state had failed to prove a compelling interest for banning same-sex marriage.[6] Three years later, Congress passed the Defense of Marriage Act, which defined marriage under federal law as a union between one man and woman and mandated that no state be required to recognize a same-sex marriage in another state. Yet another step in the evolution of the debate came in 1999, when Vermont passed the first state law recognizing civil unions between same-sex couples (Connecticut and New Jersey followed suit in 2005 and 2006, respectively).

The debate about legal recognition for same-sex couples reached full bloom in 2003. In June of that year, the United States Supreme Court struck down state sodomy laws that made homosexuality illegal. Justice Antonin Scalia's dissenting opinion argued that the decision undermined the legal basis for excluding same-sex couples from marriage. Several months later, the Massachusetts Supreme Judicial Court ruled that its state constitution mandated legal recognition for same-sex marriage. From there, the battle over same-sex marriage and civil unions continued on multiple fronts, ranging from the floor of the United States Senate to voting booths across the nation.

The political contest over gay rights played out against a backdrop of broader change. As more and more gays and lesbians "came out," growing numbers of Americans came to recognize that they had gay co-workers, friends, and family members. This new visibility in the social world was matched by a growing visibility in the media world. Through exposure to the print media, movies, and—most of all, perhaps—the television screens in their homes, Americans came into virtual contact with gays and lesbians.[7] They witnessed Pedro Zamora of MTV's reality show *The Real World* grow sick and die from AIDS. They watched comedian Ellen DeGeneres identify herself as a lesbian on the *Oprah Winfrey Show*, and then they watched her character on the sitcom *Ellen* do the same with her fictional friends. They also saw news coverage of the horrific murder of Matthew Shepard, a gay man from Laramie, Wyoming who was beaten, tied to a fence, and left to die.

In the realm of religion, some things stayed the same. Conservative evangelical Christian organizations and their leaders continued to spearhead the opposition to gay rights. Similarly, the Roman Catholic Church maintained its condemnation of gay marriages, with Pope John Paul II describing them as part of an "ideology of evil."[8] Other denominations, however, shifted their stances on gays and homosexuality. In 2003, for example, the Episcopal Church installed an openly gay man, Gene Robinson, as the bishop of the Diocese of New Hampshire in a move that led to deep divisions in both the domestic church and the worldwide Anglican Communion.[9]

Just as new developments unfolded in the world of faith, so did new advances emerge in the world of science. Perhaps the most significant discovery revolved around a potential genetic basis for homosexuality. In July 1993, Dean Hamer published an article in *Science* magazine that presented evidence of such a basis. His research sparked a wave of news stories on the possibility of a "gay gene." It also challenged an argument long advanced by opponents of gay rights—namely, that sexual orientation is both chosen and changeable.

During all of this, public opinion about gay rights and the public debate about gay rights evolved in tandem. Thus, we must understand one to understand the other. In this book, I explain how the politics of gay rights has shaped public opinion and how public opinion has shaped the politics of gay rights. Though I occasionally look back to earlier developments, I focus on the period between 1990 and 2006 because this time span witnessed the rise of the debate about gay rights to new heights of prominence on the political agenda for all branches and levels of government.

PUBLIC OPINION AND PUBLIC DEBATE

At first glance, defining public opinion may seem simple: it is what polls measure. On closer inspection, however, public opinion is not so easy to define or to measure. Poll results can vary considerably depending on such factors as the wording and even the order of the questions.[10] If we conceptualize public opinion not as Americans' responses to survey questions but as their underlying views—views that any one poll question can capture only imperfectly—then we must be prepared to deal with its complexity, its changeability, and its ambiguity. With this in mind, I look at public opinion from a variety of angles. Sometimes I examine public opinion at the aggregate level by weighing the balance of opinion among the entire adult American population as captured by multiple poll questions at multiple points in time. In other places, I divide that population into subgroups and look at opinion within each group. In still other places, I explore public opinion at the individual level by looking at the reasons why a given person might hold a particular opinion about gay rights.

I focus on public opinion because of the crucial role that it plays in democratic politics. The American system of government is founded on the notion that the people should have a voice in political decisions. Of course, observers have not always agreed on just how much faith we should place in the wisdom of the public. In the early twentieth century, for example, Walter Lippmann and George Gallup offered starkly differing assessments of the public's judgment. Lippmann, a prominent journalist, saw public opinion as capricious, irrational, and frequently uninformed.[11] Gallup, on the other hand, championed the wisdom of the public and presented his new method of scientific polling as a tool for implementing its will.[12] Wise or not, public opinion clearly matters in American politics: it can shape both the fortunes of individual politicians and the course of public policy.

The other key concept in my account is public debate, which, like public opinion, plays a central role in democratic politics. Public debate can be thought of as a "marketplace of ideas," to borrow John Stuart Mill's expression.[13] It is a place where people present information and where arguments compete with one another. In a perfect marketplace of ideas, the strongest arguments would always win in the end. Admittedly, public debate in American politics typically falls short of the ideal "public sphere" described by philosophers such as Jürgen Habermas.[14] Some voices tend to dominate the debate, while other voices are not heard at all. Be that as it may, the arena of public debate is the source of the ideas from which public opinion is formed.

In looking at the public debate about gay rights, I pay particular attention to the voices of the elites—that is, the most prominent voices. In the case at hand, the ranks of the elites included politicians such as Bill Clinton and George W. Bush; spokespeople for high-profile interest groups such as the National Gay and Lesbian Task Force, the Human Rights Campaign, and Focus on the Family; and such well-known religious figures as Reverend James Dobson, Reverend Jerry Falwell, and Pope John Paul II. At the same time, I consider less prominent voices, as well—for example, local clergy members and online grassroots activists. Moreover, I look at multiple channels for debate. Given that Americans typically get much of their information about politics through the mass media, I devote the bulk of my attention to the messages carried by the news media and the entertainment media. Even so, my account also makes room for the role of interpersonal communication and influence.

Studying public opinion and the politics of gay rights is important for its own sake. In numerous instances, the voice of the people has decided the fate of gay rights policies through the shortest possible path: direct democracy. Both sides of the debate have taken their cases to the public in campaigning for and against ballot measures on gay rights. Gay rights foes, in particular, have expended considerable effort in bringing such measures to votes.[15] In 2004 alone, voters in thirteen states cast ballots on state constitutional amendments to ban same-sex marriage (with some of the bans also including language that could affect civil unions). All thirteen amendments passed. In November 2006, voters in seven additional states approved such amendments, bringing the number of states with constitutional bans on same-sex marriage to twenty-six. From Bryant's "Save Our Children" campaign onward, the architects of anti–gay rights measures have based their political strategies on the hope that public opinion would favor their side.

Beyond the arena of direct democracy, candidates for a wide range of elected offices have followed Clinton's and Buchanan's examples by appealing to public opinion about gay rights. In 2000, for example, candidates on both sides of the issue cast the Vermont gubernatorial and legislative campaigns as referenda on the state's new civil union law.[16] Four years later, the subject of gay rights figured prominently in one of the televised presidential debates between George W. Bush and John Kerry, as well as the lone vice presidential debate between Dick Cheney and John Edwards. Voters, for their part, may weigh candidates' stances on gay rights in choosing for whom to cast their ballots. In doing so, they may indirectly shape public policy through the mechanism of representative democracy.

Outcomes in the battle over gay rights, in turn, carry substantial implications for individual citizens and the nation as a whole. Some of the consequences for gays and lesbians are obvious: public policies regarding gay rights determine whether they can serve in the military, marry, adopt children, and so forth. Other potential consequences are less obvious but important nevertheless: for example, gay rights policies may affect the physical and mental health of gays and lesbians.[17] On the national scale, public decisions regarding gay rights policies may have ramifications for the health of American democracy. Some citizens see such policies as crucial safeguards for equality, whereas others see the same policies as grave threats to the moral fabric of the nation.

Looking at the shape of this debate, as well as the public's response to it, can also provide a window into wider tensions in American politics. Many Americans who see gay rights in terms of traditional morality view the issue as part of a broader struggle over public policy, one that extends to the subjects of abortion, end-of-life issues, stem cell research, pornography, sex education, the teaching of evolution, school prayer, and birth control, among others. Thus, they see the issue as a crucial battlefield in what Buchanan described as both a "cultural war" and a "religious war" in his 1992 speech to the Republican National Convention:

> The agenda [Bill] Clinton and [Hillary] Clinton would impose on America—abortion on demand, a litmus test for the Supreme Court, homosexual rights, discrimination against religious schools, women in combat—that's change, all right. But it is not the kind of change America wants. It is not the kind of change America needs. And it is not the kind of change we can tolerate in a nation that we still call God's country.

Some scholarly accounts of American politics cast the role of gay rights in much the same way. For example, Thomas Frank's *What's the Matter with Kansas?* argues that Republicans have used appeals on gay rights and other social issues to build a successful political coalition that cuts across class lines (though other observers, such as Larry Bartels, disagree).[18]

Just as the debate about gay rights can be seen as part of a wider cultural and religious divide in American politics, so, too, can it be viewed in terms of a wider clash between prejudice and civil rights. In particular, advocates for gay rights have frequently invoked an analogy between their cause and civil rights for African Americans. In doing so, they have linked gay rights to a topic on which public opinion exhibited a startling transformation during the last sixty years of the twentieth century.[19] During this period, the proportions of white Americans who openly endorsed racial segregation and discrimination in areas such as education, job opportunities, transportation, and accommodations went from majorities to small, even single-digit, minorities. Public opposition to interracial marriage exhibited a similarly steep decline among white Americans.[20] Thus, it is not surprising that gay rights proponents have drawn rhetorical parallels between civil rights for African Americans and gay rights. Of course, neither is it surprising that many gay rights opponents have rejected the analogy.

At the level of public opinion theory, the case of gay rights provides a context in which to address questions that speak to a range of disciplines, including political science, mass communication, sociology, and social psychology. Of particular importance for my purposes, it offers a chance to answer key questions about the impact of public debate on public opinion. For example, can exposure to media images of a historically stigmatized group foster support for (or, alternatively, a backlash against) policies targeting that group? To what extent can elites—specifically, politicians, high-profile activists, and prominent religious figures—lead public opinion about policy issues, and on whom do they exert the greatest influence? Do citizens borrow the issue frames that they find in public debate to explain their own opinions and to engage in collective deliberation? If so, then to what extent do they actively and critically process (as opposed to passively accept) these frames?

The case of gay rights is especially interesting because it presents dramatic examples of movement in public opinion. Over the course of the 1990s and beyond, profound shifts took place in what Americans thought about some sorts of gay rights—most notably, employment nondiscrimination laws and gays in the military. Such shifts over time provide leverage in studying the impact of public debate on public opinion: when opinion about a political issue moves, one can look at why it moved. In particular, one can examine the extent to which changes in public opinion reflect changes in broader feelings and beliefs among the public, changes in how people weigh those feelings and beliefs in forming their opinions, or both sorts of changes. By the same token, rapid changes in public opinion provide opportunities for considering the effects of public opinion on what politicians and other political elites say and do—as well as what happens to them when they fail to keep in step with the public.

The case of gay rights also presents examples of differences across policy contexts in public opinion. During the 1990s and beyond, Americans offered substantially lower levels of support for same-sex marriage than for employment nondiscrimination laws and gays in the military. Such variations across policy contexts provide additional leverage in studying the impact of public debate on public opinion: they allow one to ask why public support varies from one sort of policy to another and whether people think about different sorts of policies in different ways. Likewise, contrasts across policy contexts in public opinion provide opportunities to examine how political elites respond to such patterns. For example, do political elites vary their messages from one aspect of gay rights to another in tune with the distinctions that citizens draw among these different aspects?

In the account that follows, I show how the nature of public debate—which encompassed news stories and television sitcoms, speeches by presidents, and sermons by local clergy—helps to explain shifts over time and differences across policy contexts in public support for gay rights. I begin with the premise that Americans based their opinions about gay rights on a diverse set of foundations. In their work on public opinion and race-related policies, Donald Kinder and Lynn Sanders argue that the "pursuit of a single sovereign theory to explain public opinion on race—or on any other topic—is misguided."[21] That is, Americans do not base their opinions about political issues on one overarching feeling or principle. Instead, they build their opinions from a variety of "opinion ingredients," such as the "sympathies and resentments that citizens feel toward those social groups implicated in the dispute, especially those groups that the policy appears to benefit or victimize" and "commitment to political principles that the policy appears to honor or repudiate."[22] In deciding what ingredients to use and how to use them, people follow "opinion recipes" that they carry in their heads.[23] They base these mental formulae on the ones that they find in public debate as conveyed, by and large, through the mass media (though sometimes through interpersonal communication, as well). The latter formulae, in turn, come from political actors who seek to shape public opinion by shaping the debate. Thus, the opinion formation process is both a psychological one and a political one.

I adopt this model in my efforts to explain public opinion about gay rights. Accordingly, my theoretical account focuses on the various foundations of public opinion about gay rights. In looking at sympathies and resentments toward groups that gay rights policies might benefit or injure, I focus on public opinion about gays, lesbians, and homosexuality. I also consider the principles that gay rights policies might honor or repudiate: partisan loyalties, ideological orientations, religious beliefs, beliefs about equality, and beliefs about traditional morality. I argue that the public debate about gay rights shaped the role that each of these elements played in the opinion formation process. Mass media messages and images not only influenced what Americans thought and felt about gays, lesbians, and homosexuality; they also influenced how Americans connected such thoughts and feelings to gay rights policies. Political and religious elites led opinion by sending signals to their followers through the media; in the process, they polarized the public along partisan, ideological, and doctrinal lines. Gay rights advocates and foes used the media to frame gay rights in terms of "equal rights" and "traditional morality"; by doing so, they provided Americans with ways to understand and discuss the topic in terms of their core values. More generally, changes over time in what and how Americans thought about gay rights reflected changes in the nature of public debate. Likewise, differences across policy contexts in what and how Americans thought about gay rights reflected differences across policy contexts in the nature of the debate.

This is not to say that elites manipulated public opinion at will. The portrait of the American public that I present falls between Gallup's idealized vision of a democratic citizenry and the "phantom public" that Lippmann and other pessimists have described.[24] When it comes to politics in general and gay rights in particular, most Americans are neither well informed and deeply engaged nor entirely passive, unreasoning, and open to manipulation.[25] I highlight the power of media messages in swaying how and what ordinary citizens thought about gay rights, but I also show that citizens sometimes resisted or reinterpreted the messages they found in public debate.

Moreover, I argue that the relationship between public opinion and public debate flowed in both directions. Though one central claim of this book is that the debate about gay rights influenced public opinion through a variety of routes, the other is that public opinion influenced the debate about gay rights. Thus, looking at patterns in public opinion can help us to understand patterns in the debate. Consider, for example, the contrast between the two quotations that open this chapter, both of which came from conservative Republican politicians. In 1992, Pat Buchanan offered a sweeping condemnation of gay rights. His stance may have won support from Republican partisans at the time, but it was already falling out of favor with the general public. Consequently, it helped to mark Buchanan as standing outside of the political mainstream. Twelve years later, President George W. Bush endorsed a Federal Marriage Amendment that would have defined marriage as being between a man and a woman, but he also advocated tolerance for same-sex relationships and hinted that states should be allowed to recognize civil unions. In doing so, he stayed in step with the trends in public opinion—a potentially advantageous position to occupy during a reelection campaign.

By shaping the strategic environment for political elites, public opinion provided them with both opportunities and obstacles.[26] In particular, public opinion helped to define the terms and boundaries of the debate about gay rights. When anti-gay sentiments declined among the public, appeals to such sentiments became less effective and riskier. When public opinion about specific gay rights policies shifted, political elites altered their messages about those policies. When opinion about a policy was divided, politicians engaged in strategic ambiguity to avoid alienating citizens on either side.[27] When some "value words" resonated more strongly with the public than did others, elites who sought to shape public opinion tailored their frames to match these resonances.[28] When the resonance of one frame faded, elites searched for new frames that the public would accept more readily.

My primary tool for testing my arguments is the public opinion poll. I use data from numerous national polls to describe aggregate trends in public opinion about gay rights. In explaining Americans' opinions at the individual level, I analyze survey data from the American National Elections Studies and the Pew Research Center for the People and the Press. I supplement my analyses of polling data with other forms of evidence. Given that one of my goals is to illuminate the nature of the public debate about gay rights, I use content analysis to provide a systematic portrait of the frames in news media coverage of this debate. Given that another of my goals is to examine the impact of public debate on public opinion, I use experimentation to establish causal relationships between the content of debate and the nature of citizens' thoughts about gay rights. Specifically, I simulate exposure to news media framing of gay rights in order to investigate the effects of such exposure on how citizens explain their opinions about the subject in their own words. By using a multimethod approach, I provide a richer account of public opinion and politics than any single approach could offer.

My findings shed new light on how the politics of gay rights has evolved in recent years and may evolve in the future. The divided state of public opinion ensures that the topic will remain contentious for years to come, but patterns in both public debate and public opinion point to further changes in the political landscape. On the subjects of employment nondiscrimination laws and military service, gay rights advocates won major victories in the battle for public opinion over the course of the 1990s and beyond, both in terms of what Americans thought and how they thought about gay rights. In response to these shifts in the terrain of public opinion, gay rights foes were forced to alter their messages and retreat to the subject of same-sex marriage. Seizing on public opposition, as well as the events that brought the topic to the foreground of the debate, they cast their fight against legal recognition for same-sex couples as a crucial struggle—even a last stand—in the "culture war." As of 2006, gay rights foes still had public opinion on their side when it came to same-sex marriage, an advantage that showed in victory after victory in votes on state constitutional amendments to ban the practice. Even here, however, the public showed signs of changing its collective mind. In November 2006, Arizona voters gave same-sex marriage advocates their first ballot box victory against a state constitutional ban. Moreover, a wide generation gap in public support for same-sex marriage pointed to the possibility of a future in which such support would approach—and perhaps attain—majority status.

THE PLAN OF THE BOOK

In chapter 2, I examine trends and patterns in public opinion about gay rights. First, I look at public opinion about what I call the "old" politics of gay rights, revolving around employment nondiscrimination laws and military service—that is, the policies that dominated the debate during the early to mid-1990s. As I show, public opinion about these policies exhibited sizable shifts over time in the direction of support for gay rights, so that an overwhelming majority of the public came to support them. I also look at the "new" politics of gay rights, revolving around same-sex marriage and civil unions—that is, the policies that came to dominate the debate in 2000 and beyond. Public support for gay rights was much lower here, particularly in the case of same-sex marriage.

Next, I explore how public opinion about gay rights differed across key social divides, including those defined by sex, race, age, education, income, religion, partisanship, ideology, and sexual orientation. In terms of its implications for the politics of gay rights, the most important demographic pattern in public opinion may be the relationship between age and support for same-sex marriage: younger Americans were much likelier than older ones to express such support. Consequently, the proportion of same-sex marriage opponents should decline and the proportion of supporters should grow as the composition of the population changes over time. I end chapter 2 by comparing trends in public opinion about gay rights to trends in public opinion about abortion and civil rights for African Americans. Though activists and observers alike have cast both gay rights and abortion as key fronts in a culture war over traditional morality, public opinion about the former has shown substantial movement whereas public opinion about the latter has been relatively stable. Thus, not all social issues have followed similar paths. The trends in public opinion about gay rights do, however, resemble historical trends in public opinion about another "equal rights" issue: civil rights for African Americans. If this parallel continues beyond 2006, then widespread public opposition to civil unions and even same-sex marriage could go the way of public opposition to racially integrated schools and interracial marriage.

In chapters 3 through 6, I go beyond describing public opinion about gay rights to explain it. In particular, I take a closer look at the building blocks of public opinion about gay rights and the ways in which Americans put together these building blocks. Along the way, I explore how politics shaped the underlying structure of public opinion about gay rights, as well as how public opinion about the topic shaped the course of public debate. In doing so, I apply, test, and extend broader theories about how images, signals, and frames in public debate influence public opinion.

In chapter 3, I consider the judgments that Americans made about homosexuality, the explanations that they offered for its origins, the stereotypes that they held about gays and lesbians, and the emotional reactions that they experienced toward gays, lesbians, and homosexuality. The evidence points to profound changes over time in such beliefs and feelings. In part, these changes reflected increased familiarity with gays and lesbians through personal contact, as well as through exposure to media images of gays and lesbians. Public opinion about gays, lesbians, and homosexuality, in turn, shaped public opinion about both the old and the new politics of gay rights. It also appeared to shape the public debate about gay rights. As the public became more accepting of gays, lesbians, and homosexuality, the costs that political elites confronted in justifying opposition to gay rights through overt expressions of anti-gay sentiment increased, just as the potential rewards for doing so decreased. Media "feeding frenzies" targeting figures ranging from House Majority Whip Dick Armey to former football star Reggie White to evangelical leader Jerry Falwell illustrate the emergence of a limited norm against "gay bashing" in public debate.[29]

The next two chapters explore how the debate over gay rights shaped the ways in which Americans used principles to form their opinions. In chapter 4, I argue that members of the public looked to opinion leaders for guidance in using partisan loyalties, ideological orientations, and religious beliefs to form their views. During the 1990s and beyond, Americans received signals about gay rights from a host of actors who sought to shape public opinion on the subject: liberal and conservative political elites; Republican and Democratic politicians (including those in the White House); and religious elites and their own clergy. I find evidence that elite signals shaped public opinion about same-sex marriage, civil unions, and a "traditional family" frame. I also find evidence that signals from the pulpit influenced what parishioners thought about gay rights. This top-down account of opinion leadership, however, must be supplemented with a bottom-up account in which public opinion sometimes worked to constrain what sorts of cues elites provided. Sending signals to the public carried risks as well as rewards for those doing the signaling, with Bill Clinton's stance on gays in the military providing one example of the risks. To complicate matters further, certain sorts of elites faced greater risks in signaling than did others, and some elites—including George W. Bush—seemingly sought to avoid risk by sending complex or ambiguous signals.

In chapter 5, I turn to two other principles that served as building blocks for public debate—and public opinion—about gay rights: egalitarianism and moral traditionalism. In particular, I look at how opponents and proponents of gay rights policies framed gay rights in terms of these values, as well as how the intended audience for such framing efforts responded. Supporters frequently justified gay rights policies by invoking the principle of equality; in contrast, opponents often framed gay rights policies as threats to traditional morality (i.e., "family values"). Using content analysis, I show that the "equal rights" and "traditional morality" frames were prominent in news media coverage of gay rights, though they did not go completely unchallenged (in particular, gay rights foes attempted to counter the equal rights frame with a "special rights" frame). I then draw on experimental data to examine how value frames in media coverage shaped the ways in which audience members explained their opinions about gay rights and discussed the topic with others. The results highlight the power of framing to shape the terms of mass deliberation, but they also illustrate the capacity of ordinary Americans to resist or recast frames in public debate. Thus, the findings reinforce the idea of framing as a two-way process in which the resonances of particular frames and the active efforts by citizens to construct political meaning constrain elite attempts to frame issues.

In chapter 6, I look at all of the various pieces of the puzzle—opinions about gays and lesbians, partisan loyalties, ideological orientations, religious beliefs, egalitarianism, and moral traditionalism—at once to assess how much each mattered in shaping public opinion about gay rights. In doing so, I address two central questions of the book. First, what lay beneath the transformation in public opinion about the old politics of gay rights? Second, what accounted for the differences between public opinion about the old politics of gay rights and public opinion about the new politics of gay rights? I find changes from the early 1990s onward in how Americans formed their opinions about employment nondiscrimination laws and gays in the military. In particular, the roles of anti-gay feelings and moral traditionalism in shaping public opinion about the policies shrank over time, even as the impact of egalitarianism remained the same. These shifts in the structure of public opinion help to explain the growth in support for employment nondiscrimination laws and gays in the military. Looking at data from 2004, I also find differences between how Americans thought about the old politics of gay rights and how they thought about same-sex marriage. Feelings toward gays and lesbians, ideological orientations, and moral beliefs played larger roles in shaping opinion about marriage than in shaping opinion about employment nondiscrimination laws and military service, whereas beliefs about equality played no discernible role in shaping support for same-sex marriage. These patterns help to explain why support for same-sex marriage was much lower than support for employment nondiscrimination laws and gays in the military.

In chapter 7, I reconsider how public opinion about gay rights influenced the course of politics. Specifically, I look at how public opinion mattered in shaping the terms of debate, the choices of political elites, and the outcomes of the political process. In some instances, the political implications of public opinion about gay rights were both obvious and substantial. For example, public votes on state same-sex marriage bans provided gay rights foes with a means for converting public opposition into gains on public policy, as well as a potential means for mobilizing citizens to wider political action. In fighting these bans, gay rights advocates were forced to respond to an unfavorable opinion climate.

Public opinion also shaped the politics of a proposed amendment to the United States Constitution that would have defined marriage as being between a man and a woman. In part, the drive to pass such an amendment reflected another attempt by same-sex marriage foes to translate current public opposition to same-sex marriage into public policy. Indeed, gay rights opponents explicitly invoked public opinion in their appeals to the public, framing the Federal Marriage Amendment as a tool for preventing "activist judges" from overturning the will of the people. At the same time, the push for such an amendment also reflected a strategy to insulate public policy from shifts toward greater public support for same-sex marriage. As gay rights advocates pointed out, the long-term trends in public opinion appear to favor the pro-marriage side of the debate.

The effects of public opinion about gay rights on races for public office, in turn, drew considerable attention from political activists and the news media but may have been smaller than advertised. The 2004 presidential election offers a case in point. Many popular accounts that drew on National Election Pool exit poll data suggested that George W. Bush's presidential election victory over John Kerry reflected the decisive influence of popular opposition to same-sex marriage. In particular, such accounts pointed to the finding that more exit poll respondents cited "moral values" as the top reason behind their vote than chose terrorism, the economy, or the war in Iraq. A look at other polling data, however, suggests a relatively modest impact of public opinion about gay rights and, more generally, cultural politics.

I conclude by presenting this book's theoretical and methodological approach as one that can be used to understand public opinion and American politics in broader terms. To be sure, the images, signals, and frames in public debate will inevitably differ from one policy area to another, as will the ways in which citizens form their opinions. The controversy over gay rights, however, may be a particularly revealing case because of its double life as both a "culture war" issue and an "equal rights" issue.

NOTES

1. Throughout this book, I use the terms "gays," "gays and lesbians," and "gay rights." I recognize, however, that these terms and their alternatives (e.g., "gay men and lesbians," "homosexuals," "homosexual rights") are, in and of themselves, potential framing tools.

2. Quoted in Colbert I. King, "Debunking the Case against Gays in the Military," *Washington Post*, 7 July 1992, A19.

3. For a more detailed account, see John Gallagher and Chris Bull, *Perfect Enemies: The Battle between the Religious Right and the Gay Movement*, updated ed. (New York: Madison Books, 2001), 47–62, 97–124.

4. For overviews of the history of the gay rights debate in the United States, see Gallagher and Bull, *Perfect Enemies*; Craig A. Rimmerman, *From Identity to Politics: The Lesbian and Gay Movement in the United States* (Philadelphia: Temple University Press, 2002); Urvashi Vaid, *Virtual Equality* (New York: Anchor Books, 1995).

5. *Bowers v. Hardwick*, 478 U.S. 186 (1986).

6. *Baehr v. Lewin*, 74 Haw. 645, 852 P.2d 44 (1993).

7. For more detailed accounts, see Edward Alwood, *Straight News: Gays, Lesbians, and the News Media* (New York: Columbia University Press, 1996); Ron Becker, *Gay TV and Straight America* (New Brunswick, N.J.: Rutgers University Press, 2006); Larry Gross, *Up from Invisibility: Lesbians, Gay Men, and the Media in America* (New York: Columbia University Press, 2001); Suzanna Danuta Walters, *All the Rage: The Story of Gay Visibility in America* (Chicago: University of Chicago Press, 2001).

8. Corky Siemaszko, "Gay Nups a New Evil, Says Pope," *New York Daily News*, 23 February 2005, 4.

9. Neela Banurjee, "U.S. Bishop, Making It Official, Throws in Lot with African Churchman," *New York Times*, 6 May 2007, A35.

10. This is true in the case of gay rights, as I show in chapter 2.

11. Walter Lippmann, *Public Opinion* (New York: Macmillan, [1922] 1965); Walter Lippmann, *The Phantom Public* (New York: Macmillan, 1925).

12. James S. Fishkin, *The Voice of the People: Public Opinion in a Democracy* (New Haven, Conn.: Yale University Press, 1997), 76–80.

13. Mill, John Stuart, *On Liberty* (Arlington Heights, Ill.: AHM Publishing, [1859] 1947).

14. Jürgen Habermas, *The Structural Transformation of the Public Sphere: An Inquiry into a Category of Bourgeois Society* (Cambridge, Mass.: MIT Press, 1989).

15. See, for example, Todd Donavan, Jim Wenzel, and Shaun Bowler, "Direct Democracy and Gay Rights Initiatives after *Romer*," in *The Politics of Gay Rights*, ed. Craig A. Rimmerman, Kenneth D. Wald, and Clyde Wilcox (Chicago: Chicago University Press, 2000), 161.

16. Michael Paulson, "Protestants Weigh Same-Sex Marriage," *Boston Globe*, 30 November 2003, B10.

17. Ellen D. B. Riggle, Jerry D. Thomas, and Sharon S. Rostosky, "The Marriage Debate and Minority Stress," *PS: Political Science & Politics* 38 (2005): 221–24.

18. Thomas Frank, *What's the Matter with Kansas? How Conservatives Won the Heart of America* (New York: Metropolitan Books, 2004); Larry Bartels, "What's the Matter with *What's the Matter with Kansas?*" *Quarterly Journal of Political Science* 1 (2006): 201–26.

19. Howard Schuman, Charlotte Steeh, Lawrence Bobo, and Maria Krysan, *Racial Attitudes in America: Trends and Interpretations*, rev. ed. (Cambridge, Mass.: Harvard University Press, 1997), 103–21.

20. Donald P. Haider-Markel and Mark R. Joslyn, "Attributions and the Regulation of Marriage: Considering the Parallels between Race and Homosexuality," *PS: Political Science & Politics* 38 (2005): 233–39; Schuman et al., *Racial Attitudes in America*, 115–18.

21. Donald R. Kinder and Lynn M. Sanders, *Divided By Color: Racial Politics and Democratic Ideals* (Chicago: University of Chicago Press, 1996), 44.

22. Kinder and Sanders, *Divided by Color*, 36.

23. Kinder and Sanders, *Divided by Color*, 45.

24. Lippmann, *Phantom Public*.

25. For more evidence regarding the general claim, see Michael X. Delli Carpini and Scott Keeter, *What Americans Know about Politics and Why It Matters* (New Haven, Conn.: Yale University Press, 1996); Benjamin I. Page and Robert Y. Shapiro, *The Rational Public: Fifty Years of Trends in American Policy Preferences* (Chicago: University of Chicago Press, 1992); Samuel L. Popkin, *The Reasoning Voter* (Chicago: University of Chicago Press, 1994).

26. For more on the concept of strategic political environments, see William A. Gamson, *Strategy of Social Protest* (Homewood, Ill.: Dorsey Press, 1975); John C. Green, James L. Guth, and Kevin Hill, "Faith and Election: The Christian Right in Congressional Campaigns 1978–1988," *Journal of Politics* 55 (1993): 80–91.

27. For more on the concept of political ambiguity, see Benjamin I. Page, "The Theory of Political Ambiguity," *American Political Science Review* 70 (1976): 742–52.

28. For more on framing and the resonance of frames, see William A. Gamson, *Talking Politics* (New York: Cambridge University Press, 1992); William A. Gamson and Andre Modigliani, "The Changing Culture of Affirmative Action," in *Research in Political Sociology*, ed. Richard D. Braungart (Greenwich, Conn.: JAI Press, 1987), 137–77; William A. Gamson and Andre Modigliani, "Media Discourse and Public Opinion on Nuclear Power: A Constructionist Approach," *American Journal of Sociology* 95 (1989): 1–37.

29. For more on the concept of the feeding frenzy, see Larry J. Sabato, *Feeding Frenzy: How Attack Journalism Has Transformed American Politics* (New York: Free Press, 1991).

2

Public Opinion about Gay Rights

On June 26, 2003, the United States Supreme Court struck down an anti-sodomy law with its ruling in *Lawrence v. Texas*, thereby overturning its 1986 decision in *Bowers v. Hardwick*.[1] In the majority opinion, Justice Anthony Kennedy wrote:

> It must be acknowledged, of course, that the Court in *Bowers* was making the broader point that for centuries there have been powerful voices to condemn homosexual conduct as immoral. The condemnation has been shaped by religious beliefs, conceptions of right and acceptable behavior, and respect for the traditional family. For many persons these are not trivial concerns but profound and deep convictions accepted as ethical and moral principles to which they aspire and which thus determine the course of their lives. These considerations do not answer the question before us, however. The issue is whether the majority may use the power of the State to enforce these views on the whole society through operation of the criminal law.[2]

Kennedy and four other justices concluded that the anti-sodomy law in question furthered "no legitimate state interest which can justify its intrusion into the personal and private life of the individual" (a sixth justice wrote a concurring opinion).

Lambda Legal, the organization that brought the suit, praised the Court for "clos[ing] the door on an era of intolerance and usher[ing] in a new era of respect and equal treatment for gay Americans."[3] Indeed, many gay rights advocates saw *Lawrence* as not only the end to legal prohibitions against sexual activity between same-sex partners but also a step toward legal recognition of same-sex marriage. For example, David Smith of the Human Rights Campaign argued that "[t]o establish a fundamental right to privacy for gay and lesbian Americans is a giant step forward, and contained in that are links to marriage."[4] Similarly, Evan Wolfson of Freedom to Marry described the decision as "a tremendous tool for moving forward to end the discrimination."[5]

More than a few gay rights foes shared the view that *Lawrence* advanced the cause of same-sex marriage. Justice Antonin Scalia's dissenting opinion cited the specter of the judiciary mandating legal recognition of same-sex marriage even in the face of public opposition:

> The people may feel that their disapprobation of homosexual conduct is strong enough to disallow homosexual marriage, but not strong enough to criminalize private homosexual acts—and may legislate accordingly. The Court today pretends that it possesses a similar freedom of action, so that that we need not fear judicial imposition of homosexual marriage. . . . Do not believe it. . . . This case "does not involve" the issue of homosexual marriage only if one entertains the belief that principle and logic have nothing to do with the decisions of this Court.[6]

Politicians and political activists who opposed same-sex marriage echoed Scalia's warning in their public statements. Ken Connor of the Family Research Council argued that the case not only constituted "yet another example of a breathtakingly activist decision where six unelected, largely unaccountable lawyers wearing black robes substituted their own political judgment for the elected representatives of the state of Texas," but also provided "the ammunition for a full-scale assault on the institution of marriage."[7] Likewise, Reverend Lou Sheldon of the Traditional Values Coalition claimed that, "We're talking about moving toward sanctioning homosexual marriage, slam dunk, across America in this decision."[8]

Gallup polls conducted in the wake of the decision pointed to a public backlash against gay rights. Whereas 39 percent of the respondents in a June 2003 Gallup poll said that "marriages between homosexuals should . . . be recognized by law as valid, with the same rights as traditional marriages," the figure was 35 percent in October 2003 and 31 percent in December 2003. Moreover, the percentage favoring "a law that would allow homosexual couples to legally form civil unions, giving them some of the legal rights of married couples" dropped from 49 percent in May 2003 to 40 percent in July 2003. Polling by the Pew Research Center for the People and the Press yielded a similar trend in public opinion about gay marriage: the percentage of Pew respondents who favored "allowing gays and lesbians to marry legally" dropped from 38 percent in late June and early July 2003 to 32 percent in October 2003 and 30 percent in November 2003. A July 31 *USA Today* story by Cathy Lynn Grossman raised the question of what the backlash portended: was it the "real turning of the tide of opinion," or "a brief statistical dip in a trend toward lasting cultural change?"[9]

In this chapter, I look at patterns in public opinion about gay rights. I begin by considering trends in public opinion about a variety of gay rights policies.[10] As I show, public support for gay rights in terms of employment and military service increased dramatically over time. Polls registered lower—if also growing—levels of support for adoption rights. Public support for same-sex marriage was lower still, though it, too, appeared to grow from the late 1980s to 2003, while support for civil unions was greater than support for same-sex marriage. As for the post-*Lawrence* backlash captured by Gallup and Pew polls, it turned out to be temporary.

Next, I examine how support for gay rights differed across key social and political divides among the public. As I demonstrate, such support varied with sex, race, education, and—most importantly, perhaps—age. Not surprisingly, gay men and lesbians expressed higher levels of support for gay rights than did heterosexuals. Support for gay rights also varied with partisan loyalties and ideological orientations, as well as with religious beliefs and practices.

Finally, I compare trends in public opinion about gay rights to trends in public opinion about two other policy areas that provide useful reference points: abortion and civil rights for African Americans. Popular accounts often grouped gay rights with abortion as key battlegrounds in a "culture war." Nevertheless, the trends in public opinion about the former differed markedly from the trends in public opinion about the latter. Public debate also included frequent analogies between gay rights and civil rights for African Americans. Here, a comparison of historical trends suggests parallels in how public opinion about each topic evolved over time.

SUPPORT FOR EMPLOYMENT NONDISCRIMINATION AND GAYS IN THE MILITARY

In 1977—the year that Anita Bryant launched her "Save Our Children" campaign against a Dade County, Florida antidiscrimination law—Gallup conducted a poll that asked, "In general, do you think homosexuals should or should not have equal rights in terms of job opportunities?" Of the respondents, 56 percent said yes and 33 percent said no. By 1992—the year of the votes on Amendment 2 in Colorado and Measure 9 in Oregon—the percentage saying yes had climbed to 74 percent, while the percentage saying no had dropped to 18 percent. As figure 2.1 shows, the shift toward greater support continued throughout the 1990s and beyond. By 2006, an overwhelming majority (86 percent) of the public agreed that gays and lesbians should have equal rights in terms of job opportunities, while opposition stood in the single digits (9 percent).

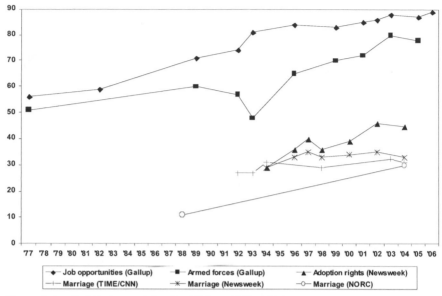

Figure 2.1.   Public Support for Gay Rights, 1977–2006

To some extent, the levels of support that the Gallup polls yielded may have reflected the wording of the question: this item included a phrase—"equal rights"—that gay rights supporters frequently used to frame the issue. Consider the results for an alternative question that was included in a series of American National Election Studies (ANES) surveys: "Do you favor or oppose laws to protect homosexuals against job discrimination?" In 1988, the first year that an ANES survey included the question, 47 percent of the respondents expressed support for such laws (with 40 percent opposed)—a clear contrast to the 1989 Gallup poll, in which 71 percent said yes (and only 18 percent said no) to equal rights for gays and lesbians in terms of job opportunities. The trend in support, however, was clear regardless of question wording: over the course of the next fifteen years, ANES surveys reported a double-digit increase in support for employment nondiscrimination laws.[11]

Public opinion about gays in the military followed the same trajectory. In 1977, 51 percent of the respondents in a Gallup poll said that "homosexuals should . . . be hired for . . . the Armed Forces," with 38 percent saying that they should not be hired. By June 1992—the year in which Bill Clinton campaigned for president on a pledge to lift the military service ban—the percentage favoring gays in the military had risen to 57 percent (see figure 2.1). Over the course of the next year—during which controversy erupted over Clinton's effort to make good on his pledge—a backlash in public opinion appeared to develop: a Gallup poll in November 1992 found only 48 percent in favor of hiring gays and lesbians for the armed forces, and a Hart and Teeter poll from June 1993 that used the same question wording found 47 percent in favor of doing so.

Though these polls may have captured a backlash, it was not a durable one. A February 1994 Princeton Survey Research Associates survey that used the Gallup wording placed support at 58 percent. In 1996, a Gallup poll put the figure at 65 percent. Over the next decade, polls from the same organization showed support for gays in the military increasing to 78 percent. Polls that used different questions yielded the same broad trend. For example, ANES surveys recorded a 23 point increase from 1992 to 2006 in the percentage of respondents saying that "homosexuals should be allowed to serve in the United States Armed Forces."[12] In Pew Research Center surveys, the percentage of respondents who favored "allowing gays and lesbians to serve openly in the military" increased from 52 percent in 1994 to 60 percent in 2006.

In short, polling on the policies that dominated the debate about gay rights during the early to mid 1990s—employment nondiscrimination protections and an end to the military service ban—points to two conclusions. First, support for these policies grew steadily from the late 1970s to 2000 and beyond. Second, such support had reached clear majority status by 2006.

SUPPORT FOR ADOPTION RIGHTS

The subject of adoption rights has not dominated the national debate about gay rights in the way that employment nondiscrimination and gays in the military did in the early to mid 1990s or same-sex marriage and civil unions did after 2000. Still, the question of whether gays and lesbians should be allowed to adopt has long been the subject of political controversy, particularly at the state level. Opponents of gay adoption have argued, among other things, that gay people are unfit parents at best and pedophiles at worst.[13] For their part, gay rights proponents have argued not only that gays and lesbians should have equal opportunities to adopt but also that allowing adoption by gay parents serves the interests of children and, thus, society as a whole.

The barriers to adoption faced by gays and lesbians have ranged from opposition on the part of adoption agencies and judges to (in some states) legal prohibitions.[14] During the 1990s and beyond, gay rights activists won some battles over adoption rights. In 1999, for example, they successfully pushed for the lifting of a New Hampshire ban on gay adoption.[15] On the other hand, neither legal challenges nor a public call by lesbian entertainer Rosie O'Donnell yielded a repeal of Florida's ban on gay adoption (a prohibition that was the product of Bryant's 1977 campaign against gay rights). For their part, gay rights opponents attempted to build on the ballot box successes of state bans on same-sex marriage by launching initiative drives to ban gay adoption. As of 2006, such drives were underway in at least sixteen states.[16]

One particularly prominent clash over gay adoption unfolded in 2006 when four Roman Catholic bishops in Massachusetts sought an exemption to a state antidiscrimination law that required them to include gay and lesbian parents in the church's adoption services. Eight board members of Catholic Charities of Boston resigned to protest the bishops' request; shortly thereafter, the board voted to shut down the organization's adoptions services.[17] Governor Mitt Romney, in turn, filed a "Protecting Religious Freedoms" bill that would have exempted religious groups, but his bill died in the legislature. Opponents criticized it as an attempt on his part to appeal to voters in the 2008 Republican presidential primaries.[18]

Polling data from the early 1990s through 2006 indicate that that public support for gay adoption was weaker than public support for employment nondiscrimination and gays in the military. The same data, however, also show that public support for adoption rights grew over time. A 1994 *Newsweek* poll found that only 29 percent of respondents favored "adoption rights" for gays and lesbians. Ten years later, support had increased to 45 percent in *Newsweek's* polling (see figure 2.1). Likewise, the percentage of ANES respondents who said that "gay and lesbian couples . . . should be legally permitted to adopt children" increased from 28 percent in 1992 to 50 percent in 2004, and the percentage of Pew respondents who favored allowing "gays and lesbians to adopt children" grew from 38 percent in 1999 to 46 percent in 2006. Thus, roughly half of the public had come to favor adoption rights for gays and lesbians by 2006.

SUPPORT FOR SAME-SEX MARRIAGE AND CIVIL UNIONS

Prior to 2000, relatively few polls had included questions measuring public support for same-sex marriage. The polls that did ask such questions revealed widespread opposition. Fully 69 percent of the respondents in a 1988 National Opinion Research Center (NORC) survey disagreed with the statement that "homosexual couples should have the right to marry," whereas only 11 percent agreed. Polls from the early and mid-1990s, in turn, suggested that less than a third of the public supported same-sex marriage. For example, 27 percent of the respondents in a 1992 *TIME*/CNN poll said that "marriages between homosexual men and between homosexual women should be recognized by law" (versus 67 percent who said no), and 29 percent of the respondents in a 1994 *Newsweek* poll said that there should be "legally sanctioned gay marriages" (versus 62 percent who said that there should not).

Poll results suggest an increase in support for same-sex marriage over time (see figure 2.1). A 2004 National Opinion Research Center survey placed such support at 30 percent, an increase of 19 percentage points from that organization's 1988 figure. The polling trends for the *TIME*/CNN and *Newsweek* measures suggest a smaller increase over the course of the 1990s and beyond: by 2003, both trends had reached the low 30s. In the meantime, the topic of same-sex marriage had risen on the public agenda, driven by events such as the 1993 Hawaii Supreme Court ruling in *Baehr v. Lewin*, the 1996 passage of the Defense of Marriage Act, and the 2000 advent of civil unions in Vermont.[19] In June 2003, Gallup and Pew polls put support for same-sex marriage at 39 percent and 38 percent, respectively.

That same month, the United States Supreme Court issued its ruling in *Lawrence v. Texas*, adding fuel to the debate about same-sex marriage and triggering an apparent backlash against gay rights in public opinion (see above). The controversy continued over the next year, as Massachusetts recognized same-sex marriages and gay rights foes pushed for a Federal Marriage Amendment. The backlash did not last, however. By May 2006, public support for same-sex marriage had rebounded from a low of 31 percent to 39 percent in Gallup polling and from a low of 30 percent to 37 percent in Pew polling (see figure 2.2). Thus, the events of 2003 produced only a temporary

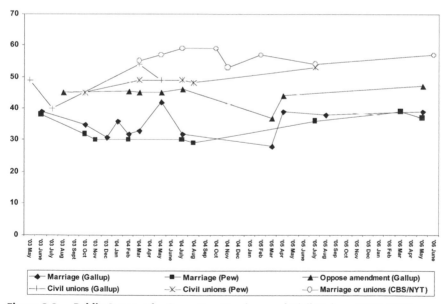

Figure 2.2.   Public Support for Same-Sex Marriage and Civil Unions, 2003–2006

decline in support for same-sex marriage, just as the 1993 controversy over Clinton's effort to lift the military ban had produced only a temporary reversal of the trend toward greater support for gays in the military.

Though majority opinion continued to tilt against legal recognition for same-sex marriages, public opinion about a federal amendment to ban such marriages was more evenly divided. A series of Gallup polls conducted between July 2003 and May 2006 found that the percentage of respondents who favored "a constitutional amendment that would define marriage as being between a man and a woman, thus barring marriages between gay or lesbian couples" fluctuated around the 50 percent mark, while slightly smaller percentages opposed such an amendment (see figure 2.2). Results from other polls indicate that variations in question wording produced variations in support. Four polls by CBS News and the *New York Times* (*NYT*; one from 2003 and three from 2004) that omitted any specific mention of barring same-sex marriages found solid majorities in support of an amendment that would "allow marriage only between a man and a woman." In contrast, a series of 2004 polls by ABC News and the *Washington Post* found that more respondents favored "each state mak[ing] its own laws on homosexual marriage" than favored "amending the U.S. Constitution to make it illegal for homosexual couples to get married anywhere in the U.S." Similarly, a pair of 2004 polls by CBS News and the *New York Times* found solid majorities who saw "defining marriage as a union only between a man and a woman" as not being the "kind of issue" that was "important enough to be worth changing the Constitution."

Public support for civil unions was stronger than public support for same-sex marriage, as data from both Gallup and Pew indicate (see figure 2.2). Polls from these organizations showed that close to half of the public supported recognition for "civil unions" between "homosexual couples" (Gallup) or "legal agreements" between "gay and lesbian couples . . . that would give them many of the same rights as married couples" (Pew). Two Gallup polls and four Pew polls conducted between 2003 and 2006 included questions about both civil unions and same-sex marriage; in these six polls, the average difference between support for the former and support for the latter was 16 percentage points. Gallup's results also suggest an increase over time in support for civil unions: a 2000 poll put such support at 42 percent, whereas a poll conducted four years later put it at 49 percent.

Other survey results point to even higher levels of support for legal recognition of same-sex relationships. When respondents in a series of CBS News/ *New York Times* polls were presented with a three-way choice between allowing "gay couples . . . to legally marry," allowing them to "form civil unions but not legally marry," and offering "no legal recognition of a gay couple's relationship," small majorities endorsed either same-sex marriage or civil unions (see figure 2.2). These results suggest, once again, that question wording can shape survey responses regarding gay rights. On a deeper level, such question wording effects point to the potential influence of framing on public opinion about gay rights.

Question order can matter, as well. Both Pew (October 2003) and Gallup (May 2004) conducted survey-experiments in which respondents were asked about civil unions either before or after being asked about same-sex marriage. Respondents expressed higher levels of support for civil unions when the question came after one about marriage (45 percent versus 37 percent for Pew; 56 percent versus 49 percent for Gallup).[20] One possible explanation for this pattern is that respondents who were asked about marriage first subsequently saw civil unions as a compromise choice.[21]

GROUPS DIFFERENCES IN SUPPORT FOR GAY RIGHTS

Thus far, I have focused on support for gay rights among the public as a whole. Public opinion is not always uniform across the various social and political groups in the American population, however. With this in mind, I present a closer look at the opinions held by members of groups defined by sex, race, age, sexual orientation, education, partisan loyalties, ideology, and religion.[22] Support for gay rights varies—sometimes dramatically—with each of these characteristics.

Sex and Support for Gay Rights

Scholars and commentators alike have paid considerable attention to differences between the political opinions of women and men. Such differences are commonly known as "gender gaps," though "sex gaps" may be a more precise term.[23] One persistent gap between women and men revolves around partisanship. In every presidential election from 1980 to 2004, women were more likely than men to support the Democratic nominee (and, thus, men were more likely to support the Republican).[24] Another gap revolves around public opinion regarding what some scholars have labeled "compassion" issues, such as child care, education, and health care.[25] For example, women tend to express more support for social welfare spending than do men.

Evidence from a variety of sources indicates that women are also more supportive of gay rights than are men. Looking at data from a 1999 survey, Gregory Herek found that women were more likely than men to support employment protection, adoption rights, and legal recognition of same-sex relationships.[26] In the 2004 ANES survey, women were significantly more likely than men to support gays in the military and adoption rights (the sex gaps for employment nondiscrimination and same-sex marriage were not significant, however). An analysis of seven pooled Pew surveys from July 2003 to August 2004 revealed a statistically significant difference between men and women in support for same-sex marriage, and an analysis of four pooled Pew surveys from the same time period showed a similar gap between men and women in support for civil unions.[27] Likewise, a 2006 Pew survey found that women were more likely than men to favor adoption rights and gays in the military.[28]

In part, the sex gap on gay rights could reflect the sex gap in partisanship. Women are more likely than men to be Democrats, and Democrats are (as I explain below) more likely to support gay rights than are Republicans. The sex gap in support for gay rights could reflect the broader gap on "compassion issues," as well. Herek points to a third explanation: the distinctively unfavorable opinions about gay rights that heterosexual men offer may reflect the distinctively unfavorable evaluations of gay men that they also offer.[29]

Race and Support for Gay Rights

Research on race and American public opinion has focused heavily (though not exclusively) on differences between the opinions of African Americans and whites. Poll results point to a profound racial divide on many aspects of politics, particularly those that are overtly or implicitly related to race. For example, African Americans are more likely than whites not only to support policies explicitly intended to advance racial equality (such as affirmative action) but also to support social welfare spending and to oppose capital punishment.[30] In addition, African Americans are far more likely than whites to identify as Democrats and to support Democratic candidates.

The relationship between race and public opinion about gay rights appears to have been complex (as has the role of race in the politics of gay rights; see below). Drawing on an analysis of thirty-one surveys from 1973 to 2000, Gregory Lewis found that African Americans were more likely than whites to disapprove of homosexuality but just as likely as whites to support gays in the military and more likely than whites to support a law against employment discrimination.[31] Then again, Jeffrey Koch found that the gap between African Americans and whites on support for an employment nondiscrimination law had essentially disappeared by 2000.[32] To further complicate matters, white respondents in the 2004 ANES survey were significantly more likely than African American respondents to support adoption rights and same-sex marriage. Similarly, white respondents were significantly more likely than African American respondents to support same-sex marriage in seven pooled Pew surveys from 2003 and 2004 and to support civil unions in four pooled Pew surveys from the same period.

These divides in public opinion may reflect a shifting racial divide in feelings toward gays and lesbians.[33] In the 1992 ANES survey, African American respondents rated gays and lesbians more favorably than did white respondents.[34] By 2004, however, the pattern had reversed, with white respondents rating gays and lesbians more favorably than did African American respondents.[35] The reasons behind this change are unclear, though Koch speculates that a burgeoning rate of AIDS cases among the African American population may have fueled hostility toward gays on the part of some African Americans.[36]

Age and Support for Gay Rights

Polls point to a variety of differences across age in public opinion. Of particular relevance for my purposes is the finding that young Americans are more liberal than their older counterparts on a host of social issues. Such age gaps in public opinion could reflect two sorts of effects: life-cycle effects resulting from experiences that are part of the typical process of growing older and generational effects resulting from experiences shared by members of a particular age cohort.[37] The age gaps in public opinion about social issues appear to reflect the latter sort of effect, as members of each succeeding generation have expressed more socially liberal views than members of older generations at every stage of the life cycle. Thus, Baby Boomers are more socially liberal than pre–Baby Boomers, members of Generation X are more liberal than Baby Boomers, and members of Generation Y are more liberal than members of Generation X.[38]

Public opinion about gay rights not only fits this pattern; it provides a particularly striking example of it. Both the 1992 ANES and the 2004 ANES surveys showed that younger respondents were more likely than older respondents to support employment nondiscrimination, gays in the military, and adoption rights. Moreover, the 2004 ANES survey revealed an especially strong connection between youth and support for same-sex marriage. Along the same lines, Pew surveys from 2003 to 2006 showed that younger respondents were more likely than older respondents to support gays in the military, adoption rights, same-sex marriage, and civil unions. One 2003 Pew survey found that respondents in their late teens and twenties were evenly divided between supporting and opposing same-sex marriage while those in their forties and fifties opposed it by a two-to-one margin and those in their sixties and seventies opposed it by a four-to-one margin.[39]

The explanation for the generation gap in support for gay rights may lie in the differing experiences of younger and older Americans. Americans who were sixty years old in 2006 came of age in the pre-Stonewall era, a time in which gays and lesbians were deeply marginalized and stigmatized in almost every aspect of public life.[40] This was a period, for instance, during which the

American Psychiatric Association still labeled homosexuality as a mental illness and the *New York Times* ran headlines such as "Homosexuals Proud of Deviancy, Medical Academy Study Finds."[41] In contrast, Americans who were twenty years old in 2006 came of age in an era during which a president (Bill Clinton) advocated for gay rights (even if he did so in a limited and not entirely successful way); a prime-time sitcom (*Ellen*) starred an openly lesbian woman playing an openly lesbian character (even if the show was cancelled in relatively short order); and growing numbers of Americans came to realize that they had gay friends, co-workers, and family members. Given all of this, it makes sense that younger respondents in Pew and ANES surveys rated gays and lesbians more favorably than did their older counterparts. Such age differences in public opinion about gays and lesbians may help to account for the generation gap in support for gay rights. The latter gap, in turn, may carry important implications for both the contemporary politics of gay rights and the future of public opinion on the subject.

Sexual Orientation and Support for Gay Rights

We know relatively little about differences between the political opinions of gay and heterosexual Americans. This lack of knowledge may stem from both neglect on the part of scholars and practical limitations. One obstacle to studying "sexual orientation gaps" in public opinion is the scarcity of national polls that include questions about sexual orientation. Polls of the general public that include such questions typically yield small samples of gays and lesbians due to the small percentage of respondents (typically no more than 5 percent) who self-identify as gay or lesbian. Moreover, not all respondents who are gay or lesbian may be willing to identify themselves as such to pollsters, and those who choose to identify as gay or lesbian may differ in their opinions from those who do not disclose their sexual orientation. Even so, it is safe to say that gays and lesbians are more Democratic and liberal than are heterosexuals. Both gaps emerged clearly in national exit polls from 1992 through 2004 that included substantial numbers of self-identified gay and lesbian respondents due to large overall sample sizes.[42] The gap on party loyalties may reflect responses on the part of gays and lesbians to the relatively pro–gay rights rhetoric of Democratic leaders, but it may also reflect the high priority that both gays and the Democratic Party attach to social welfare programs.[43]

Given the pulls of self-interest and group consciousness on gays and lesbians, one might expect them to express particularly high levels of support for gay rights. Just such a pattern emerged from the responses to a 2004 National Election Pool exit poll question on legal recognition for same-sex relationships.[44] Of the heterosexual respondents, 25 percent said that gay and lesbian couples "should be allowed to legally marry," 35 percent said that they "should be allowed to form civil unions but not marry," and 38 percent said that there "should be no legal recognition of their relationships." Among gay respondents, the percentages were 51 percent, 31 percent, and 17 percent, respectively. Note, however, that gays were not monolithic in their endorsement of same-sex marriage or even legal recognition in either form. Building on the finding that support for marriage was especially pronounced among younger gays, Patrick Egan and Kenneth Sherrill suggest that "a strong generational effect may be in place among [gays] that will lead same-sex marriage to become an issue of steadily increasing priority."[45]

Education and Support for Gay Rights

More educated and less educated Americans diverge in their opinions on a wide range of political topics. Generally speaking, higher levels of education are positively related to support for greater social and political equality. For example, the highly educated are more likely than the less educated to favor gender equality and civil rights for African Americans.[46] This pattern extends to gay rights, as evidenced by results from numerous polls. One Pew poll from 2003 found that college-educated respondents were almost evenly divided on the question of whether to recognize same-sex marriages, whereas those without a college degree were opposed by a two-to-one margin.[47] The same poll found that the gap on civil unions was almost as wide. Likewise, level of education was positively and strongly related to support for employment nondiscrimination, gays in the military, adoption rights, and same-sex marriage among 2004 ANES respondents and to support for gays in the military and adoption rights among 2006 Pew respondents.[48]

One potential explanation for the differences across education in support for gay rights rests with the impact of the educational process itself. It could be that pro–gay rights messages—as well as more general pro-equality messages—in the classroom foster support for gay rights among students. The gay rights foes who decry a perceived "gay agenda" in the schools would presumably argue that this is the case (just as the advocates of pro-tolerance curricula may seek to produce such an impact). Then again, differences across education in opinion can also reflect the association between education and exposure to information in the broader public debate. An overwhelming body of evidence indicates that better educated members of the public are particularly attuned to messages from political, social, and scientific elites.[49] In the case at hand, the public debate may carry messages about homosexuality, gay people, and gay rights that serve to bolster support for gay rights. Consistent with this notion, higher levels of education go hand in hand with a variety of beliefs that reinforce support for gay rights, including the belief that acceptance of gays is good for the country and the belief that sexual orientation is something people are born with and cannot be changed.[50]

Partisanship, Ideology, and Support for Gay Rights

Partisanship is one of the key dividing lines in American public opinion. From the early days of survey research onward, polls have shown that self-identified Democrats and Republicans hold sharply contrasting opinions not only on candidates for public office but also on many of the policy issues that dominate the political agenda.[51] Similar gaps divide self-labeled liberals and conservatives. Furthermore, Americans' partisan loyalties often overlap with their ideological orientations: Democrats are much more likely than Republicans to label themselves liberals, whereas Republicans are far more likely to call themselves conservatives. To be sure, not all Americans have strong, well developed, and internally consistent partisan loyalties and ideological views.[52] Taken individually or together, however, partisanship and ideology provide many citizens with starting points for organizing their views on more specific policy areas. By looking at which side party leaders and ideological elites take in a political dispute, partisan and ideological self-identifiers among the public can draw inferences about which side they should take.[53] Put another way, partisan loyalties and ideological orientations provide citizens shortcuts for making sense of the political world.[54]

Clear partisan and ideological divisions emerge in polling on gay rights, with Democrats and liberals expressing greater support for such rights than do Republicans and conservatives. These differences are not only wide; they also cut across policy areas. For example, they emerged among ANES respondents on employment nondiscrimination, gays in the military, adoption rights, and same-sex marriage. Likewise, they emerged among Pew respondents on gays in the military, adoption rights, same-sex marriage, and civil unions. Conservative Republicans tend to be especially opposed to gay rights, whereas liberal Democrats express the strongest support. For example, a 2006 Pew poll found that almost half of the former opposed gays in the military, compared to only one in ten of the latter.[55] The same poll revealed that three-fourths of self-identified conservative Republicans opposed adoption rights, compared to only one in five liberal Democrats.

Religion and Support for Gay Rights

Scholars have looked at religion and public opinion in several different ways. One approach is to search for differences across religions and religious denominations—for example, by comparing the opinions of Protestants, Catholics, Jews, and those who profess no religion. Another approach is to compare the opinions of those who endorse a particular religious doctrine or identity (e.g., those who identify as evangelical or "born again" Christians) to those who do not. Yet another approach is to compare across religious practices—for example, by comparing those who regularly attend religious services to those who do not. This mix of approaches has uncovered religious divides in public opinion on a number of issues. Consider the case of abortion. Opposition to legal abortion tends to be stronger among white evangelicals than among other Protestants, Catholics, or (particularly) secular respondents; it also tends to be stronger among those who attend religious services regularly than among those who do not.[56] Such "religion gaps" may reflect the influence of interpersonal communication with clergy and co-religionists, as well as the impact of mass-mediated messages from religious leaders.

Like public opinion about abortion, public opinion about gay rights is characterized by divides along religious lines. Pew polling from 2003 showed that white evangelical Protestants were more likely than other Protestants or Catholics to oppose same-sex marriage and civil unions, while secular respondents expressed by far and away the highest levels of support for each.[57] A 2006 Pew poll found similar patterns for gays in the military and adoption rights.[58] Support for gay rights also varies with attendance at religious service, as evidenced by ANES and Pew survey results. Compared to those who regularly attended services, respondents who seldom or never did so were more supportive of employment nondiscrimination, gays in the military, adoption rights, same-sex marriage, and civil unions. In addition, 2004 ANES respondents who endorsed a literal interpretation of the Bible were more opposed to gay rights across the board than were respondents who did not endorse such an interpretation.

TWO REFERENCE POINTS: ABORTION AND CIVIL RIGHTS FOR AFRICAN AMERICANS

No two issues are exactly alike when it comes to public opinion or to public debate. Public opinion follows a unique course in each policy domain, and every policy debate has its own set of images, signals, and frames that people use to make sense of it.[59] At the same time, politicians, activists, and citizens often compare one policy debate to another. Perhaps the two most common issue comparisons in the debate about gay rights have been the analogies to abortion and to civil rights for African Americans. Thus, it is useful to consider whether—and if so, how—trends in public opinion about gay rights resemble trends in public opinion about these two issues. In the case of abortion, the comparison reveals sharp differences that belie any notion of a simplistic and uniform culture war over social policy. In the case of civil rights for African Americans, the comparison reveals similarities that carry suggestions about what the future may hold for public opinion about gay rights.

Public Opinion about Abortion

If there is a culture war going on in American politics, then the debate over abortion is undoubtedly one of its central fronts. The defining moment of this dispute came in 1973 with *Roe v. Wade*, the United States Supreme Court ruling that struck down restrictions on abortion and provided a legal foundation for abortion rights.[60] In the wake of the decision, activists on both sides of the issue—commonly framed as the "pro-choice" and "pro-life" positions—mobilized to influence abortion policy. Those on the pro-life side argued that life begins at conception and that abortion is murder; they often invoked moral and religious principles in making their case. Meanwhile, those on the pro-choice side argued that the choice to have an abortion is a fundamental right for women; they frequently framed their position in terms of personal freedom and gender equality.

The battle lines on abortion overlapped with the battle lines on gay rights. Many of the politicians and activists who organized on the pro-life side also advocated against gay rights. For example, Pat Buchanan's August 17 address to the 1992 Republican National Convention cast both "abortion on demand" and "homosexual rights" as parts of a "religious war going on in this country for the soul of America." Almost a decade later, Reverend Jerry Falwell included both "the abortionists" and "the gays and lesbians who are actively trying to make that an alternative lifestyle" on the list of people at whom he would "point the finger . . . and say, 'You helped [the terrorist attacks of September 11, 2001] happen.'"[61] By the same token, many of those who organized on the pro-choice side endorsed gay rights. For the most part, the Democratic Party aligned itself with the advocates of abortion rights, while the Republican Party took the side of abortion foes.

In 1972—the year before *Roe*—the National Opinion Research Center's General Social Survey (GSS) measured public support for allowing abortion under a range of circumstances. The results indicated that support varied considerably across situations. Under some scenarios—a pregnancy that endangers the health of the mother, fetal defects, or rape—support approached consensus levels; in other circumstances—when the family is too poor to support the child, the mother is unmarried, or a married couple does not want another child—less than half of the respondents supported allowing an abortion.[62] Subsequent GSS surveys revealed similar distinctions in respondents' views. Thus, public opinion about abortion resembled public opinion about gay rights in one regard: namely, its complexity. Just as support for gay rights depended on what sort of right was at stake (employment, military service, adoption, civil unions, or marriage), support for allowing an abortion depended on what the reason for it was.

In another key respect, however, public opinion about abortion looked quite different from public opinion about gay rights. Whereas support for gay rights grew over time, support for abortion rights changed little from the early 1970s to 2000 and beyond. Even as the debate about abortion raged on and key abortion-related political events—including the United States Supreme Court's 1989 decision in *Webster v. Reproductive Health Services* and its 1992 decision in *Planned Parenthood v. Casey*—unfolded, public opinion remained largely static.[63] For example, the percentage of GSS respondents who favored allowing an abortion to protect a pregnant woman's health was 87 percent in 1972 and 83 percent in 2005. Likewise, the percentage of GSS respondents who favored allowing an abortion for a single mother was 43 percent in 1972 and 40 percent in 2005. Nor did Pew polls from 1987 to 2006 yield any clear trends in support for "making it more difficult for a woman to get an abortion."[64]

To the extent that abortion and gay rights are both parts of a broader war over religious principles, traditional morality, and "family values," it seems clear that not all battles in the culture war have turned out the same way. On abortion, the competing sides have reached a long-running stalemate in the arena of public opinion. The battle over public opinion about gay rights, in contrast, has tended to favor one side over the other, with proponents of such rights making substantial gains in the polls.

Public Opinion about Civil Rights for African Americans

In 1954, the United States Supreme Court ruled that racial segregation in the public schools was unconstitutional.[65] The decision, which marked the culmination of a long-running legal effort by the National Association for the Advancement of Colored People (NAACP), pushed the debate about civil rights for African Americans to new heights of prominence on the national agenda (just as later court decisions would do for gay rights). It also provided a rallying point for the burgeoning civil rights movement. In the years that followed *Brown v. Board of Education of Topeka*, civil rights activists organized a series of challenges to racial segregation, including the 1955 bus boycott in Montgomery, the 1960 sit-in in Greensboro, and the 1963 protest in Birmingham.[66] On August 28, 1963, Dr. Martin Luther King, Jr., stood on the steps of the Lincoln Memorial in front of hundreds of thousands of demonstrators and called for racial equality in his "I Have a Dream" speech. Major national legislation came shortly thereafter with the passage of the Civil Rights Act of 1964 and the Voting Rights Act of 1965, as the "equal rights" frame of the civil rights movement triumphed over the "states' rights" rhetoric of its opponents. The focus of the debate over racial equality subsequently shifted to a variety of methods—from school busing to college admissions policies to set-asides in government spending—for ensuring greater racial equality in social and economic life. Though supporters of such "race-conscious" policies won victories in pushing for their implementation, their opponents fought back—sometimes successfully—by arguing that these policies led to "reverse discrimination" rather than equality.[67]

From the early years of the gay rights movement onward, its proponents drew the analogy between civil rights for African Americans and civil rights for gays and lesbians. Moreover, they echoed the civil rights movement by framing their stance in terms of equal rights. For their part, gay rights opponents sought to refute the analogy. They also emulated the opponents of affirmative action in claiming the principle of equality for their own side. Specifically, they cast gay rights policies as tools to create "special rights" for gays and lesbians. African American leaders and activists, in turn, offered a mixed reaction to the argument that gay rights are equivalent to civil rights for African Americans. Chairman of the Joint Chiefs of Staff (and later United States Secretary of State) Colin Powell, who spoke out against lifting the military ban in 1993, recalled in his memoir two years later that the "Congressional Black Caucus favored removing the ban. . . . But other [African American] leaders were telling me that they resented having the civil rights crusade appropriated—hijacked, some of them put it—by the gay community for its ends."[68] Even Reverend (and former presidential candidate) Jesse Jackson, an advocate for civil unions and other sorts of gay rights policies, drew the line at same-sex marriage, stating, "In my culture, marriage is a man-woman relationship."[69] He also called the analogy between gay rights and civil rights for African Americans a "stretch," arguing that "gays were never called three-fifths human in the Constitution."[70]

In any event, it is no stretch to draw a parallel between the growth over time in support for African Americans' civil rights and the growth over time in support for gay rights. Polls on civil rights for African Americans go back for more than half of a century, and their results point to a profound shift in white Americans' opinions about the principle of racial equality.[71] National Opinion Research Center polls from the 1940s found that over half of white respondents endorsed segregated public transportation and preferential treatment for whites in employment; two-thirds of white respondents endorsed segregated schools.[72] By 1972, however, around nine in ten white respondents favored integrated schools, equal opportunity in employment, and desegregated public transportation.[73] Along the same lines, white public opinion about interracial marriage went from near-universal condemnation to wide majority support. A 1958 Gallup poll found that 96 percent of white respondents disapproved of interracial marriage, and the 1970 GSS found that half supported a ban on interracial marriages.[74] In contrast, less than a third of the white respondents in a 1997 Gallup poll disapproved of interracial marriage, and only a tenth of all respondents in the 2000 GSS favored banning interracial marriages.[75]

On some policies, such as employment nondiscrimination and gays in the military, support for gay rights has approached the near-consensus levels attained by support for the principle of racial equality. For same-sex marriage (and, to a lesser extent, civil unions), the picture is different; here, support falls short of even majority status. Note, however, that not all aspects of support for African Americans' civil rights reached near-consensus levels at the same time. In particular, support for racial equality in employment opportunity attained such levels well before opposition to banning interracial marriage did. If the parallel between trends in public opinion about civil rights for African Americans and trends in public opinion about gay rights were to persist, then support for same-sex marriage would eventually follow the same path as opposition to banning interracial marriage. The generation gap on gay marriage also points in this direction: recall that young people are much more likely than their older counterparts to endorse gay marriage. As employment nondiscrimination goes today, then, marriage may go tomorrow.

NOTES

1. *Lawrence v. Texas*, 539 U.S. 558 (2003); *Bowers v. Hardwick*, 478 U.S. 186 (1986).

2. *Lawrence v. Texas*.

3. Lambda Legal, "Landmark Ruling for Gay Civil Rights: U.S. Supreme Court Strikes Down Texas 'Homosexual Conduct' Law" (New York: Lambda Legal, 2003).

4. Quoted in Carolyn Lochhead, "High Court Ruling Likely to Usher in New Era for Gays; Decision's Logic to Have Impact on Other Rights," *San Francisco Chronicle*, 29 June 2003, A4.

5. Quoted in Sarah Kershaw, "Adversaries on Gay Rights Vow State-by-State Fight," *New York Times*, 6 July 2003, A8.

6. *Lawrence v. Texas*.

7. Quoted in Karen Branch-Brioso, "Court Strikes Down Texas' Ban on Gay Sex; Ruling Expected to Bring End to Other Anti-Sodomy Laws," *St. Louis Post-Dispatch*, 27 June 2003, A1.

8. Quoted in Carolyn Lochhead, "Gay Rights Affirmed in Historic Ruling; 6–3 Decision: Supreme Court Throws Out Sodomy Laws," *San Francisco Chronicle*, 27 June 2003, A1.

9. Cathy Lynn Grossman, "Is the Recent Backlash Against Homosexuality Just a 'Blip?'" *USA Today*, 31 July 2003, 6D.

10. In describing these trends, I draw on the poll archive of the Roper Center for Public Opinion Research, as well as the following summaries: Karlyn Bowman, "Attitudes about Homosexuality and Gay Marriage" (Washington, DC: American

Enterprise Institute, 2006); Paul R. Brewer and Clyde Wilcox, "Trends: Same-Sex Marriage and Civil Unions," *Public Opinion Quarterly* 69 (2005): 599–616; Oscar Torres-Reyna and Robert Y. Shapiro, "Trends: Women and Sexual Orientation in the Military," *Public Opinion Quarterly* 66 (2002): 618–32; Alan S. Yang, "Trends: Attitudes toward Homosexuality," *Public Opinion Quarterly* 61 (1997): 477–507.

11. See chapter 6 for details.

12. See chapter 6 for details.

13. See, for example, John Gallagher and Chris Bull, *Perfect Enemies: The Battle between the Religious Right and the Gay Movement*, updated ed. (New York: Madison Books, 2001), 216–17.

14. Clyde Wilcox and Robin Wolpert, "Gay Rights in the Public Sphere: Public Opinion on Gay and Lesbian Equality," in *The Politics of Gay Rights*, ed. Craig A. Rimmerman, Kenneth D. Wald, and Clyde Wilcox (Chicago: University of Chicago Press, 2000), 409–32.

15. John DiStaso, "Sheehan Steamroller Leaves GOP in the Dust," *Union Leader*, 24 June 1999, A2.

16. Andrea Stone, "Drive to Ban Gay Adoption Heats Up in 16 States," *USA Today*, 20 February 2006, 1A.

17. Marie Szaniszlo, "Catholic Charities Caves; Bowing to Pressure, Agency Drops All Adoptions to Exclude Gays," *Boston Herald*, 11 March 2006, 5.

18. Jonathan Saltzman, "Romney Eyes Bill Exempting Religious Groups on Bias Laws," *Boston Globe*, 11 March 2006, A4.

19. *Baehr v. Lewin*, 74 Haw. 645, 852 P.2d 44 (1993).

20. Pew Research Center for the People and the Press, "Republicans Unified, Democrats Split on Same-Sex Marriage; Religious Beliefs Underpin Opposition to Homosexuality" (Washington, DC: Pew Research Center for the People and the Press, 2003); David W. Moore and Joseph Carroll, "Support for Gay Marriage/Civil Unions Edges Upward; Public Remains Divided on Constitutional Amendment to Ban Gay Marriage" (Washington, DC: Gallup Organization, 2003).

21. Brewer and Wilcox, "Trends: Same-Sex Marriage," 603.

22. For additional evidence regarding group differences in public opinion about gay rights, see Steven H. Haeberle, "Gay and Lesbian Rights: Emerging Trends in Public Opinion and Voting Behavior," in *Gays and Lesbians in the Democratic Process*, ed. Ellen D. B. Riggle and Barry L. Tadlock (New York: Columbia University Press, 1999), 146–69; Gregory B. Lewis and Marc A. Rogers, "Does the Public Support Equal Employment Rights For Gays and Lesbians?" in *Gays and Lesbians in the Democratic Process*, ed. Riggle and Tadlock, 118–45; Laura Olson, Wendy Cadge, and James T. Harrison, "Religion and Public Opinion about Same-Sex Marriage," *Social Science Quarterly* 87 (2006): 340–60; Clyde Wilcox and Barbara Norrander, "Of Moods and Morals: The Dynamics of Opinion on Abortion and Gay Rights," in *Understanding Public Opinion*, 2nd ed., ed. Barbara Norrander and Clyde Wilcox (Washington, DC: Congressional Quarterly Press, 2002), 121–48; Clyde Wilcox and Robin Wolpert, "President Clinton, Public Opinion, and Gays in the Military," in *Gay Rights, Military Wrongs: Political Perspectives on Lesbians and Gays in the Military*, ed. Craig A. Rimmerman (New York: Garland Publishing, 1996), 127–45; and Wilcox and Wolpert, "Gay Rights in the Public Sphere."

23. R. Michael Alvarez and Edward J. McCaffery, "Are There Sex Gaps in Fiscal Policy Preferences?" *Political Research Quarterly* 56 (2003): 5–17.

24. See, for example, Karen M. Kaufmann and John R. Petrocik, "The Changing Politics of American Men: Understanding the Sources of the Gender Gap," *American Journal of Political Science* 43 (1999): 864–87; Barbara Norrander, "The Evolution of the Gender Gap," *Public Opinion Quarterly* 63 (1999): 566–76.

25. See, for example, Carol Gilligan, *Understanding the Gender Gap: An Economic History of American Women* (Cambridge, Mass.: Harvard University Press, 1990); Benjamin I. Page and Robert Y. Shapiro, *The Rational Public: Fifty Years of Trends in American Policy Preferences* (Chicago: University of Chicago Press, 1992).

26. Gregory M. Herek, "Gender Gaps in Public Opinion about Lesbians and Gay Men," *Public Opinion Quarterly* 66 (2002): 40–66.

27. See Appendix A for details about the surveys.

28. Pew Research Center for the People and the Press, "Less Opposition to Gay Marriage, Adoption, and Military Service; Only 34% Favor South Dakota Abortion Law" (Washington, DC: Pew Research Center for the People and the Press, 2006).

29. Herek, "Gender Gaps."

30. Donald R. Kinder and Lynn M. Sanders, *Divided By Color: Racial Politics and Democratic Ideals* (Chicago: University of Chicago Press, 1996); Donald R. Kinder and Nicholas Winter, "Exploring the Racial Divide: Blacks, Whites, and Opinion on National Policy," *American Journal of Political Science* 45 (2001): 439–53; Howard Schuman, Charlotte Steeh, Lawrence Bobo, and Maria Krysan, *Racial Attitudes in America: Trends and Interpretations*, rev. ed. (Cambridge, Mass.: Harvard University Press, 1997).

31. Gregory B. Lewis, "Black-White Differences in Attitudes toward Homosexuality and Gay Rights," *Public Opinion Quarterly* 67 (2003): 59–78.

32. Jeffrey W. Koch, "The Changing Black and White Divide on Americans' Attitudes toward Gays," paper presented at the annual meeting of the American Political Science Association, Chicago, September 2004.

33. For more on the relationship between such feelings and support for gay rights, see chapter 3.

34. See chapter 6 for details on question wording.

35. See also Koch, "Changing Black and White Divide."

36. Koch, "Changing Black and White Divide."

37. Page and Shapiro, *Rational Public*, 302.

38. Pew Research Center for the People and the Press, "Trends in Political Values and Core Attitudes: 1987–2007; Political Landscape More Favorable to Democrats" (Washington, DC: Pew Research Center for the People and the Press, 2007).

39. Pew Research Center, "Republicans Unified."

40. See, for example, Edward Alwood, *Straight News: Gays, Lesbians, and the News Media* (New York: Columbia University Press, 1996); Larry Gross, *Up from Invisibility: Lesbians, Gay Men, and the Media in America* (New York: Columbia University Press, 2001).

41. Alwood, *Straight News*, 31.

42. Patrick J. Egan, "Lesbian and Gay Voters in the 1990s," paper presented at the annual meeting of the American Political Science Association, Chicago, September 2004; Mark Hertzog, *The Lavender Vote: Lesbians, Gay Men, and Bisexuals in American*

Politics (New York: New York University Press, 1996); Brian Schaffner and Nenad Senic, "Rights or Benefits? Explaining the Sexual Identity Gap in American Political Behavior," *Political Research Quarterly* 59 (2006): 123–32.

43. Schaffner and Senic, "Rights or Benefits?"

44. Patrick J. Egan and Kenneth Sherrill, "Marriage and the Shifting Priorities of a New Generation of Lesbians and Gays," *PS: Political Science & Politics* 38 (2005): 229–32.

45. Egan and Sherrill, "Marriage and the Shifting Priorities," 231.

46. Page and Shapiro, *Rational Public*, 313–18.

47. Pew Research Center, "Republicans Unified."

48. Pew Research Center, "Less Opposition."

49. See, for example, Page and Shapiro, *Rational Public*; John Zaller, *The Nature and Origins of Mass Opinion* (New York: Cambridge University Press, 1992). For more evidence on this point in the context of gay rights, see chapter 4.

50. See chapter 3.

51. See, for example, Angus Campbell, Philip E. Converse, Warren E. Miller, and Donald E. Stokes, *The American Voter* (Chicago: University of Chicago Press, 1960); Page and Shapiro, *Rational Public*, 307–13.

52. See, for example, Philip E. Converse, "The Nature of Belief Systems in Mass Publics," in *Ideology and Discontent*, ed. David E. Apter (New York: Free Press, 1964), 206–61.

53. Anthony Downs, *An Economic Theory of Democracy* (New York: HarperCollins, 1957); Zaller, *Nature and Origins of Mass Opinion*.

54. Samuel L. Popkin, *The Reasoning Voter* (Chicago: University of Chicago Press, 1994).

55. Pew Research Center, "Less Opposition."

56. Pew Research Center, "Less Opposition."

57. Pew Research Center, "Republicans Unified."

58. Pew Research Center, "Less Opposition to Gay Marriage, Adoption, and Military Service."

59. William A. Gamson and Andre Modigliani, "The Changing Culture of Affirmative Action," in *Research in Political Sociology*, ed. Richard D. Braungart (Greenwich, Conn.: JAI Press, 1987), 137–77; William A. Gamson and Andre Modigliani, "Media Discourse and Public Opinion on Nuclear Power: A Constructionist Approach," *American Journal of Sociology* 95 (1989): 1–37.

60. *Roe v. Wade*, 410 U.S. 113 (1973).

61. Quoted in John F. Harris, "Falwell Apologizes for Remark," *Washington Post*, 18 September 2001, C4.

62. Page and Shapiro, *Rational Public*, 105–10; Wilcox and Norrander, "Of Moods and Morals," 130.

63. *Webster v. Reproductive Health Services*, 492 U.S. 490 (1989); *Planned Parenthood v. Casey*, 505 U.S. 833 (1992).

64. Pew Research Center, "Trends in Political Values."

65. *Brown v. Board of Education of Topeka*, 347 U.S. 483 (1954).

66. For an overview of these events, see Schuman et al., *Racial Attitudes in America*, 20–27.

67. Gamson and Modigliani, "Changing Color of Affirmative Action"; Kinder and Sanders, *Divided by Color*.

68. Colin L. Powell with Joseph E. Persico, *My American Journey* (New York: Random House, 1995), 533.

69. Quoted in Kevin Duchschere, "Is Gay Marriage a Civil-Rights Issue? Five Black Leaders Say It's Not the Same," *Star Tribune*, 26 March 2004, 1B.

70. Quoted in Lynette Clemetson, "Both Sides Court Black Churches in the Battle over Gay Marriage," *New York Times*, 1 March 2004, A1.

71. Trends in public support for policies designed to implement racial equality (e.g., affirmative action) followed a different path. Specifically, support for such policies was not nearly as strong and did not exhibit the same growth over time. See, for example, Kinder and Sanders, *Divided by Color*, 21–27; Page and Shapiro, *Rational Public*, 74–75; Schuman et al., *Racial Attitudes in America*, 170–83.

72. Schuman et al., *Racial Attitudes in America*, 104.

73. Schuman et al., *Racial Attitudes in America*, 104.

74. Schuman et al., *Racial Attitudes in America*, 106.

75. Donald P. Haider-Markel and Mark R. Joslyn, "Attributions and the Regulation of Marriage: Considering the Parallels between Race and Homosexuality," *PS: Political Science & Politics* 38 (2005): 233–39.

3

Whose Rights?
Public Opinion about Gays, Lesbians, and Homosexuality

The movie *Brokeback Mountain* tells the story of two Wyoming cowboys who fall in love with one another. Following its release in 2005, the film won widespread critical acclaim, including an Academy Award nomination for Best Motion Picture of the Year (its director, Ang Lee, won the Academy Award for Best Achievement in Directing). It also did well at the box office, grossing over $80 million.[1] In the process, the "gay cowboy movie" (as it was widely known) became a media phenomenon. The film even made its way onto the national evening news when a Kansas State University student asked President George W. Bush for his opinion about it. "I'd be glad to talk about ranching, but I haven't seen the movie," Bush responded.[2]

The success of *Brokeback Mountain* suggests that many Americans were prepared to accept not only a Western that centered on a same-sex relationship but also same-sex relationships in real life. According to some observers, the movie had additional significance for the debate about gay rights: they saw a political agenda behind the movie and the media coverage of it. Consider Bill O'Reilly's comments on the December 20, 2005 episode of his FOX News Channel talk show, *The O'Reilly Factor*:

> The *New York Times* and the *L.A. Times* have each, each, run six articles on *Brokeback Mountain*. Some believe these newspapers want to spin the film positive to help the gay cause in this country. . . . I couldn't care less about the gay cowboys. I'm confused by straight cowboys. I don't need gay cowboys. I don't get it, OK? So, let the gay cowboys be gay. Let them be happy. Let them do whatever they want. That's my philosophy. But when I see . . . all of these articles, I'm going, "They definitely want to mainstream this kind of stuff, because then it becomes easier to pass gay marriage and things like that."

O'Reilly sounded two themes that frequently appeared in public discussion of the movie. First, he took the opportunity to state his personal tolerance of "gay cowboys." Thus, he stayed in step with a public that had grown increasingly inclined to endorse such tolerance. Second, he argued that media messages, public opinion about same-sex relationships, and the politics of gay rights are interconnected. Specifically, he suggested that media images of gays and lesbians shape mainstream public opinion—which, in turn, shape the political environment surrounding same-sex marriage. Though O'Reilly presented this argument in criticizing the movie (and same-sex marriage), defenders of the movie (and of same-sex marriage) advanced similar claims.

In this chapter, I take a closer look at what Americans thought and felt about gays, lesbians, and homosexuality during the latter part of the twentieth century and beyond. In doing so, I begin my examination of the foundations on which Americans based their opinions about gay rights (in the following chapters, I turn my attention to another set of foundations: principles such as partisanship, ideology, religious beliefs, egalitarianism, and moral traditionalism). My initial step is to identify various aspects of public opinion about gays, lesbians, and homosexuality that may have shaped public opinion about gay rights. These include feelings about gays, lesbians, and homosexuality; beliefs about the nature and changeability of homosexuality; beliefs about whether homosexuality is wrong, sinful, or against God's will; stereotypes of gays and lesbians; and beliefs about whether society should accept gays, lesbians, and homosexuality. I also look at trends in these aspects of public opinion and consider explanations for such trends.

Next, I examine how public opinion about gays, lesbians, and homosexuality shaped public opinion about two sets of gay rights policies. I use survey data from 1993 to analyze public opinion about two gay rights policies that dominated the debate about gay rights in the early 1990s: gays in the military and employment nondiscrimination laws. I then use survey data from ten years later to analyze public opinion about two gay rights policies that were relative newcomers to the public agenda: same-sex marriage and civil unions. I find that beliefs about the nature of homosexuality and feelings toward gays and lesbians shaped public support for all four policies. Other aspects of public opinion about gays, lesbians, and homosexuality also influenced support for some of the policies. In addition, the 2003 data reveal that two forms of contact with gay men and lesbians were tied to public opinion about gays, lesbians, homosexuality, and gay rights: personal contact with gay family members, friends, or co-workers and virtual contact through exposure to gay figures in the media.

I conclude by considering the implications of my findings for the public debate about gay rights. In particular, I argue that shifting beliefs and feelings about gays, lesbians, and homosexuality may have altered the rules for public debate by contributing to a growing norm against overt "gay bashing." I also suggest that the politics of gay rights may have carried implications for public opinion about gays, lesbians, and homosexuality.

DIMENSIONS OF PUBLIC OPINION ABOUT GAYS, LESBIANS, AND HOMOSEXUALITY

Appearing as a guest on the aforementioned episode of *The O'Reilly Factor*, film critic Michael Medved related the following story about *Brokeback Mountain*:

> As a matter of fact, even in very liberal Seattle at a screening, there were people who were very uncomfortable. About 15 minutes into the movie, as the infamous pup tent scene. And for most guys . . . the idea of two guys going at it in a pup tent, there's an "eww!" factor where there are people, and this has been reported, who are actually heading for the doors at that point.

Regardless of whether Medved's account was accurate, it illustrates the sort of visceral negative reactions to gay people and to homosexuality that some Americans report experiencing. Many observers label such reactions "homophobic," and some scholars argue that they are an important influence on public opinion about gay rights.[3] In surveys from the 1980s through 2004, sizable percentages of Americans reported visceral negative reactions to gays and lesbians.[4] These surveys also showed, however, that the percentage doing so declined over time. Consider the trend from *Los Angeles Times* polls that asked respondents whether they felt uncomfortable when they were around "gay men" or "lesbian women." In 1983, only 40 percent of respondents said that they felt uncomfortable around neither gay men nor lesbians (see figure 3.1). Over the next two decades, this percentage increased by twenty points. Even so, a sizable minority of respondents continued to express discomfort at being around gay men, lesbians, or both.

American National Election Studies (ANES) data reflected a similar trend, though the ANES surveys used a different approach in measuring feelings toward "gay men and lesbians": a "feeling thermometer" that asked respondents to rate the group on a scale from 0 to 100, where higher numbers indicated warmer feelings.[5] Whereas the *Los Angeles Times* item captures a specific sort of negative visceral response, the ANES item provides a general measure of affect toward gays and lesbians. In 1984, the mean rating on the thermometer was 30 degrees.[6] By 2004, it had climbed to 49 degrees. If one defines prejudice toward gays and lesbians as negative affect toward this group, then such prejudice appears to have declined substantially

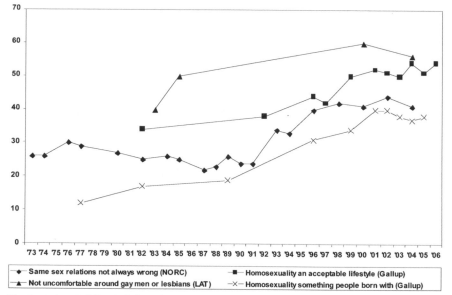

Figure 3.1. Public Opinion about Gays, Lesbians, and Homosexuality, 1973–2006

over time (though it hardly disappeared).[7] For example, 35 percent of the 1984 respondents offered the lowest possible rating (0 degrees), whereas only 14 percent of the 2004 respondents did so. Like visceral responses, general affect toward gays and lesbians may influence public opinion toward gay rights policies.[8]

In addition to experiencing emotional reactions toward gays, lesbians, and homosexuality, Americans hold beliefs about these subjects. Indeed, beliefs about the nature of homosexuality may be particularly important in shaping public opinion about gay rights.[9] Some Americans attribute homosexuality to biology, seeing it as something with which people are born; others attribute it to developmental factors or individual choice. Along similar lines, some Americans believe that homosexuality is a changeable lifestyle preference, whereas others view it as a fixed orientation. To those who hold them, such beliefs may carry implications regarding whether homosexual is "natural" or whether gay men and lesbians should be "held responsible" for their sexual orientation.[10] As with feelings toward gays and lesbians, public opinion about the nature of homosexuality shifted over time. Only 12 percent of respondents in a 1977 Gallup poll said that "homosexuality is something a person is born with," whereas 56 percent said that it is "due to other factors such as upbringing or environment." Over the course of the 1980s and especially the 1990s, the percentage choosing the former option increased. By 2001, it had reached 40 percent, while the percentage choosing "upbringing or environment" had dropped to 36 percent (see figure 3.1).

Another belief divide that may be crucial in shaping public opinion about gay rights is the one revolving around whether homosexuality is wrong—or, in more explicitly theological terms, a sin and against God's will.[11] Beliefs about the morality of homosexuality underwent a sizable shift over a three-decade period, as illustrated by the trend for an item in the National Opinion Research Center's General Social Surveys (see figure 3.1). In 1973, 70 percent of GSS respondents said that "sexual relations between two adults of the same sex" are "always wrong," while only 11 percent said that such relations are "not wrong at all." Throughout the 1970s and 1980s, these percentages remained relatively stable. Beginning in the early 1990s, the proportion of respondents choosing the "always wrong" option declined while the proportion choosing the "not wrong at all" increased. Even so, the former remained a majority: in 2004, 57 percent chose the "always wrong" option, while 29 percent chose the "not wrong at all" option.

Just as Americans hold beliefs about the nature and morality of homosexuality, so, too, do they hold a variety of beliefs about gays and lesbians. In particular, many Americans hold stereotypical beliefs about members of this group that may shape how they judge gay rights policies.[12] Walter Lippmann famously described stereotypes as pictures "we carry about in our heads" that tell us "about the world before we see it."[13] Some of the most enduring stereotypes of gays and lesbians cast them as threatening, sexualized, and socially deviant.[14] For example, gays and lesbians have been stereotyped as carrying diseases (particularly AIDS), as eager to seduce heterosexuals (or even molest children), and as unable to maintain stable relationships (or preferring promiscuity). Gay rights opponents invoked these stereotypes from the early years of the gay rights debate onward. For example, those who opposed military service by gays and lesbians often invoked the "seducer" stereotype through "images of shared pup tents and showers."[15] Likewise, they invoked the "diseased" stereotype through such specters as "gay bowel syndrome."[16] Given the other trends in public opinion about gays, lesbians, and homosexuality, it seems likely that popular endorsement of such stereotypes faded over the latter part of the twentieth century. Nevertheless, stereotypes of gays and lesbians clearly persisted through 2000 and beyond (as will soon become clear).

Yet another aspect of public opinion toward gays, lesbians, and homosexuality involves societal acceptance of homosexuality. For those who favor such acceptance, supporting gay rights policies may be a relatively easy next step. To those who reject such acceptance, however, gay rights policies may seem to endorse the unacceptable. Polling data indicate a trend toward greater acceptance of homosexuality (see figure 3.1). Beginning in 1982, Gallup conducted a series of polls that asked respondents, "Do you think that homosexuality should be considered an acceptable alternative lifestyle or not?" That year, 34 percent said yes and 51 percent said no. By 2006, opinion had tilted in the other direction, with 54 percent saying yes and 41 percent saying no.

Taken as a whole, the polls point to two conclusions. On the one hand, sizable proportions of the American public continued, as of 2006, to express negative feelings toward gays and lesbians, support for the notion that homosexuality is a choice that can be changed, support for the idea that homosexuality is wrong, and opposition to social acceptance of homosexuality. On the other hand, these feelings and opinions became less common among the public over the course of the late twentieth century and beyond.

ELITE MESSAGES, PERSONAL CONTACT, AND MEDIA IMAGES

One potential explanation for the transformation in public opinion about gays, lesbians, and homosexuality lies with changes in the messages that political, social, and scientific elites put forth in public debate. During the 1990s and beyond, Americans received a different mix of messages about gays, lesbians, and homosexuality than they had in previous decades. The debate about the origins of homosexuality provides one example. A key moment in this debate came in 1994, when *Science* magazine published a National Institute of Health study that endorsed a genetic explanation for homosexuality.[17] Such a message—amplified by media coverage—could have served to undermine public beliefs that homosexuality was a choice (and a changeable one at that) while reinforcing "nature" attributions for homosexuality.

A second explanation for the shift in public opinion about gays, lesbians, and homosexuality revolves around the growing percentage of Americans who said that they knew a gay man or lesbian. From 1992 to 2000, a series of Princeton Research Survey Associates/*Newsweek* polls asked respondents whether they had "a friend or acquaintance who is gay," "work[ed] with someone who is gay," and "had a gay person in your family." In 1992, the percentages saying yes to these questions were 22 percent, 20 percent, and 9 percent, respectively. Over the next eight years, they rose to 56 percent, 32 percent, and 23 percent. If social contact erodes stereotypes and prejudice, then such a dramatic increase in contact with gays and lesbians (or, more likely, in *self-awareness* of contact with gays and lesbians) could have influenced public opinion about gays, lesbians, and homosexuality.[18] Furthermore, this increase in social contact could have carried implications for public opinion about gay rights policies. If personal contact with gays and lesbians shapes public opinion about such policies—either directly or indirectly through its impact on public opinion about gays, lesbians, and homosexuality—then rising levels of contact should have produced rising levels of support for gay rights.

A third explanation for the transformation in public opinion about gays, lesbians, and homosexuality lies with the increasing visibility of gays and lesbians in the mass media. Throughout most of the twentieth century, gays and lesbians were largely invisible in the media world; when they did appear, the media often presented them as deviant.[19] Gradually, however, the media began to depict gays and lesbians more frequently, more positively, and in more diverse ways. In 1989, the *Brattleboro Reformer* became the first newspaper to publish notices of same-sex weddings.[20] Popular movie star Tom Hanks played a gay man in 1993 in the movie *Philadelphia* and won an Academy Award for Best Actor. On prime time television, sitcom protagonist Ellen came out as lesbian in 1997—as did Ellen DeGeneres, who portrayed her. In her wake came numerous gay figures on television. Among them were Richard Hatch, the winner on the first season of the reality television show *Survivor*; Will and Jack, lead characters on the sitcom *Will & Grace*; Patty, a cartoon character on *The Simpsons*; and the five makeover specialists from the cable show *Queer Eye for the Straight Guy*. The gay cowboys in *Brokeback Mountain* were part of a broader media phenomenon, one that many Americans would have found difficult to overlook or avoid. Exposure to these gay media figures could have shaped public opinion in the direction of greater favorability toward gays, lesbians, and homosexuality. Consistent with this argument, research conducted by Edward Schiappa and his colleagues found that exposure to *Will & Grace* predicted positive attitudes toward gay men.[21] Such findings also suggest that virtual or "parasocial" contact could have influenced public opinion toward gay rights policies— again, either directly or indirectly through its effects on public opinion about gays, lesbians, and homosexuality.

Of course, it is possible—even likely—that changes in elite messages, personal contact, and media images reinforced one another. For example, the increased visibility of gays and lesbians in the media could have encouraged gays and lesbians to disclose their homosexuality to people who knew them, thereby leading to increased awareness of personal contact. Similarly, the growing numbers of "out" gays and lesbians among the public could have encouraged media organizations to change how—and how often— they presented gays and lesbians. At the same time, the transformation in public opinion about gays, lesbians, and homosexuality could have reinforced changes in elite messages, personal contact, and media images.

EMPLOYMENT NONDISCRIMINATION AND GAYS IN THE MILITARY: 1993

In 1993, the debate over gay rights loomed large on the public agenda: the controversy over President Clinton's effort to overturn the ban on military service had reached its peak, and the battle over employment nondiscrimination was playing out on multiple fronts. That same year, the ANES Pilot Study included a series of questions measuring public opinion about gays, lesbians, homosexuality, and gay rights, thereby yielding a dataset that allows me to examine the relationships among these various aspects of public opinion at a particularly important moment in time.

The 750 respondents in the 1993 Pilot Study were asked a series of questions that captured their feelings toward gays and lesbians, their beliefs about homosexuality, and their stereotypes of gays and lesbians (see table 3.1). A sizable minority reported that they found "the very idea of homosexuality disgusting," and the average feeling thermometer score was colder than it was warm. The respondents who said that homosexuality was the "natural sexuality" of some people outnumbered those who said that "homosexuality is unnatural," but not by a wide margin. The sample was closely divided between those who believed that "being homosexual is something people choose to be" and those who believed that "it is something they cannot change." Respondents were almost evenly divided between those who believed that "homosexuality is against the will of God" and those who did not. Relatively small percentages believed that "many homosexuals will try to seduce people who are not homosexuals" or were worried about "getting AIDS or some other disease" from "working with a gay or lesbian" (a sizable minority of respondents, however, were only "somewhat confident" that "working with a homosexual person poses no special danger of disease"). The various aspects of public opinion about gays, lesbians, and homosexuality were all positively related to one another ($p < .01$ in every case).[22] Given that responses to the "natural" and "cannot change" were conceptually intertwined and strongly correlated, I combined them into an index.

To measure support for gay rights, I used a pair of items. The first asked respondents whether they strongly favored (39 percent), favored (24 percent), opposed (14 percent), or strongly opposed (23 percent) "laws to protect homosexuals against job discrimination."[23] The second asked respondents whether they strongly favored (45 percent), favored (17 percent), opposed (8 percent), or strongly opposed (30 percent) allowing "homosexuals . . . to serve in the United States Armed Forces." In each case, a majority favored the policy.

I then examined how the various aspects of public opinion about gays, lesbians, and homosexuality were related to support for each policy after controlling for a host of other factors that might have shaped such support: party identification, ideology, belief in a literal interpretation of the Bible, attendance at religious services, sex, race, age, education, and income.[24] As table 3.2 reports, positive feelings toward gays and lesbians and beliefs that homosexuality is natural and cannot be changed emerged as powerful predictors of support for both an employment nondiscrimination law and gays

Table 3.1. Public Opinion about Gays, Lesbians, and Homosexuality (ANES Pilot Study, 1993)

Emotional reaction to homosexuality	
Disgusted—strongly	34%
Disgusted—not strongly	6%
Uncomfortable but not disgusted	12%
Not uncomfortable	44%
Don't know/refused	4%
Mean feeling thermometer score for gay men and lesbians (range 0–100)	39
Which of the following statements comes closest to your view:	
For some people, homosexuality is their natural sexuality—believe strongly	38%
For some people, homosexuality is their natural sexuality—believe not strongly	14%
Homosexuality is unnatural—believe not strongly	6%
Homosexuality is unnatural—believe strongly	37%
Don't know/refused	5%
Do you think being homosexual is something people choose to be, or do you think it is something they cannot change?	
Choose to be—believe strongly	32%
Choose to be—believe not strongly	10%
Cannot change—believe not strongly	13%
Cannot change—believe strongly	33%
Don't know/refused	12%
Do you feel that . . .	
Homosexuality is against the will of God—believe strongly	43%
Homosexuality is against the will of God—believe not strongly	4%
Homosexuality can be acceptable to God—believe not strongly	4%
Homosexuality can be acceptable to God—believe strongly	10%
Homosexuality should have nothing to do with God or religion	32%
Don't know/refused	8%
Which comes closer to your view: Homosexuals . . .	
Will try to seduce people who are not homosexual—believe strongly	12%
Will try to seduce people who are not homosexuals—believe not strongly	5%
Don't make sexual advances on people who are not interested—believe not strongly	18%
Don't make sexual advances on people who are not interested—believe strongly	59%
Don't know/refused	7%
If I had a job working with a gay or lesbian . . .	
I would be worried about getting AIDS or some other disease—worry a lot	8%
I would be worried about getting AIDS or some other disease—worry a little	5%
Working with a homosexual poses no special danger of disease—somewhat confident	30%
Working with a homosexual poses no special danger of disease—very confident	53%
Don't know/refused	3%

Note: N = 750

Table 3.2.   Influences on Support for Employment Nondiscrimination Law and Gays in the Military (ANES Pilot Study, 1993)

	Employment nondiscrimination	Gays in the military
Comfortable with homosexuality	−.05	.10*
	(.05)	(.05)
Feelings toward gay men and lesbians	.35**	.37**
	(.08)	(.08)
Belief that homosexuality is natural and cannot	.23**	.22**
be changed	(.05)	(.05)
Belief that homosexual behavior is not against	−.09*	−.01
the will of God	(.04)	(.04)
Belief that homosexuals do not try to seduce	.18**	.09†
people who are not homosexuals	(.05)	(.05)
Confident that working with a homosexual poses	.17**	.13*
no special danger of disease	(.06)	(.06)
N	481	475

Notes: Table entries are unstandardized OLS coefficients. Standard errors are in parentheses. Models also included controls for party identification, ideology, belief that the Bible should be taken literally, attendance at religious services, sex, self-identification as African American, age, education, and income.
†Significant at the .10 level
*Significant at the .05 level
**Significant at the .01 level

in the military. Rejection of the "seducer" stereotype and lack of concern about getting a disease from a gay or lesbian co-worker were positively related to support for each policy, as well. In contrast, beliefs that homosexuality is not against the will of God failed to foster support for either policy. Feeling comfortable with homosexuality predicted support for the gays in the military but was not significantly related to support for an employment nondiscrimination law.

The results from the 1993 data suggest that feelings and beliefs about gays, lesbians, and homosexuality shaped support for gay rights. Beliefs about the nature of homosexuality and feelings toward gays and lesbians appear to have played particularly important roles in doing so. Yet these findings came from a particular moment in time and revolved around a specific pair of gay rights policies. It may be that the relationships between public opinion about gays, lesbians, and homosexuality and public opinion about gay rights changed over time, varied across policy contexts, or both.

SAME-SEX MARRIAGE AND CIVIL UNIONS: 2003

With this point in mind, I turned to data collected a decade later. In October 2003, the Pew Research Center for the People and the Press conducted a survey that included a series of questions about gays, lesbians, and homosexuality, as well as the two gay rights policies that had come to dominate the public agenda by that time: same-sex marriage and civil unions.[25] Thus, the Pew data allow me to examine public support for gay rights at a different point in time and in two "newer" policy contexts.

Like the respondents in the 1993 ANES Pilot Study, the 1,515 respondents in the Pew survey were asked questions that measured their visceral responses, their beliefs about whether homosexuality is natural and whether it is unchangeable, and their beliefs about the morality of homosexuality (see table 3.3). Of the Pew respondents, only a small minority said that they were "uncomfortable [being] around homosexuals." A larger minority said that homosexuality is "something that people are born with," and the sample was evenly split between those saying that a person's sexual orientation can be changed and those saying that it cannot. A majority said that "it is a sin . . . to engage in homosexual behavior."

The Pew survey did not include a measure of general feelings toward gays and lesbians. It did, however, include a pair of questions that asked respondents for their "overall opinion of gay men" and their "overall opinion of lesbian women." The distributions for these two items were virtually identical, with unfavorable opinions outnumbering favorable opinions.[26] By a 2–1 margin, respondents rejected a stereotype of gays and lesbians as being "less likely to have stable, long term relationships" than "people in general."[27] The percentage of respondents saying that "more acceptance of gays and lesbians" would be bad for the country outnumbered the percentage saying that it would be good, but the percentage saying that it would not make much difference was larger than either.

I combined responses to the "born with" and "cannot be changed" items to create an index.[28] Given that opinions toward gay men and opinions toward lesbian women were strongly correlated, I combined these into an index, as well. As in 1993, the various aspects of public opinion about gays, lesbians, and homosexuality were all positively related to one another ($p < .01$ in every case).

To measure support for same-sex marriage, I used a question that asked respondents whether they strongly favored (10 percent), favored (26 percent), opposed (26 percent), or strongly opposed (39 percent) "allowing gays and lesbians to marry legally." To measure support for civil unions, I used a question that asked respondents whether they strongly favored (15 percent), favored (31 percent), opposed (22 percent), or strongly opposed (33 percent) "allowing gay and lesbian couples to enter into legal agreements with each other that would give them many of the same rights as married couples."

My models of support for the two policies included all of the various measures for public opinion about gays, lesbians, and homosexuality (see

Table 3.3. Public Opinion about Gays, Lesbians, and Homosexuality (Pew Research Center, October 2003)

Would you say . . .	
It doesn't bother you to be around homosexuals	76%
It makes you uncomfortable to be around homosexuals	20%
Don't know/refused	4%
Would you say that your overall opinion of gay men is . . .	
Very favorable	8%
Mostly favorable	30%
Mostly unfavorable	21%
Very unfavorable	29%
Don't know/refused	12%
Would you say that your overall opinion of lesbian women is . . .	
Very favorable	9%
Mostly favorable	30%
Mostly unfavorable	22%
Very unfavorable	26%
Don't know/refused	13%
In your opinion . . . when a person is homosexual is it . . .	
Something that people are born with	30%
Something that develops because of the way people are brought up	14%
Just the way that some people prefer to live	42%
Don't know/refused	14%
Do you think a gay or lesbian person's sexual orientation can be changed or cannot be changed?	
Can be changed	42%
Cannot be changed	42%
Don't know/refused	16%
Do you think that it is a sin, or not, to engage in homosexual behavior?	
Is a sin	55%
Is not a sin	33%
Don't know/refused	12%
Compared to people in general, are gays and lesbians . . .	
Less likely to have stable, long term relationships	24%
Don't think so	52%
Don't know/refused	24%
Do you think more acceptance of gays and lesbians would be . . .	
Good for country	23%
Bad for country	31%
Wouldn't make much difference	42%
Don't know/refused	4%

Note: N = 1,515

table 3.4). These models also included controls for party identification, ideology, self-identification as "born again," attendance at religious services, sex, race, age, education, and income. Neither comfort levels with gays and lesbians nor beliefs about the relative instability of gay and lesbian relationships were significantly related to support for either same-sex marriage or civil unions. Favorable opinions toward gays and lesbians were significant and powerful predictors of support for each policy, however, as were beliefs that homosexuality is innate and cannot be changed. Beliefs that "homosexual behavior" is not a sin and that acceptance of gays and lesbians would be good also played substantial roles in predicting support for both same-sex marriage and civil unions.

Differences in question wording for the independent variables preclude me from directly comparing the predictors of support for an employment nondiscrimination law and gays in the military in 1993 to the predictors of support for same-sex marriage and civil unions in 2003. Even so, the findings suggest some patterns. One is that general attitudes toward gays and lesbians (as measured by the 1993 feeling thermometer or by the 2003 opinion items) were strongly related to support for all four policies. Another pattern is that beliefs about the nature of homosexuality were related to support for all four policies. A third pattern is that visceral responses to homosexuality or to gays and lesbians exerted relatively little impact on support for the four policies. Of course, it is possible that such responses

Table 3.4. Influences on Support for Same-Sex Marriage and Civil Unions (Pew Research Center, October 2003)

	Same-sex marriage	Civil unions
Comfortable around gays and lesbians	.03	.04
	(.02)	(.03)
Favorable opinions about gays and lesbians	.25**	.28**
	(.04)	(.04)
Belief that homosexuality is something that	.07**	.11**
people are born with and cannot be changed	(.03)	(.03)
Belief that homosexual behavior is not a sin	.21**	.17**
	(.03)	(.03)
Belief that gays and lesbians are just as likely	.02	.002
to have stable relationships	(.02)	(.02)
Belief that acceptance of gays and lesbians	.21**	.24**
would be good for country	(.03)	(.03)
N	685	689

Notes: Table entries are unstandardized OLS coefficients. Standard errors are in parentheses. Models also included controls for party identification, ideology, self-identification as "born again," attendance at religious services, sex, self-identification as African American, age, education, and income.
†Significant at the .10 level
*Significant at the .05 level
**Significant at the .01 level

exerted indirect effects on support for gay rights by shaping other aspects of public opinion about gays, lesbians, and homosexuality. A final pattern is that the relationship between beliefs about the sinfulness of homosexuality and support for gay rights was stronger for same-sex marriage and civil unions in 2003 than for employment nondiscrimination and gays in the military in 1993. To the extent that this pattern is not merely an artifact of question wording, it may reflect differences between how Americans thought about the former set of policies and how they thought about the latter set of policies.

PERSONAL CONTACT, MEDIA IMAGES, AND SUPPORT FOR GAY RIGHTS

In addition to capturing public opinion about gays, lesbians, homosexuality, and gay rights, the October 2003 Pew survey provides a window into personal and virtual contact with gays and lesbians. Half of the respondents were asked, "Who is the first homosexual person that comes to your mind?" Around a fourth of these respondents said that they could not think of anyone (24 percent) or refused to answer (2 percent). Another 39 percent mentioned someone with whom they had personal contact, with 1 percent mentioning themselves or their partner, 8 percent mentioning a relative, and 30 percent mentioning a friend, acquaintance, co-worker, or neighbor. The remaining 35 percent named a public figure, with entertainment media figures dominating the roster of names. Of the 735 respondents in the split sample, fully 9 percent mentioned one person, Ellen DeGeneres. Other frequently mentioned entertainment media figures included Rosie O'Donnell, Will from *Will & Grace*, Rock Hudson, Liberace, and Elton John. Respondents were much less likely to name political figures, though a handful cited United States Representative Barney Frank or slain San Francisco politician Harvey Milk.

In looking at public opinion about gays, lesbians, homosexuality, and gay rights, a clear pattern emerges across respondents whose answers reflected personal contact, those whose answers reflected virtual contact, and those whose answers reflected neither form of contact (see figure 3.2). Compared to respondents who did not mention a gay person, those who mentioned a public figure were more likely to say that they felt comfortable around gays and lesbians ($p < .01$), to hold positive opinions about gay men and lesbians ($p < .01$), to believe that homosexuality is innate and unchangeable ($p < .10$), to believe that homosexual behavior is not a sin ($p < .01$), to reject the notion that same-sex relationships are particularly unstable ($p < .10$), and to say that acceptance of homosexuality would be good

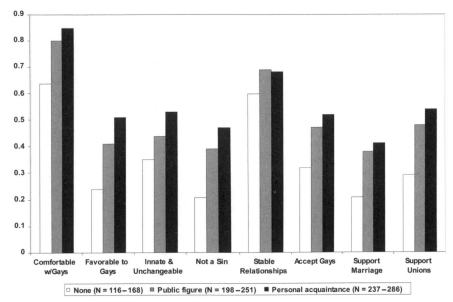

Figure 3.2. Public Opinion about Gays and Lesbians, Homosexuality, Same-Sex Marriage, and Civil Unions by Choice of "First Homosexual Person That Comes to Mind" (Pew Research Center, October 2003)

for the country (p <.01). They were also more likely to support same-sex marriage (p <.01) and civil unions (p <.01).

Respondents who mentioned personal contact, in turn, tended to hold more positive opinions than did those who mentioned virtual contact. Specifically, the former were more likely than the latter to say that they felt comfortable around gays and lesbians (p <.10), to hold positive opinions about gay men and lesbians (p <.01), to believe that homosexuality is innate and unchangeable (p <.05), to believe that homosexual behavior is not a sin (p <.10), and to support civil unions (p <.10). Significant differences between these two groups did not emerge on beliefs about the relative stability of same-sex relationships, the acceptance of homosexuality, or support for same-sex marriage. Compared to respondents who did not mention a gay person, however, those who mentioned personal contact were significantly more accepting of homosexuality (p <.01) and supportive of same-sex marriage (p <.01).

To be sure, neither personal contact nor virtual contact was evenly distributed across the sample. Female respondents, younger respondents, and highly educated respondents were more likely to mention personal contact than were male respondents, older respondents, and less educated respondents; moreover, younger respondents were more likely to mention virtual contact.[29] Even when I controlled for such background characteristics, however, I found similar patterns of relationships between contact—be it personal or virtual—and favorable opinions about gays, lesbians, homo-sexuality, and gay rights.[30]

It seems reasonable to assume that at least part of each relationship be-tween contact and opinion reflected the impact of the former on the latter. Then again, it is also plausible that the latter could have influenced the for-mer, at least in some cases. For example, respondents with favorable opin-ions toward gays and lesbians may have been more inclined than those with unfavorable opinions to seek out (or at least not avoid) contact with gay men and lesbians or to watch television shows with gay characters. Then again, it seems less plausible that views on specific policies—for example, opinions about same-sex marriage or civil unions—would have influenced contact with gays and lesbians, rather than the other way around. An addi-tional complication comes from the potential for indirect effects. Personal or virtual contact could have shaped public opinion about gay rights by shaping public opinion about gays, lesbians, and homosexuality; at the same time, public opinion about gays, lesbians, and homosexuality could have influenced support for gay rights by influencing contact.

Though the data did not allow me to disentangle such relationships, the Pew survey included a question specifically about media images of gays and lesbians. Respondents were asked, "Do you think the entertainment media are including too many gay themes and characters these days, not enough gay themes and characters, or about the right amount?" Only 3 percent said "not enough." Another 40 percent said "the right amount," but a plurality of 48 percent said "too many." The results stood in contrast to those from a 2000 Kaiser Family Foundation poll in which 52 percent said "the right amount" and 37 percent said "too many."[31] At first glance, such a pattern suggests the possibility that the increasing visibility of gays and lesbians in the media produced a backlash in public opinion. Indeed, respondents who said that there were "too many gay themes and characters" were par-ticularly likely to hold unfavorable views on every aspect of public opinion toward gays, lesbians, and homosexuality, even after controlling for back-ground characteristics. Curiously, however, these same respondents were not particularly likely to mention public figures when asked to name the first gay person who came to mind.[32] Thus, it may be that opinions about gay themes and characters in the media merely reflected opinions about gays, lesbians, and homosexuality.

Another potential explanation for the pattern of poll results on this ques-tion involves the nature of elite messages in public debate. Gay rights op-ponents expended considerable effort in promoting the argument that gays, lesbians, and homosexuality receive too much attention in the media, with the debate over *Brokeback Mountain* representing but one battle in a larger

campaign. Perhaps no figure drew more attention for advancing this argument than Reverend Jerry Falwell. In addition to calling Ellen DeGeneres
"Ellen DeGenerate," he accused children's television character Tinky Winky
(of *Teletubbies*) of "role-modeling the gay lifestyle [that is] damaging to
children" and denounced beer company Anheuser-Busch for running an
advertisement that "presents two Bud-drinking homosexual men in a hand-
holding posture."[33] In the same vein, James Dobson of Focus on the Family
argued that children's television characters such as SpongeBob SquarePants,
the Muppets, and Barney were "being hijacked to promote an agenda that involves teaching homosexual propaganda to children."[34] In a study of public
opinion about media bias, Mark Watts and his colleagues concluded that perceptions of a liberal bias reflected elite messages about such bias rather than
the nature of news coverage itself.[35] By a similar logic, opinions about gay
themes and characters in entertainment television may have reflected elite
messages about these themes and characters rather than (or in addition to)
their actual presence.

SHIFTING OPINIONS AND SHIFTING NORMS
IN PUBLIC DEBATE

Public opinion about gays, lesbians, and homosexuality was a key influence
on public opinion about gay rights during the 1990s and beyond. In 1993,
beliefs about homosexuality and feelings toward gays and lesbians helped
to explain support for an employment nondiscrimination law and gays in
the military. In 2003, these beliefs and feelings helped to explain support
for same-sex marriage and civil unions. The presence of such relationships
highlights one potential reason behind the increase in public support for a
range of gay rights policies during the same period: the transformation in
public opinion toward gays, lesbians, and homosexuality may have helped
to produce a parallel transformation in public opinion about gay rights. In
chapter 6, I revisit this possibility.

For now, however, I focus on how the first of these transformations may
have altered the nature of public debate not only regarding gays, lesbians,
and homosexuality but also gay rights. One potential outgrowth of the de-
crease in negative feelings toward gays and lesbians—and the accompany-
ing increase in acceptance of homosexuality—was an emergent norm
against "gay bashing" in public debate. During the early years of the debate
over gay rights, opponents frequently appealed to anti-gay sentiments.
Anita Bryant's "Save Our Children" campaign of 1977 was a case in point.
In one fundraising letter, she wrote, "I don't hate the homosexuals! But as
a mother, I must protect my children from their evil influence. When homosexuals burn the holy Bible in public, how can I stand by silently?"[36]

Such appeals persisted through the 1990s and beyond, yet this period also saw a number of public figures receive widespread opprobrium for engaging in what appeared to be overt appeals to anti-gay sentiment. When House Majority Whip Dick Armey referred to fellow Congressman Barney Frank as "Barney Fag" in 1995, he suffered a barrage of negative publicity that prompted him to explain his choice of words as a slip of the tongue.[37] In 1998, former National Football League star Reggie White faced a similar fallout from a speech to the Wisconsin Assembly in which he called homosexuality "one of the biggest sins," said that he was offended that homosexuals "compare their plight with the plight of black people," and stated that "homosexuality is a decision."[38] Jerry Falwell and Pat Robertson were subjected to particularly fierce criticism for remarks that they made on the Christian Broadcasting Network's *700 Club* program shortly after the terrorist attacks of September 11, 2001. Falwell said, "I really believe that the pagans, and the abortionists, and the feminists, and the gays and the lesbians who are actively trying to make that an alternative lifestyle, the ACLU, People for the American Way—all of them who have tried to secularize America—I point the finger in their face and say, 'You helped this happen,'" to which Robertson responded, "I totally concur."[39] Two years later, MSNBC fired talk show host Michael Savage for telling a caller, "Oh, you're one of those sodomites! You should get AIDS and die, you pig!"[40]

In broader terms, the shifting terrain of public opinion about gays, lesbians, and homosexuality presented challenges to politicians and other political actors who had to negotiate it. Two illustrations of this came in the third presidential debate between George W. Bush and John Kerry, which took place on October 13, 2004. Moderator Bob Schieffer asked Bush a question about the nature of homosexuality: "Both of you are opposed to gay marriage. But to understand how you have come to that conclusion, I want to ask you a more basic question. Do you believe homosexuality is a choice?" The question placed Bush in a difficult situation, as an answer in either direction would have contradicted the views of a substantial proportion of the public. He responded as follows:

> You know, Bob, I don't know. I just don't know. I do know that we have a choice to make in America and that is to treat people with tolerance and respect and dignity. It's important that we do that. And I also know in a free society people, consenting adults can live the way they want to live. And that's to be honored. But as we respect someone's rights, and as we profess tolerance, we shouldn't change—or have to change—our basic views on the sanctity of marriage.

Thus, he avoided taking any position on the origins of homosexuality while endorsing the increasingly popular stance of accepting homosexuality (and rejecting the less-popular stance of favoring same-sex marriage).

In contrast, Bush's opponent answered the question. Specifically, he rebutted the notion that homosexuality is a choice (and advocated social acceptance of gays and lesbians) by citing what he had learned from personal contact:

> We're all God's children, Bob. And I think if you were to talk to Dick Cheney's daughter [Mary Cheney], who is a lesbian, she would tell you that she's being who she was, she's being who she was born as. I think if you talk to anybody, it's not choice. I've met people who struggled with this for years, people who were in a marriage because they were living a sort of convention, and they struggled with it. And I've met wives who are supportive of their husbands or vice versa when they finally sort of broke out and allowed themselves to live who they were, who they felt God had made them. I think we have to respect that.

Kerry's answer may have backfired, however, as figures in the Bush campaign—first, Lynn Cheney (Mary Cheney's mother), then Dick Cheney, and finally Bush himself—criticized him for mentioning the vice president's daughter. A *Washington Post* poll found that two in three likely voters viewed Kerry's mention of Mary Cheney as "inappropriate."[41] Some of Kerry's critics even argued that his invocation of her sexual orientation was, in itself, a covert appeal to anti-gay feelings and beliefs.[42]

A final point to consider is that the politics of gay rights may have shaped public opinion about gays, lesbians, and homosexuality, in addition to the latter shaping the former. One piece of evidence for such an impact comes from Gallup polls conducted before and after the June 2003 United States Supreme Court decision in *Lawrence v. Texas*.[43] Recall from chapter 2 that public support for same-sex marriage and civil unions exhibited short-term declines in the immediate aftermath of the decision and the wave of media coverage that accompanied it, a pattern that indicates a public backlash. During the same period, Gallup polls also showed evidence of a decline in the percentage of Americans who said that "homosexuality should be considered an acceptable alternative lifestyle." In May 2003, 54 percent of the respondents said yes and 44 percent said no, whereas 46 percent said yes and 49 percent said no in July 2003.[44] This backlash in social acceptance of homosexuality was temporary; by 2004, the percentage saying yes had rebounded to 54 percent. Nevertheless, its emergence suggests that a key development in the politics of gay rights carried implications for what Americans thought about homosexuality. The same logic may work in the other direction, as well: changes in the political landscape surrounding gay rights could also produce shifts in the direction of more favorable beliefs and feelings regarding gays, lesbians, and homosexuality.

NOTES

1. According to the Internet Movie Database (www.imdb.com), *Brokeback Mountain* grossed $83,025,853 domestically.

2. *NBC Nightly News* aired Bush's reply on January 23, 2006.

3. Clyde Wilcox and Robin Wolpert, "President Clinton, Public Opinion, and Gays in the Military," in *Gay Rights, Military Wrongs: Political Perspectives on Lesbians and Gays in the Military*, ed. Craig A. Rimmerman (New York: Garland Publishing, 1996), 127–45; Clyde Wilcox and Robin Wolpert, "Gay Rights in the Public Sphere: Public Opinion on Gay and Lesbian Equality," in *The Politics of Gay Rights*, ed. Craig A. Rimmerman, Kenneth D. Wald, and Clyde Wilcox (Chicago: University of Chicago Press, 2000), 409–32; Peter B. Wood and John P. Bartkowski, "Attribution Style and Public Policy Attitudes Toward Gay Rights," *Social Science Quarterly* 85 (2004): 58–74. For a critical perspective on the term "homophobia," see Gregory M. Herek, "Stigma, Prejudice, and Violence against Lesbians and Gay Men," in *Homosexuality: Research Implications for Public Policy*, ed. John C. Gonsiorek and James D. Weinrich (Newbury Park, Calif.: Sage, 1991), 60–80.

4. For additional evidence on trends in public opinion about gays, lesbians, and homosexuality, see Karlyn Bowman, "Attitudes about Homosexuality and Gay Marriage" (Washington, DC: American Enterprise Institute, 2006); Alan S. Yang, "Trends: Attitudes toward Homosexuality," *Public Opinion Quarterly* 61 (1997): 477–507.

5. See chapter 6 for additional details.

6. Alan S. Yang, "Trends: Attitudes toward Homosexuality," 491.

7. For the seminal discussion of prejudice as a psychological construct, see Gordon W. Allport, *The Nature of Prejudice* (New York: Doubleday, 1954).

8. Paul R. Brewer, "The Shifting Foundations of Public Opinion about Gay Rights," *Journal of Politics* 65 (2003): 1208–20; Stephen C. Craig, Michael D. Martinez, James G. Kane, and Jason Gainous, "Core Values, Value Conflict, and Citizens' Ambivalence about Gay Rights," *Political Research Quarterly* 58 (2005): 5–17; Douglas Alan Strand, "Civil Liberties, Civil Rights, and Stigma: Voter Attitudes and Behavior in the Politics of Homosexuality," in *Stigma and Sexual Orientation: Understanding Prejudice against Lesbians, Gay Men, and Bisexuals*, ed. Gregory M. Herek (Thousand Oaks, Calif.: Sage, 1998), 108–37; Wilcox and Wolpert, "President Clinton"; Wilcox and Wolpert, "Gay Rights in the Public Sphere."

9. Donald P. Haider-Markel and Mark R. Joslyn, "Attributions and the Regulation of Marriage: Considering the Parallels between Race and Homosexuality," *PS: Political Science & Politics* 38 (2005): 233–39; Gregory B. Lewis and Marc A. Rogers, "Does the Public Support Equal Employment Rights For Gays and Lesbians?" in *Gays and Lesbians in the Democratic Process*, ed. Ellen D. B. Riggle and Barry L. Tadlock (New York: Columbia University Press, 1999), 118–45; Clyde Wilcox and Barbara Norrander, "Of Moods and Morals: The Dynamics of Opinion on Abortion and Gay Rights," in *Understanding Public Opinion*, 2nd ed., ed. Barbara Norrander and Clyde Wilcox (Washington, DC: Congressional Quarterly Press, 2002), 121–48; Wilcox and Wolpert, "President Clinton"; Wilcox and Wolpert, "Gay Rights in the Public Sphere"; Bernard E. Whitley, "The Relationship of Heterosexuals' Attributions

for the Causes of Homosexuality to Attitudes toward Lesbians and Gay Men," *Personality and Social Psychology Bulletin* 16 (1990): 369–97; Wood and Bartkowski, "Attribution Style."

10. Haider-Markel and Joslyn, "Attributions and the Regulation of Marriage"; Wood and Bartkowski, "Attribution Style."

11. Lewis and Rogers, "Equal Employment Rights"; Wilcox and Norrander, "Of Moods and Morals."

12. Wilcox and Wolpert, "President Clinton"; Wilcox and Wolpert, "Gay Rights in the Public Sphere."

13. Walter Lippmann, *Public Opinion* (New York: Macmillan, [1922] 1965), 59.

14. Herek, "Stigma, Prejudice, and Violence against Lesbians and Gay Men"; Gregory M. Herek, "Gender Gaps in Public Opinion about Lesbians and Gay Men," *Public Opinion Quarterly* 66 (2002): 40–66.

15. Wilcox and Norrander, "Of Moods and Morals," 140.

16. David Ari Bianco, "Echoes of Prejudice: The Debates Over Race and Sexuality in the Armed Forces," in *Gay Rights, Military Wrongs: Political Perspectives on Lesbians and Gays in the Military*, ed. Craig A. Rimmerman (New York: Garland Publishing, 1996), 47–70.

17. Wilcox and Norrander, "Of Moods and Morals"; Wood and Bartkowski, "Attribution Style."

18. Gregory M. Herek and John P. Capitanio, "'Some of My Best Friends': Intergroup Contact, Concealable Stigma, and Heterosexuals' Attitudes toward Gay Men and Lesbians," *Personality and Social Psychology Bulletin* 22 (1996): 414–24; Lewis and Rogers, "Equal Employment Rights"; Wilcox and Norrander, "Of Moods and Morals"; Wilcox and Wolpert, "President Clinton"; Wilcox and Wolpert, "Gay Rights in the Public Sphere"; Wood and Bartkowski, "Attribution Style."

19. Edward Alwood, *Straight News: Gays, Lesbians, and the News Media* (New York: Columbia University Press, 1996); Larry Gross, *Up from Invisibility: Lesbians, Gay Men, and the Media in America* (New York: Columbia University Press, 2001); Suzanna Danuta Walters, *All the Rage: The Story of Gay Visibility in America* (Chicago: University of Chicago Press, 2001).

20. Gross, *Up from Invisibility*, 112.

21. Edward Schiappa, Peter B. Gregg, and Dean A. Hewes, "Can One TV Show Make a Difference? *Will & Grace* and the Parasocial Contact Hypothesis," *Journal of Homosexuality* 51 (2006): 15–37.

22. See appendix B for details on coding.

23. Nonrespondents were excluded from the analyses in this chapter.

24. See chapter 2.

25. Pew Research Center for the People and the Press, "Republicans Unified, Democrats Split on Same-Sex Marriage; Religious Beliefs Underpin Opposition to Homosexuality" (Washington, DC: Pew Research Center for the People and the Press, 2003).

26. For a discussion of distinctions between public opinion about gay men and public opinion about lesbians, see Herek, "Gender Gaps."

27. The Pew survey included two additional questions that captured stereotypes of gays and lesbians. The first asked, "Do most gay men have a better sense of style

than most heterosexual men [34 percent], or don't you think so [44 percent; don't know/refused, 22 percent]?" The second asked, "Do you think most gays and lesbians are unhappier than most people [24 percent], or don't you think so [57 percent; don't know/refused, 19 percent]?" When I included these measures in the models described below, neither emerged as a significant predictor of support for same-sex marriage or civil unions.

28. See appendix B for coding details.

29. These findings came from logistic regression analyses that also included race, income, party identification, ideology, endorsement of evangelical doctrine, and attendance at religious services. None of these other variables was significantly related to personal contact or virtual contact.

30. Specifically, I estimated models for each aspect of opinion that included sex, race, age, education, income, party identification, ideology, endorsement of evangelical doctrine, and attendance at religious services, as well as dummy variables for personal contact and virtual contact. All of the coefficients for personal contact and virtual contact had the expected positive signs. These coefficients were also statistically significant except in a few cases (personal contact for the "stable" item; virtual contact for the "nature" index, the "sin" item, and the "stable" item).

31. Pew Research Center for the People and the Press, "Republicans Unified, Democrats Split on Same-Sex Marriage."

32. As one might expect, personal contact was negatively related to saying that there are too many gay themes and characters.

33. Quoted in Christine Sparta, "Falwell: Teletubby Looks Way Too Gay for Kids' Well-Being," *USA Today*, 11 February 1999, 2D; Twila Decker, "With Rants, Falwell Outs Products to Popularity," *St. Petersburg Times*, 15 May 1999, 3 (Citrus Times Section).

34. Quoted in Jean Torkelson, "SpongeBob Flap Sends Dobson on Media Blitz: Focus on Family Founder Says Video's Agenda Is 'Sinister,'" *Rocky Mountain News*, 1 February 2005, 20A.

35. Mark D. Watts, David Domke, Dhavan V. Shah, and David P. Fan, "Elite Cues and Media Bias in Presidential Campaigns: Explaining Public Perceptions of a Liberal Press," *Communication Research* 26 (1999): 144–75.

36. John Gallagher and Chris Bull, *Perfect Enemies: The Battle between the Religious Right and the Gay Movement*, updated ed. (New York: Madison Books, 2001), 16.

37. Gallagher and Bull, *Perfect Enemies*, 252. Frank replied that he "turned to my own expert, my mother, who reports that in fifty-nine years of marriage, no one ever introduced her as Elsie Fag."

38. Quoted in Amy Rinard, "Speech by White Upsets Assembly with Views on Race, Homosexuality," *Milwaukee Journal Sentinel*, 26 March 1998, 1. White also received condemnation for endorsing a variety of racial and ethnic stereotypes in his speech.

39. Quoted in John F. Harris, "Falwell Apologizes for Remark," *Washington Post*, 18 September 2001, C4.

40. Quoted in Dan Fost, "Savage Says He's Sorry—But Stays Fired; Talk Show Host Insists Epithets Not Aimed at People with AIDS," *San Francisco Chronicle*, 9 July 2003, A2.

41. Richard Morin, "Singling Out Mary Cheney Wrong, Most Say; 2 in 3 Find Kerry's Comment 'Inappropriate,'" *Washington Post*, 17 October 2004, A5.

42. See, for example, William Safire, "The Lowest Blow: The Kerry Campaign Believes Cheney's Daughter Is 'Fair Game,'" *New York Times*, 18 October 2004, A17. In the vice presidential debate on October 5, 2004, Democratic nominee John Edwards had responded to a question about a constitutional ban on same-sex marriage with a similar reference to Mary Cheney: "Now, as to this question, let me say first that I think the vice president and his wife love their daughter. I think they love her very much. And you can't have anything but respect for the fact that they're willing to talk about the fact that they have a gay daughter, the fact that they embrace her. It's a wonderful thing. And there are millions of parents like that who love their children, who want their children to be happy." Cheney replied by saying, "Let me simply thank the senator for the kind words he said about my family and our daughter. I appreciate that very much." Unlike Kerry's response, Edwards's comments stirred little controversy at the time.

43. *Lawrence v. Texas*, 539 U.S. 558 (2003).

44. Frank Newport, "Public Shifts to More Conservative Stance on Gay Rights; Change Comes in Aftermath of Supreme Court Decision" (Washington, DC: Gallup Organization, 2003). Figure 3.1 presents the average of the two 2003 figures for the "acceptable" option.

4

From the Podium and the Pulpit: Opinion Leadership and Gay Rights

SENATOR SANTORUM: You say, well, it's my individual freedom. Yes, but it destroys the basic unit of our society because it condones behavior that's antithetical to strong healthy families. Whether it's polygamy, whether it's adultery, where it's sodomy, all of those things, are antithetical to a healthy, stable, traditional family. Every society in the history of man has upheld the institution of marriage as a bond between a man and a woman. Why? Because society is based on one thing: that society is based on the future of the society. And that's what? Children. Monogamous relationships. In every society, the definition of marriage has not ever to my knowledge included homosexuality. That's not to pick on homosexuality. It's not, you know, man on child, man on dog, or whatever the case may be. It is one thing. And when you destroy that you have a dramatic impact on the quality—

REPORTER: I'm sorry, I didn't think I was going to talk about "man on dog" with a United States senator, it's sort of freaking me out.

—Associated Press interview with U.S. Senator Rick Santorum (R-Pa.), April 7, 2003

On April 7, 2003, Senator Rick Santorum signaled his opposition to same-sex marriage in no uncertain terms. In doing so, he also advanced a specific rationale for his position: the argument that legal recognition of same-sex marriage would undermine the "traditional family." Even before he made these remarks, the junior senator from Pennsylvania was known in Washington circles for his social conservatism. After the interview was published on April 21, however, Santorum's views on same-sex marriage received a new level of attention not only from his fellow politicians but also from the mass media.

Not surprisingly, gay rights activists condemned his statement. The Human Rights Campaign, for example, labeled it "deeply hurtful"; spokesperson David Smith called it "one of the most egregiously anti-gay statements that I have ever heard."[1] Prominent Democrats—including Senate Majority Leader Tom Daschle, House Minority Leader Nancy Pelosi, Senator (and presidential contender) John Kerry, and Vermont Governor (and presidential contender) Howard Dean—also castigated Santorum for his remarks.[2] Some went on to argue that the senator should step down from his position as the chairman of the Republican conference in the Senate, the number three leadership position in that body. In effect, Santorum's critics argued that he had violated a norm against gay bashing in public debate.

Conservative activists came to the senator's defense, however, rebutting the charge of gay bashing and casting his remarks as principled opposition to same-sex marriage. Ken Connor of the Family Research Council said that those condemning Santorum were trying "to intimidate defenders of marriage and silence critics of the homosexual political agenda."[3] Likewise, Paul Weyrich of the Free Congress Foundation said that the senator was "defending the sanctity of marriage" and "family values as defined by the Bible."[4]

Santorum's own party showed signs of division. Some Republicans—including Senator Majority Leader Bill Frist (TN) and the senior senator from Pennsylvania, Arlen Specter—quickly rallied to his side.[5] Others, however, expressed disapproval of his remarks; their ranks included Senators Lincoln Chafee (R-RI), Gordon Smith (R-OR), and Olympia Snowe (R-ME).[6] Connor and the Family Research Council, in turn, criticized Republican leaders for failing to provide a "spirited defense" of Santorum.[7] On April 25, after four days of silence, President George W. Bush signaled support for Santorum—if not necessarily for his comments—through White House Press Secretary Ari Fleischer, who stated, "The president believes that the senator is an inclusive man."[8] This vote of confidence did not satisfy Connor, who said, "The administration has offered only timid support to Senator Rick Santorum, but little defense of marriage against the ugly attacks of the extremist homosexual lobby."[9] In the end, the senator kept his leadership post.

The statements made by Santorum, his critics, and his defenders illustrate the sorts of messages regarding gay rights that would-be shapers of opinion sent to the public during the 1990s and beyond. Moreover, Santorum's claim that same-sex marriage would undermine the traditional family reflected one of the most common frames in the public debate about gay rights. In this chapter, I consider the signals about gay rights that Americans received from liberal and conservative political elites; from Republican and Democratic politicians, including those in the White House; and from national religious figures and their own clergy. In doing so, I focus on a crucial two-year period in the debate about same-sex marriage and civil unions. I then provide evidence that signals in this debate shaped public opinion about gay rights and public acceptance of frames for gay rights. I also argue, however, that sending signals about gay rights carried potential costs for some political elites.

OPINION LEADERSHIP

In *The Reasoning Voter*, Samuel Popkin highlights three lines of research that have shaped our understanding of the ways in which political and social elites lead public opinion.[10] The first comes from sociology: the seminal research on mass persuasion conducted by scholars in the "Columbia school."[11] Their work emphasizes the social and indirect nature of influence. According to the "two-step flow of communication" model that they developed, opinion elites (e.g., politicians and leaders of prominent organizations) influence opinion leaders—that is, particularly active, attentive, and socially connected citizens—who then influence ordinary members of the public. For example, a national religious figure might sway the opinions of local clergy, who, in turn, might sway members of their congregations. The work of the Columbia scholars also emphasizes how political predispositions such as partisan loyalties shape—and often limit— the impact of mass communication. Put another way, citizens are not empty vessels; they approach signals from would-be persuaders with their own filters in the form of self-reinforcing prior beliefs.

The second line of research that Popkin highlights comes from economics— specifically, Anthony Downs's economic theory of democracy.[12] According to Downs, few people devote the time and energy necessary to become well informed about public affairs because the rewards of doing so rarely match the costs. Instead, most people rely on information shortcuts in making their political decisions. For example, they reduce politics into ideological and partisan terms—liberals versus conservatives, Republicans versus Democrats—and base their decisions on who stands where in this simplified political world. Building on both the Columbia school's model of mass persuasion and Downs's notion of information shortcuts, Popkin argues that citizens use what he calls "low-information rationality" to behave as though they are informed: in reaching specific judgments, they rely on cues, or signals, from sources who share their general viewpoints.

Popkin also highlights a third line of research, the study of framing. As he observes, people's decisions depend in part on what frames of reference they use. Here, I focus on the sociological understanding of frames as definitions of what controversies "are about."[13] For example, Santorum sought to frame the dispute over same-sex marriage as being about the preservation of the "traditional family," rather than, say, equal marriage rights for gays and lesbians. When frames in elite debate reach the public, they can shape not only what opinions people hold but also how they form those opinions.[14] The mass audience for elite framing is not a completely passive one, however. Instead, people bring their own beliefs to the frames that they encounter.[15] For example, they can judge frames on the basis of their sources, accepting those that come from trusted sources and rejecting those that do not.[16]

Bill Clinton and Public Opinion about Gays in the Military

President Bill Clinton's ill-fated 1993 push to overturn the ban on gays in the military provides one opportunity to look at the impact of elite leadership on public opinion about gay rights. During the 1992 presidential campaign, Clinton had pledged to lift the ban. Shortly after his inauguration, he attempted to make good on this promise. His decision to do so sparked considerable controversy, with the ensuing debate about gays in the military drawing the attention of a substantial proportion of the public. In August 1993, 81 percent of the respondents in a Pew survey said that they were following the issue "very" or "fairly" closely. Thus, news of President Clinton's stance regarding the issue undoubtedly reached many citizens. To test the impact of this signal, Michael Bailey and his colleagues took advantage of an American National Election Studies panel survey in which respondents were interviewed during the 1992 presidential campaign and then reinterviewed in 1993.[17] The researchers found that Clinton's stand shifted public opinion toward greater support, particularly among those who strongly supported him. They also found, however, that Clinton's popularity declined among those who opposed allowing gays and lesbians to serve in the military. In short, the president was able to lead opinion, but at a cost.

Elite Signals and Polarization Effects

In *The Nature and Origins of Mass Opinion*, John Zaller provides another approach for thinking about—and capturing—the effects of elite signals on public opinion.[18] He begins with the notion that people form their opinions partly on the basis of messages from elites who are on "their side" of a belief spectrum. For example, conservatives among the public should tend to follow conservative elites' signals about whether to favor gay rights while rejecting liberal elites' signals regarding the same subject. Liberals among the public, in turn, should tend to do just the opposite. Thus, contrasts between the signals of conservative and liberal elites should be reflected in contrasts between the opinions of conservative and liberal members of the public. By the same logic, Republican and Democratic partisans should diverge when Republican and Democratic elites send contrasting signals. Extending the argument even further, those who support and oppose the president may diverge in how they respond to signals from the White House, just as evangelical Christians and nonevangelicals may diverge in how they respond to signals from evangelical elites.

Zaller's account focuses on signals that flow from elites to the public through the mass media, rather than through the two-step flow of interpersonal influence. Accordingly, he argues that the potential impact of elite signals on people's opinions should depend not only on who is doing the signaling but also on how much attention audience members pay to public debate, especially as covered in the mass media. Specifically, Zaller posits that "people tend to resist arguments that are inconsistent with their political predispositions, but they do so only to the extent that they possess the contextual information necessary to perceive a relationship between the message and their predispositions."[19] In other words, increased awareness translates into an increased propensity to reject signals from opposing elites but *not* an increased propensity to reject signals from elites on one's own side of the belief spectrum. Thus, elite polarization along partisan, ideological, or doctrinal lines should be reflected more strongly in the opinions of the politically aware than in the opinions of the relatively unaware.[20] By a similar logic, opinion gaps between the president's supporters and opponents may be widest among the most politically aware. Testing for such "polarization effects" provides an indirect means for demonstrating the impact of elite signals on opinion.

ELITE SIGNALS ABOUT SAME-SEX MARRIAGE AND CIVIL UNIONS

Not long after the controversy over Santorum's comments, a series of high-profile events brought increased media attention to same-sex marriage and civil unions. In June 2003, the United States Supreme Court struck down sodomy laws as unconstitutional in *Lawrence v. Texas*.[21] In November, the Massachusetts Supreme Judicial Court ruled in *Goodridge v. Department of Public Health* that the state had no right to deny gay and lesbian couples the right to marry.[22] Within a few months, public officials in several locales—including San Francisco—were performing same-sex marriages (which would later be ruled invalid), and proposals to amend the United States Constitution and a number of state constitutions to define marriage as being between a man and a woman were winding their way through the political process.

During this time, prominent conservative organizations and activists signaled opposition to same-sex marriage and civil unions, while many of their liberal counterparts signaled support. A number of conservative groups—including the Family Research Council, the Free Congress Foundation, James Dobson's Focus on the Family, Gary Bauer's American Values, and William Bennett's Empower America—formed the Arlington Group to campaign against both same-sex marriage and civil unions.[23] Other conservative organizations, including those belonging to the Alliance for Marriage, chose to focus their efforts on same-sex marriage rather than civil unions. Even these organizations, however, tended to cast the latter in unfavorable terms; for example, Institute for Marriage and Public Policy president Maggie Gallagher labeled them an "unwise step."[24] On the other side of the ideological spectrum, People for the American Way hailed the *Goodridge* decision as "victory in Massachusetts."[25] Similarly, the American Civil Liberties Union issued a press release titled, "ACLU Cheers Massachusetts High Court Decision Not to Deny Same-Sex Couples Right to Marry."[26] Kim Gandy, president of the National Organization for Women, declared that sex was not "relevant to the right to marry."[27]

Though the signals on these topics from conservative and liberal elites clearly diverged, Republican and Democratic politicians did not necessarily present such a sharp contrast. On the Republican side, opposition to same-sex marriage was widespread and unambiguous. President Bush issued a statement proclaiming that, "Marriage is a sacred institution between a man and a woman."[28] Senate Majority Leader Frist took a similar stance, as did numerous other prominent Republicans.[29] Leading Democrats, however, also publicly stated their opposition to same-sex marriage (just as President Clinton had supported the Defense of Marriage Act in 1996). For example, all of the "major" contenders for the 2004 Democratic presidential nomination—General Wesley Clark, Governor Howard Dean, Senators John Edwards, Joseph Lieberman, and eventual nominee John Kerry—came out against legal marriage for gay and lesbian couples; only the "minor" contenders—Senator Carol Moseley Braun (IL), Rep. Dennis Kucinich (OH), and Reverend Al Sharpton—favored it.[30]

On the subject of civil unions, all of the Democratic presidential hopefuls were united in support. Here, however, leaders of the Republican Party took opaque stances, thereby blurring the contrast with the Democrats. In a December 16, 2003 interview, President Bush said that he would, "if necessary . . . support a constitutional amendment which would honor marriage between a man and a woman," but he also said that the "position of this administration is that whatever legal arrangements people want to make, they're allowed to make, so long as it's embraced by the state or start at the state level."[31] To some observers, the latter statement not only sounded like an implicit endorsement of civil unions; it also recalled Vice President Dick Cheney's comment in the October 5, 2000 vice presidential debate that "we ought to do everything we can to tolerate and accommodate whatever kind of relationships people want to enter into."

Religious elites entered the debate, as well. Prominent evangelicals, including religious broadcaster Reverend Pat Robertson, Reverend Jerry Falwell, and Reverend Franklin Graham (the president of the Billy Graham Evangelistic Association), spoke out against same-sex marriage, civil unions, or both.[32] Furthermore, many of the conservative organizations that made up the Arlington Group had ties to evangelical Christianity.[33] The evangelical Southern Baptist Convention, representing over 16 million church members, also condemned same-sex marriage.[34] In contrast, mainline Protestant denominations such as the Episcopal Church USA, the Evangelical Lutheran Church in America, the United Church of Christ, and the United Methodist Church sent mixed or supportive signals regarding same-sex marriage and civil unions.[35]

TESTING FOR POLARIZATION EFFECTS

Half of the respondents in an August 2003 Pew survey said that they were following "the issue of gay and lesbian marriage" very or fairly closely. By February 2004, three months after the *Goodridge* decision in Massachusetts, that figure had risen to 58 percent. In March 2004, it stood at 62 percent. Thus, it seems reasonable to assume that some—but not all—Americans received the signals about same-sex marriage and civil unions that various elites sent during this period. Following Zaller's model, it also seems plausible to assume that politically attentive Americans would have been particularly likely to receive these signals.[36]

If so, then the sorts of polarization effects described by Zaller should have emerged among the public when—but perhaps only when—elites on opposing sides of a given belief divide clearly diverged in the signals that they sent to the public. Using data from a series of Pew surveys, I tested for such patterns in public opinion about same-sex marriage and civil unions.[37] On both of these subjects, one would expect more favorable opinions among liberals than among conservatives, among Democrats than among Republicans, among Bush opponents than among Bush supporters, and among nonevangelicals than among evangelicals.[38] For the purpose at hand, however, the central question is whether these opinion divides were wider among the politically attentive than among the less attentive.

Elite Signals and Public Opinion about Same-Sex Marriage

Given the clear contrast between conservative and liberal elites on same-sex marriage, I expected political attentiveness to magnify the gap between liberal and conservative Americans on support for legal recognition of marriages between same-sex couples. In light of the overwhelming opposition to same-sex marriage among evangelical elites combined with the more diverse range of signals from nonevangelical elites, I also expected polarization along doctrinal lines to be greatest among the most attentive Americans. In light of Bush's clear position on the issue, I expected political attentiveness to magnify an opinion gap between Bush supporters and opponents. I did not necessarily expect such a polarization effect along party lines, however, given that both Republican and Democratic elites opposed same-sex marriage.

Between June 2003 and August 2004, the Pew Research Center for the People and the Press conducted seven surveys that included the same question about same-sex marriage: "Do you strongly favor, favor, oppose, or strongly oppose allowing gays and lesbians to marry legally?" Support ranged from 29 percent to 38 percent, with opposition ranging from 53 percent to 63 percent. Each survey also included measures for ideology, partisanship, approval of the president's job performance, and endorsement of evangelical religious doctrine.[39] Furthermore, each survey included measures of key background characteristics: attendance at religious services, sex, self-identification as African American, age, education, and income. I pooled the data from all seven surveys for my analysis.[40]

Testing for polarization effects requires a measure of political attentiveness. The Pew surveys did not include the sorts of items that Zaller identifies as ideal measures of the concept: namely, questions assessing factual knowledge of politics.[41] Nor did all seven surveys include the item asking respondents how closely they had been following "the issue of gay and lesbian marriage." Instead, I used education as a proxy for political attentiveness—a reasonable strategy given that education is a powerful and robust predictor of political knowledge.[42] I multiplied my measures of ideology, partisanship, presidential approval, and religious doctrine by education to create terms that would capture the extent to which the impact of each variable differed across education and, by extension, political attentiveness.

These multiplicative terms captured the polarization effects that I expected (see table 4.1, first column). Consider, for example, the negative coefficient for ideology x education, which indicates that the impact of ideology varied across education levels. Among the least educated respondents, conservatives were significantly less supportive of same-sex marriage than were liberals.[43] This divide was four times as wide, however, among the most educated respondents—that is, the ones most likely to receive the diverging signals from conservative and liberal elites. Figure 4.1A illustrates the pattern by showing the predicted level of support among very conservative and very liberal respondents across levels of education, holding all other variables constant at their means.

If figure 4.1A depicts evidence of a polarization effect, then the virtually parallel lines in figure 4.1B—which substitutes partisanship for ideology—

show the absence of evidence for such an effect. The least educated Republicans were less supportive of same-sex marriage than were the least educated Democrats, but the partisan gap was not discernibly wider among the most educated (and, by implication, attentive) respondents. This makes sense given the absence of a clear contrast between the signals from Republican elites and those from Democratic elites. Still, the signals from one politician—President Bush—may have affected public opinion, particularly among the most educated respondents. The least educated Bush supporters were only slightly less favorable toward same-sex marriage than were the least educated Bush opponents, whereas the size of this gap tripled among the respondents most likely to be aware of Bush's stance (see figure 4.1C). Yet another polarization effect emerged along doctrinal lines. As figure 4.1D illustrates, a shift from the minimum level of education to the maximum magnified the gap between evangelicals and nonevangelicals by a factor of four. The contrast between the oppositional signals from evangelical elites and the mixed signals from nonevangelical elites provides a plausible explanation for this pattern in public opinion.

Table 4.1.   Influences on Support for Same-Sex Marriage and Civil Unions (Pew Research Center, 2003–2004)

	Favor Same-Sex Marriage (June 2003–August 2004)	Favor Civil Unions (October 2003–August 2004)
Ideology	−.12**	−.05
	(.03)	(.05)
Ideology x education	−.37**	−.41**
	(.05)	(.07)
Party identification	−.07**	−.05**
	(.01)	(.02)
Party identification x education	−.02	−.02
	(.02)	(.02)
Presidential approval	−.03†	−.06*
	(.02)	(.02)
Presidential approval x education	−.07**	−.001
	(.03)	(.03)
Evangelical	−.04*	−.11*
	(.02)	(.02)
Evangelical x education	−.13**	−.06†
	(.03)	(.03)
Education	.45**	.48**
	(.03)	(.04)
N	8,234	5,324

Notes: Table entries are OLS coefficients. Standard errors are in parentheses. Models also included controls for attendance at religious services, sex, self-identification as African American, age, and income.
†Significant at the .10 level
*Significant at the .05 level
**Significant at the .01 level

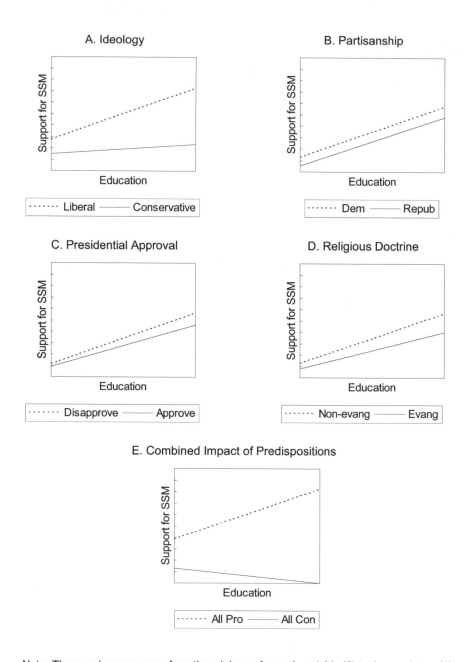

Note: The x and y axes range from the minimum for each variable (0) to the maximum (1)

Figure 4.1.   Support for Same-Sex Marriage by Predispositions and Education

To illustrate the full potential impact of elite signals on public support for same-sex marriage, consider two hypothetical respondents: one, a conservative, Republican, Bush supporter, and evangelical; the other, a liberal, Democrat, Bush opponent, and nonevangelical. If both of these respondents had the minimum level of education, then they would, all else being equal, differ in their opinions. Specifically, the former would fall between opposition and strong opposition; the latter, between opposition and support. If both of these respondents had the maximum level of education, however, then a wide gulf would separate them (see figure 4.1E). The highly educated, nonevangelical, Bush-opposing liberal Democrat would fall somewhere between support and strong support, whereas the highly educated, evangelical, Bush-supporting conservative Republican would strongly oppose same-sex marriage.

Elite Signals and Public Opinion about Civil Unions

Turning to civil unions, I anticipated polarization effects along ideological and doctrinal lines. Given that conservative and liberal elites sent sharply contrasting signals regarding such unions, I expected political attentiveness to magnify the opinion gap between liberals and conservatives among the public. Considering the diverging signals of evangelical elites and nonevangelical elites, I also expected attentiveness to magnify the opinion gap between evangelicals and nonevangelicals among the public. On the other hand, I did not necessarily expect such polarization effects along partisanship or presidential approval given the fuzzier nature of the signals about civil unions from Republican elites in general and the president in particular.

Of the seven Pew surveys that asked about same-sex marriage, four also included a question about civil unions: "Do you strongly favor, favor, oppose, or strongly oppose allowing gays and lesbian couples to enter into legal agreements with each other that would give them many of the same rights as married couples?" The first of these surveys was conducted in October 2003, the last in August 2004. Public opinion was more favorable toward civil unions than toward same-sex marriage, with support for the former ranging from 45 percent to 49 percent and opposition from 43 percent to 47 percent.

I used the same approach to test for polarization effects in public opinion about civil unions that I used to test for such effects in opinion about same-sex marriage (see table 4.1, second column). As expected, I found evidence of polarization along ideological and doctrinal lines. Among the least educated respondents, conservatives were not significantly more supportive of civil unions than were liberals; among the most educated respondents, the ideological divide on civil unions was almost as wide as it was for same-sex marriage. The polarization along doctrinal lines was less pronounced: the gap between the most educated evangelicals and nonevangelicals was only half again as large as the gap between the least educated members of these two groups. I found little evidence of polarization along partisanship or presidential approval: Republicans and Bush supporters expressed less support for civil unions than did Democrats and Bush opponents, respectively, but neither gap varied in magnitude with education. These patterns are consistent with predictions derived from my account of elite signals regarding civil unions.

All in all, my findings regarding polarization effects suggest that elite signals shaped public opinion about both policies. To be sure, my evidence on this point is circumstantial and, thus, subject to alternative explanations. In particular, one might argue that the role of education in conditioning the impact of Americans' beliefs on their opinions reflected not the power of elite signals but rather the power of formal education to enhance reasoning skills and, thus, belief consistency. The latter explanation, however, would not account for why education conditions the effects of some beliefs (i.e., ideology and religious doctrine) but not others (i.e., partisanship) and on some topics (i.e., presidential approval for same-sex marriage) but not others (i.e., presidential approval for civil unions). In contrast, an explanation based on elite signaling fits all of the findings.

CLERGY AS CUE-GIVERS ON SAME-SEX MARRIAGE AND CIVIL UNIONS

Though signals from elites that reached the public through the mass media appear to have influenced public opinion about same-sex marriage and civil unions, opinion leadership on these subjects could have taken place through interpersonal communication as well as through mass communication. Indeed, studies suggest that congregation members follow cues from their clergy in forming their political opinions, particularly when the latter regularly address issues.[44] Thus, clergy may have influenced their parishioners' opinions about same-sex marriage and civil unions through signals from the pulpit.

The Cooperative Clergy Study Project surveys provide portraits of the views on gay rights held by American clergy.[45] In each of these surveys—all of which were conducted in the aftermath of the 2000 election campaign— randomly selected clergy from a particular denomination were interviewed. Respondents were asked whether they agreed that, "Homosexuals should have all the same rights and privileges as other American citizens."[46] Clergy from nine evangelical Protestant denominations were interviewed. Within six of these samples, agreement was at 37 percent or below. In the other three, the agreement rates were 44 percent, 54 percent, and 55 percent.[47] In contrast, agreement ranged from 60 percent to 85 percent within the samples of clergy from the six mainline Protestant denominations studied.[48] The study also measured agreement among Roman Catholic priests (71 percent), American rabbis (84 percent total, ranging from 52 percent for Orthodox rabbis to 100 percent for Reconstructionist rabbis), and Unitarian-Universalist clergy (99 percent).

The Pew Research Center's October 2003 survey, in turn, presents a portrait of the signals that Americans recalled receiving from their clergy.[49] Respondents who said that they attended religious services at least once or twice a month were asked "whether or not the clergy at your place of worship speaks out on . . . issues related to homosexuality." Among these respondents, 55 percent said yes and 44 percent said no. Those who said yes were then asked, "When your clergy has spoken about homosexuality, do they say it is something that should be accepted, something that should be discouraged, or don't they take a position on the issue?" Only 4 percent said "accepted," while 76 percent said "discouraged." Among evangelical Protestants, the percentages were even more lopsided, with 86 percent reporting that their clergy discouraged homosexuality and only 2 percent reporting that their clergy advocated acceptance. Among Catholics, the percentages were 67 percent and 5 percent, respectively; among mainline Protestants, they were 48 percent and 10 percent. In short, the views that clergy held and the signals that parishioners received matched along denominational lines: evangelical parishioners were especially likely to receive oppositional cues on issues related to homosexuality, just as their clergy were especially likely to report opposition to gay rights. Indeed, more than half of the respondents who said that their clergy spoke out on the subject were evangelical Protestants.

Using the data from the October 2003 Pew survey, I tested whether respondents' reports of clergy signals on homosexuality were related to their opinions about same-sex marriage and civil unions, taking into account all of the other factors described above: political beliefs, endorsement of evangelical doctrine, attendance at religious services, and demographics. The key independent variable in this analysis captured whether respondents received signals from their clergy that discouraged homosexuality, received no signals on homosexuality (because they did not attend, because their clergy did not speak on the issue, or because their clergy took no position), or received signals to accept homosexuality.[50] As the first two columns of table 4.2 report, clergy support for homosexuality was positively related to respondent support for same-sex marriage and civil unions. Given the distribution of signals that respondents reported receiving, however, any net

Table 4.2. Influences on Support for Same-Sex Marriage, Civil Unions, and the "Traditional Family" Frame for Same-Sex Marriage (Pew Research Center, October 2003)

	Favor Legal Marriage	*Favor Civil Unions*	*Disagree: Undermine Family*
Ideology	−.11	−.02	−.23**
	(.09)	(.09)	(.12)
Ideology x education	−.39**	−.54**	−.32†
	(.15)	(.15)	(.19)
Party identification	−.10†	−.06	.003
	(.06)	(.06)	(.08)
Party identification x education	.08	.03	−.11
	(.09)	(.10)	(.12)
Presidential approval	−.04	−.03	−.06
	(.05)	(.05)	(.07)
Presidential approval x education	−.03	−.03	−.05
	(.08)	(.08)	(.10)
Evangelical	−.05	−.03	.01
	(.04)	(.05)	(.05)
Evangelical x education	−.07	−.12†	−.19*
	(.07)	(.07)	(.07)
Clergy support for homosexuality	.18**	.21**	.22**
	(.04)	(.05)	(.06)
Education	.35**	.53**	.45**
	(.08)	(.09)	(.10)
N	1,153	1,167	1,189

Notes: Table entries are OLS coefficients. Standard errors are in parentheses. Models also included controls for attendance at religious services, sex, self-identification as African American, age, and income.
†Significant at the .10 level
*Significant at the .05 level
**Significant at the .01 level

effect of clergy signals would have been to produce greater opposition to same-sex marriage and civil unions.[51] Caution is in order in drawing a causal interpretation here: it may be that some respondents projected their own opinions about these topics onto their clergy, rather than being persuaded by their clergy. Still, the results suggest that clergy signals mattered in shaping public opinion on both policies.[52]

FRAMES AND THEIR SOURCES: THE "TRADITIONAL FAMILY" FRAME

As the story of Rick Santorum illustrates, would-be opinion leaders have done more than just signal their opposition to or support for gay rights.

They have also promoted frames for understanding and talking about gay rights. The particular frame that Santorum endorsed presented same-sex marriage as threatening the traditional family. Nor was the senator alone in his effort to promote this frame; many conservative and evangelical elites invoked it in their criticisms of same-sex marriage. What impact, then, might elite messages have had on public acceptance of the frame? Here, I derived my expectations from Zaller's notion of polarization effects and James Druckman's argument that acceptance or rejection of a frame depends in part on the credibility of its source.[53] For conservatives and evangelicals, the sources of the "traditional family" frame should have been highly credible. For liberals and nonevangelicals, its sources should have been less credible. Thus, I expected the impact of ideology and religious doctrine on acceptance of the frame to be greater among the highly educated than among the less educated. In addition, I suspected that clergy signals about homosexuality may have shaped acceptance of the traditional family frame given that many clergy who discouraged homosexuality presumably promoted this frame in their messages from the pulpit.

The October 2003 Pew survey included a question about the traditional family frame: "Do you completely agree, somewhat agree, somewhat disagree, or completely disagree with this statement: Allowing gay or lesbian couples to marry would undermine the traditional family?" A clear majority of respondents agreed, with 40 percent agreeing completely and 16 percent agreeing somewhat, whereas 24 percent disagreed completely and 15 percent disagreed somewhat. Among the least educated respondents, liberals were more likely than conservatives to disagree. Higher levels of education, however, magnified the ideological divide over the frame (see table 4.2, third column). Similarly, the impact of religious doctrine varied with education. Among the least educated, no discernible difference emerged between evangelicals and nonevangelicals. Among the most educated, evangelicals were more likely than nonevangelicals to endorse the traditional family frame. Agreement also varied with the signals that respondents reported receiving from their clergy. Those reporting signals to accept homosexuality were especially likely to reject the frame, while those reporting signals that discouraged homosexuality were especially likely to endorse it.

THE REWARDS AND RISKS OF SIGNALING

For political actors who seek to shape public opinion about gay rights, the potential reward for sending signals to the public is clear: people sometimes follow such cues. One piece of evidence for the impact of elite signals is the finding that President Clinton was able to shape public opinion about gays in the military, particularly among his supporters. My findings of polarization effects along ideology, religious doctrine, and presidential approval provide evidence that elite signals also shaped public opinion about same-sex marriage and civil unions. Moreover, the relationships between Americans' reports of clergy signals about homosexuality and their own opinions on same-sex marriage and civil unions suggest that signals from the pulpit influenced what parishioners thought about gay rights. Taken as a whole, these results provide a compelling case for how signals can matter in shaping public opinion about gay rights.

Yet sending signals to the public can carry risks as well as rewards. Again, President Clinton is a case in point: in leading public opinion toward greater support for allowing gays and lesbians to serve in the military, he also spent political capital in the form of his own approval rating. Santorum's strongly worded signal on same-sex marriage likewise put his political fortunes at risk, as the Pennsylvania senator learned the hard way that ordinary citizens can send signals of their own. One sort of signal from the public came from the online grassroots activists who "Google-bombed" him. Following a call to action by sex columnist and same-sex marriage advocate Dan Savage, they worked to publicize an unflattering redefinition of Santorum's name by manipulating the results produced by the popular search engine Google. As a result of their efforts, a web page presenting Savage's definition swiftly overtook the senator's own official web page as the first result in a search for "Santorum."[54] In November 2006, Rick Santorum received another sort of signal from ordinary citizens: he was defeated in his reelection bid by almost 20 percentage points.[55] His loss undoubtedly reflected a variety of factors, but his image as an ideological extremist—an image fueled, in part, by his comments on same-sex marriage—may have contributed to the outcome.

Of course, not everyone who seeks to lead opinion faces the same risks. For some signal-senders, the risks may be relatively small. The conservative and evangelical elites who signaled opposition to same-sex marriage and civil unions probably faced few potential costs in taking these stances given that their political capital depended more on maintaining and mobilizing committed supporters than on appealing to swing voters. Similarly, the 2004 Democratic presidential contenders who endorsed same-sex marriage probably did so at little cost to their political fortunes: Braun, Kucinich, and Sharpton were widely regarded not only as the most liberal candidates in the race but also as the ones with the smallest chances of winning.

In contrast, actors who depend on widespread political support face greater risks in sending signals on gay rights, particularly when they send signals with which large numbers of citizens may disagree. President Bush's public stance against legal recognition for same-sex marriage was not particularly risky for him given that a clear majority of the public opposed such recognition (it also helped that Bush worded his opposition in less inflammatory terms than did

Santorum). A stance against (or for) civil unions, however, would have been riskier given the more even distribution of opinion on that subject. On civil unions, then, Bush may have engaged in strategic ambiguity.[56] By the same logic, the pro–civil unions stance taken by the major Democratic contenders in 2004 was not as risky for them as a pro-same-sex marriage stance would have been. In broader terms, the signals that politicians send regarding gay rights may shape public opinion, but public opinion can also serve as a constraint on the signals that politicians send.

Though this chapter focused on looking at how political actors shaped public opinion about gay rights by taking positions, it provided hints about another route of influence: framing the subject in terms of citizens' core values. I showed that many Americans endorsed the traditional family frame that Santorum and other gay rights opponents worked to disseminate. At the same time, I demonstrated that not all citizens were equally likely to endorse this frame. Instead, the frame appeared to resonate most strongly among conservatives and evangelicals who closely followed the public debate over gay rights, as well as among those who received antihomosexuality signals from their clergy. In the following chapter, I take a closer look at the framing of gay rights in news media coverage and at Americans' responses to the frames that they encountered in public debate.

NOTES

1. Quoted in James O'Toole, "Santorum: No Apology; Remarks on Sodomy Case Continue to Draw Fire from Gays, Democrats," *Pittsburgh Post-Gazette*, 23 April 2003, A1; Marc Sandalow, "Gay Uproar May Not Hurt Senator; Condemnation by GOP's Santorum Seen as Offending Only Small Group of Voters," *San Francisco Chronicle*, 23 April 2003, A3.

2. Ann McFeatters, "GOP Colleagues Put Heat on Santorum; But Conservatives Back Remarks on Gays," *Pittsburgh Post-Gazette*, 25 April 2003, A13; O'Toole, "Santorum: No Apology"; Sandalow, "Gay Uproar."

3. Quoted in O'Toole, "Santorum: No Apology," A1.

4. O'Toole, "Santorum: No Apology," A1.

5. Alan Cooperman, "Frist and Specter Defend Santorum; Remarks on Gays Should Not Be Misconstrued, Leaders Say," *Washington Post*, 24 April 2003, A6.

6. O'Toole, "Santorum: No Apology."

7. Quoted in McFeatters, "GOP Colleagues Put Heat on Santorum," A13.

8. Quoted in Ann McFeatters, "White House Backs Santorum," *Pittsburgh Post-Gazette*, 26 April 2003, A1.

9. Quoted in McFeatters, "White House Backs Santorum," A1.

10. Samuel L. Popkin, *The Reasoning Voter* (Chicago: University of Chicago Press, 1994).

11. Bernard Berelson, Paul Lazarsfeld, and William McPhee, *Voting: A Study of Opinion Formation in a Presidential Campaign* (Chicago: University of Chicago Press,

1954); Elihu Katz and Paul Lazarsfeld, *Personal Influence: The Part Played by People in the Flow of Mass Communications* (New York: Free Press, 1964); Paul Lazarsfeld, Bernard Berelson, and Hazel Gaudet, *The People's Choice: How the Voter Makes Up His Mind in a Presidential Campaign* (New York: Columbia University Press, 1948).

12. Anthony Downs, *An Economic Theory of Democracy* (New York: HarperCollins, 1957).

13. William A. Gamson and Andre Modigliani, "The Changing Culture of Affirmative Action," in *Research in Political Sociology*, ed. Richard D. Braungart (Greenwich, Conn.: JAI Press, 1987), 143.

14. See, for example, Thomas E. Nelson, Rosalee A. Clawson, and Zoe M. Oxley, "Media Framing of a Civil Liberties Conflict and its Effect on Tolerance," *American Political Science Review* 91 (1997): 567–83.

15. William A. Gamson, *Talking Politics* (New York: Cambridge University Press, 1992).

16. James N. Druckman, "On the Limits of Framing Effects: Who Can Frame?" *Journal of Politics* 63 (2001): 1041–66.

17. Michael Bailey, Lee Sigelman, and Clyde Wilcox, "Presidential Persuasion on Social Issues: A Two-Way Street?" *Political Research Quarterly* 56 (2004): 49–58.

18. John Zaller, *The Nature and Origins of Mass Opinion* (New York: Cambridge University Press, 1992).

19. Zaller, *The Nature and Origins of Mass Opinion*, 44.

20. Zaller, *The Nature and Origins of Mass Opinion*, 100–101.

21. *Lawrence v. Texas*, 539 U.S. 558 (2003).

22. *Goodridge v. Department of Public Health*, 798 N.E. 2d 941 (Mass. 2003).

23. Alan Cooperman, "Opponents of Gay Marriage Divided; At Issue Is Scope of an Amendment," *Washington Post*, 29 November 2003, A1.

24. Quoted in Cooperman, "Opponents of Gay Marriage Divided," A1.

25. People for the American Way, "Victory in Massachusetts: State's High Court Rejects 'Gay Exception' to State Constitution's Declaration of Rights" (Washington, DC: People for the American Way, 2003).

26. American Civil Liberties Union, "ACLU Cheers Massachusetts High Court Decision Not to Deny Same-Sex Couples Right to Marry" (New York: American Civil Liberties Union, 2003).

27. Quoted in Bob Deans, "Bush: Ban Gay Marriage; An Amendment Is Needed, the President Says, but He Doesn't Preclude Civil Unions," *Atlanta Journal-Constitution*, 25 February 2004, 1A.

28. Quoted in Susan Page, "Gay Marriage Looms Large for '04," *USA Today*, 19 November 2003, 3A.

29. Sheryl Gay Stolberg, "Democratic Candidates Are Split on the Issue of Gay Marriage," *New York Times*, 16 July 2003, A14.

30. Marc Sandalow, "Dean Supports Gay Unions but Wavers on Saying, 'I Do'; Presidential Hopeful Stresses Equal Rights over Choice of Words," *San Francisco Chronicle*, 2 December 2003, A1.

31. Quoted in Carolyn Lochhead, "Bush Plays Both Sides in Debate over Gay Marriage; He Says He'll Back Constitutional Ban—If Necessary," *San Francisco Chronicle*, 18 December 2003, A1.

32. Joan Biskupic, "Court's Opinion on Gay Rights Reflects Trends," *USA Today*, 18 July 2003, 2A; Mary Leonard, "Gay Marriage Stirs Conservatives Again; Right Wing Braces for Mass. Ruling," *Boston Globe*, 28 September 2003, A1; "Talk Ranges from Gay Marriage to Iraq," *St. Petersburg Times*, 31 July 2003, 5A.

33. Cooperman, "Opponents of Gay Marriage Divided."

34. Leonard, "Gay Marriage Stirs Conservatives."

35. Michael Paulson, "Protestants Weigh Same-Sex Marriage," *Boston Globe*, 30 November 2003, B10.

36. Zaller, *Nature and Origins of Mass Opinion*.

37. See appendix A for details on these surveys.

38. See chapter 2.

39. See appendix A for details on question wording and coding.

40. I found no consistent patterns across time in the effects of ideology, partisanship, presidential approval, or religious doctrine. Nor did I find any consistent patterns across time in the extent to which the effects of these variables were moderated by education (see below).

41. Zaller, *The Nature and Origins of Mass Opinion*, 333–39.

42. Michael X. Delli Carpini and Scott Keeter, *What Americans Know About Politics and Why It Matters* (New Haven, Conn.: Yale University Press, 1996).

43. The coefficients for ideology, party identification, presidential approval, and evangelical doctrine capture the effects of these variables when education equals zero.

44. For a summary of relevant research, see Corwin E. Smidt, *Pulpit and Politics: Clergy in American Politics at the Advent of the Millennium* (Waco, Tex.: Baylor University Press, 2004).

45. Smidt, *Pulpit and Politics*.

46. Note that this question did not specifically address same-sex marriage or civil unions. Note also that the Cooperative Clergy Study Project was conducted well before the debate about these topics reached the intensity that it did in 2003–4.

47. The denominations, with agreement rates, were as follows: Assemblies of God (23 percent), Churches of Christ (31 percent), Southern Baptist Convention (33 percent), Church of the Nazarene (35 percent), Lutheran Church—Missouri Synod (37 percent), Presbyterian Church in America (37 percent), Evangelical Free Church of America (44 percent), Christian Reformed Church (54 percent), and Mennonite Church USA (55 percent).

48. The denominations, with agreement rates, were as follows: American Baptist Convention (60 percent), Reformed Church in America (65 percent), United Methodist Church (68 percent), Presbyterian Church (USA) (76 percent), Disciples of Christ (79 percent), and Evangelical Lutheran Church of America (85 percent).

49. Pew Research Center for the People and the Press, "Republicans Unified, Democrats Split on Same-Sex Marriage; Religious Beliefs Underpin Opposition to Homosexuality" (Washington, DC: Pew Research Center for the People and the Press, 2003).

50. See appendix A for coding details.

51. When I treated accepting and discouraging signals as two separate dichotomous variables, I found that the former predicted greater support while the latter predicted greater opposition.

52. The results for the other key variables paralleled the results from the pooled datasets, though in some cases they fell short of statistical significance. Attendance at religious services also shaped support for same-sex marriage and civil unions, suggesting that my account does not exhaust the ways in which religion mattered here.

53. Zaller, *Nature and Origins of Mass Opinion*; Druckman, "On the Limits of Framing Effects."

54. The website, spreadingsantorum.com, defined "santorum" as "the frothy mixture of lube and fecal matter that is sometimes the byproduct of anal sex."

55. Jason DeParle, "A High-Profile Ouster in Pennsylvania," *New York Times*, 8 November 2006, P5.

56. Benjamin I. Page, "The Theory of Political Ambiguity," *American Political Science Review* 70 (1976): 742–52.

5

Using Values to Frame Gay Rights: Traditional Morals, Equal Rights, or Special Rights?

> All animals are equal, but some animals are more equal than others.
>
> —George Orwell, *Animal Farm*

> "The question is," said Alice, "whether you can make words mean so many different things."
>
> "The question is," said Humpty Dumpty, "which is to be master—that's all."
>
> —Lewis Carroll, *Through the Looking-Glass*

The United States Supreme Court decision *Romer v. Evans* illustrates three frames in the debate about gay rights. In the majority opinion—which struck down Amendment 2, a Colorado initiative to ban gay rights laws—Justice Anthony Kennedy framed the Court's position in terms of equality. "Central both to the idea of the rule of law and our own Constitution's guarantee of equal protection," he wrote, "is the principle that government and each of its parts remain open on impartial terms to all who seek its assistance . . . Amendment 2 classifies homosexuals not to further a proper legislative end but to make them unequal to everyone else."[1] In a dissent, Justice Antonin Scalia framed opposition to gay rights in terms of morality, writing that the initiative was a "reasonable effort to preserve traditional American moral values."[2] At the same time, Scalia also framed gay rights policies as *inegalitarian* measures. To him, the dispute was not over "equal rights" for gays and lesbians, but over "special treatment."[3]

Each of these frames revolves around an abstract value that many Americans cherish. The "equal rights" frame and the "special rights" frame invoke the principle of equality; the "traditional morality" frame invokes moral values. In this chapter, I examine the "double lives" that frames played in the politics of gay rights.[4] In one sense, frames exist within communicating texts—conversational statements, newspaper articles, television news broadcasts, and other transmissions of information.[5] In another sense, they exist in the minds of individual citizens.[6] The twin lives of frames also interact with one another, as political elites frequently invoke values to forge common frames of reference among the public.[7]

I begin by looking at how value frames set the terms of the debate about gay rights in news media coverage from the early 1990s (when this debate focused on employment nondiscrimination and gays in the military) to 2000 and beyond (by which time the focus of the debate had shifted to same-sex marriage and civil unions). I highlight how political elites competed with one another in their efforts to define the issue in terms of the public's core values. I also show how value words took on varied—even mutually contradictory—meanings in public debate depending on who used them and for what purpose. In doing so, I follow George Orwell, who argues in "Politics and the English Language" that words such as "democracy," "freedom," and "equality" "have each of them several different meanings which cannot be reconciled with one another."[8]

Next, I examine the effects of value frames on public opinion about gay rights. Specifically, I show that exposure to such frames in public debate shaped how Americans explained their views on the topic and deliberated with one another about it. I also argue, however, that ordinary citizens have the capacity to resist elite attempts to define issues in terms of values. Elite competition in issue framing provides citizens with opportunities to choose among frames. Moreover, people can use the frames that they find in media coverage not only in ways that echo the conclusions presented in the frames but also in ways that challenge those conclusions. In short, there are limits to the power of framing.

VALUES, FRAMING, AND THE DEBATE ABOUT GAY RIGHTS

News media coverage of politics often contains frames that define what political controversies "are about."[9] Such frames are typically introduced into public debate by political elites in the hope that the media will disseminate them and that citizens will receive them, accept them, and use them to make judgments.[10] As William Jacoby observes, the "ability to frame issues . . . is undoubtedly one of the most important 'tools' that political elites have at their disposal. Therefore, they do so in ways that shine the best possible light on their own preferred course of action."[11] When competing sets of elites prefer opposing courses of action, they often introduce competing frames into public debate.[12] Given the tendency of citizens to understand political issues in terms of core values, it is not surprising that those frames sometimes link a position on an issue (e.g., support for or opposition to gay rights) to an abstract value (e.g., equality or traditional morality).[13]

I conducted a content analysis to examine what value frames dominated media coverage of gay rights from 1990 to 1997.[14] During this period, controversies over employment nondiscrimination and military service occupied the center of the public debate about the issue, though the topic of same-sex marriage was also beginning to rise on the agenda. My data source was the All News file of the LexisNexis database, which contained the full text of media reports (i.e., newspaper and magazine articles, as well as television and radio transcripts) from a wide range of outlets. I chose this source because it provided a broad cross-section of items to which ordinary citizens might have been exposed. It did not contain every item in the universe of media reports, but it offered the closest approximation of that population available. I generated citations by searching for "gay rights" in the headlines of all items in the archive from 1990 to 1997. I chose this search term after ruling out alternatives that were either too vague (as was "homosexuality," which would have produced citations for a higher proportion of articles that did not specifically discuss gay rights policies) or too uncommon (as were "gay and lesbian rights," "gay issues," "homosexual rights," and "gay agenda," which would have produced too few citations). For my analysis, I randomly sampled four hundred items from the 4,237 citations generated by the search.

For each item (i.e., article or transcript) in the sample, I coded a frame as being present if it appeared at least once in the entire text of the item.[15] Each individual item could contain one frame, multiple frames, or no frame at all. A secondary coder coded a subset of one hundred items randomly selected from among the four hundred. Intercoder reliability coefficients indicated satisfactory to high levels of reliability in coding.

The coding scheme captured four frames. The *anti–gay rights morality frame* cast opposition to gay rights in terms of support for traditional morals, as in the following examples:

> [The U.S. Supreme Court ruling in *Romer v. Evans*] makes you wonder, you know, what it takes for people of traditional values to get a Supreme Court justice to agree with them. . . . The justices are clearly out of control and contemptuous of the moral heritage of America.[16]

> But many of those who oppose gay rights legislation, including lifting the military ban, argue that homosexuality goes against traditional family values. They regard homosexuality as immoral.[17]

This frame was fairly common, appearing in 16 percent of the four hundred items analyzed.

By contrast, the *pro–gay rights morality frame*—which rebutted any linkage between support for traditional morality and opposition to gay rights— occurred in only 2 percent of the items. The following quotation is one of the rare examples of this frame:

> One does not have to support homosexuality or its morality to support [a bill to ban job discrimination against homosexuals].[18]

The imbalance here indicates that there was little contest over the meaning of traditional morality in the public debate about gay rights.

The framing of the other value was more contentious. The *pro–gay rights equality frame* connected equality to support for gay rights through the language of equal rights, equal opportunity, or equal protection. For example:

> Mr. Clinton is the first president to attend a homosexual-rights event. Mr. Truman was the first to attend a National Association for the Advancement of Colored People event. There, Mr. Truman pledged to support equality for all Americans. "And when I say all Americans, I mean all Americans." At the banquet . . . Mr. Clinton said: "Well, my friends, all Americans still means all Americans."[19]

This frame appeared in almost a quarter of the items in the sample.

It did not go unchallenged, however. A rival equality frame revolved around the argument that gay rights policies are inegalitarian because they provide special rights, special privileges, or preferential treatment to gays and lesbians. Consider the following example:

> Opponents of homosexual rights argue that homosexuals should not be equated with blacks and other oppressed minorities. By adding sexual orientation to such lists [of protected groups], homosexuals are given potential access to a host of "special rights" they don't deserve, foes say.[20]

Though less prominent than the pro–gay rights equality frame, this *anti–gay rights equality frame* was also common, appearing in 16 percent of the items.

It may be that a different approach would have produced somewhat different results. For example, a sample produced by searching for "gay rights" in the text, rather than the headlines, of items might have produced a sample containing smaller percentages of frames. Similarly, searches for different terms might have altered the frequencies of the frames (though there is a strong case for using "gay rights" as a search term, given that it appears to have been the dominant term in public debate for denoting the issue). Given these points, I make no strong claims about the exact percentages reported above. My conclusions are simpler: namely, that the anti–gay rights morality frame was effectively undisputed, that the pro–gay rights equality frame was the dominant interpretation of equality in the debate, and that the anti–gay rights equality frame was a prominent challenge.

I also examined the sources to which the media attributed these frames. Here, the most striking finding was prominence of organized interests in shaping the terms of the debate as conveyed through news coverage. Interest groups not only entered the public debate by providing value frames through spokespeople; they also did so by choosing names for themselves. On one side of the issue, pro–gay rights groups such as Equality Washington, the Ypsilanti Campaign for Equality, the Equality Foundation of Greater Cincinnati, Housing Opportunities Made Equal, and Prince Georgians for Equal Rights wove the pro–gay rights equality frame into the names of their organizations. On the other side of the issue, the Coalition to End Special Rights, the Campaign Opposing Special Treatment, Yes for Equal Rights, Equal Rights Not Special Rights, and San Diego Citizens for Equal Rights campaigned against gay rights, as did Colorado for Family Values, the Traditional Values Coalition, the Committee on Moral Concerns, and Citizens for Community Values. The courts accounted for the second largest share of source attributions, due in part to coverage of *Romer v. Evans.* Other sources for the frames included the White House, members of Congress, state and local government officials, and "people on the street."

After 1997, the gay rights debate—and news coverage of it—began to shift from the "old" politics of employment nondiscrimination and gays in the military to the relatively "new" politics of same-sex marriage and civil unions. For the most part, however, the same frames continued to dominate coverage of gay rights. When Ann Gordon and her colleagues conducted a content analysis of frames for same-sex marriage and civil unions in twenty-six newspapers, they found that two frames dominated coverage from November 4, 2002 to November 4, 2003.[21] One was a traditional values frame arguing against same-sex marriage and civil unions. The other was an equality frame arguing for gay marriage and civil unions. Among the articles in the authors' sample, 20 percent included the traditional values frame by itself, 16 percent included the equality frame by itself, and 29 percent included both frames. In contrast, the authors found few mentions of frames that pitted equality against gay rights or that used traditional morality to justify gay rights.

FRAMING EFFECTS ON PUBLIC OPINION

In forming issue opinions, citizens must typically choose from an array of potentially ambiguous or contradictory considerations.[22] For example, Americans could base their opinions about gay rights on their moral beliefs, their beliefs about equality, or both. In doing so, they would also need to decide what the value(s) at stake implied in the context of gay rights. Does faith in equality demand support for or opposition to gay rights? Similarly, what stance does adherence to family values demand in this context? Confronted with such dilemmas, citizens may rely on the frames that they receive from the mass media in deciding which values to connect to issues and how to interpret those values.[23]

Experimental studies have shown that exposure to frames embedded in television news broadcasts, newspaper articles, and survey questions can alter the weights that citizens attach to specific values in forming their issue opinions.[24] Such exposure can even reverse the implications that citizens attach to a particular value within a particular context. For example, Donald Kinder and Lynn Sanders demonstrated that survey respondents exposed to one frame saw egalitarianism as a reason for supporting affirmative action, whereas respondents exposed to an alternative frame saw egalitarianism as a reason for opposing affirmative action.[25] Put another way, each of these frames led citizens toward a different interpretation of equality's meaning in the context of affirmative action.

Along similar lines, experimental studies have shown that exposure to value frames in media coverage can shape how people use value language to explain their issue opinions. As a case in point, Paul Brewer and Kimberly Gross found that exposure to a pro–school vouchers equality frame led participants to explain their opinions about this issue in terms of equality.[26] The researchers found a similar effect for exposure to an anti–school vouchers equality frame and an even stronger effect for exposure to both frames at once.

Framing effects on public opinion can also extend beyond the expression of individual opinions. William Gamson's focus group research showed that citizens use the frames that they find in media coverage not only to form their own issue opinions but also to engage in conversations about issues.[27] Likewise, Katherine Cramer Walsh's participant observation research highlighted the role that frames play in shaping citizens' political discussions.[28] Gamson calls such effects "effects *in use*," arguing that, when citizens "use elements from media discourse to make a conversational point of view, we are directly observing a media effect."[29]

Studies of framing and public opinion offer two alternative psychological explanations as to why exposure to value frames in mass media coverage might influence how people link their values to issues. Early studies of framing effects often argued that such exposure increases the accessibility of particular values in citizens' memories, thereby making those values easier to recall in the opinion formation process.[30] This explanation suggests that such effects emerge through a passive and automatic psychological process. Later studies, however, argued that framing effects emerge because exposure to frames influences the importance that citizens attach to specific values.[31] This explanation suggests that such effects can reflect a more deliberate process.

The latter account also provides a psychological foundation for considering potential limitations on framing effects.[32] Experimental studies have identified a variety of factors on which framing effects can depend.[33] Most importantly for my purposes, such studies have shown that exposure to a competing frame can dampen the impact of a frame on public opinion.[34] Furthermore, Gamson's focus group research revealed that citizens sometimes draw on "counterframes" (i.e., frames that criticize dominant media frames), popular wisdom, and their own reasoning skills in responding to frames in media coverage.[35] Thus, citizens who encounter value frames in such coverage may borrow the ideas in the frames to make their own points about the issue at hand.

Taken as a whole, the literature on framing effects suggests two key points about the value frames that dominated media coverage of gay rights. First, these frames may have shaped public opinion about gay rights. Second, the ordinary Americans who received these frames may have responded to them in active—and sometimes critical—ways.

FRAMING EFFECTS ON STATEMENTS ABOUT GAY RIGHTS

An October 2003 Pew survey provides evidence that many Americans used the anti–gay rights morality frame to understand same-sex marriage.[36] In this survey, respondents who said that they opposed "allowing gays and lesbians to marry legally" were asked an open-ended follow-up question: "What would you say is the MAIN reason you object to allowing gays and lesbians to marry?" Interviewers coded responses into a variety of categories. The most common theme was that same-sex marriage was "morally wrong," a "sin," or contrary to biblical injunctions, with 28 percent of respondents providing answers that fit this category. Another 2 percent said that same-sex marriage "opens the door to other immoral behavior," and 1 percent said that it "undermines the traditional family."

Still, these findings do not establish that the frame's presence in media coverage fostered its use by citizens. One could just as easily argue that political elites responded to public opinion by trying to latch onto a frame that already resonated among citizens. With this in mind, I tested the effects of exposure to two value frames—the pro–gay rights equality frame and the anti–gay rights morality frame—on how recipients understood gay rights.[37] Specifically, I examined whether exposure to these frames influenced how recipients explained their thoughts about the issue in their own words. To do so, I conducted an experiment. By controlling the conditions under study—in this case, exposure to frames—and randomly assigning participants to conditions, I was able to isolate the effects of framing in a laboratory setting.[38]

I expected the experimental participants who received the pro–gay rights equality frame to be more likely than those who did not to invoke equality when they expressed their thoughts about gay rights in their own words. Exposure to media coverage containing this frame should have made the principle of equality more accessible in their memories, more important in their judgments, or both—and, thus, more likely to appear in their explanations. By a similar logic, participants who received the anti–gay rights morality frame should have been more likely than those who did not to invoke morality when they explained their views on gay rights.

I also tested whether exposure to these frames led participants to adopt the interpretations of equality and morality offered by the frames, competing interpretations, neither, or both. The pro–gay rights equality frame suggests that those who endorse equality should endorse gay rights; thus, exposure to the frame could have encouraged participants to use equality language in ways that justified gay rights policies. Similarly, exposure to the anti–gay rights morality frame could have encouraged participants to invoke morality as a basis for opposing gay rights. Alternatively (or additionally), exposure to these frames could have encouraged participants to discuss the implications of equality and morality in ways that challenged the pro–gay rights interpretation of equality and the anti–gay rights interpretation of morality.

Lastly, I examined whether the anti–gay rights morality frame and the pro–gay rights equality frames interfered with one another. I tested whether participants who were exposed to the equality frame and the morality frame in conjunction with one another were less likely to invoke equality than those who were exposed only to the pro–gay rights equality frame. Similarly, I tested whether those who were exposed to both frames were less likely to invoke morality than those who were exposed only to the anti–gay rights morality frame.

Experimental Procedure

The experiment, which I conducted in 1999, simulated exposure to value frames embedded in news coverage. The procedure consisted of four stages: a pretest; a treatment, which involved the presentation of one, two, or no value frames for gay rights; a distractor task; and a posttest. I recruited participants at a public university in the southeastern United States. The results presented here are based on data from the 224 participants who completed all four stages of the experiment. My reliance on a student participant pool raises questions, of course, about the generalizability of my results—a point that I revisit later.

In the first stage of the experimental procedure, participants completed a written pretest, presented as "a questionnaire designed to measure your opinions toward and knowledge about a variety of public figures, groups, and issues." This pretest included questions on a range of topics, including demographic characteristics.

After an interval ranging from no less than one full week to no more than two months, participants completed the remaining stages of the procedure, which took place in a laboratory. Upon arrival, participants were seated at a computer and asked to follow the instructions presented on the screen. Their first task was to read four short articles "taken from real newspapers." Each article was presented as text on the screen. The instructions introduced the first one as a "warm-up article" and explained that the other three would "all be about current political controversies." In truth, both the first article (about the discovery of water on the moon) and the second article (about a Native American whale hunt) were included to acclimate participants to the reading task. Once they had read the practice articles, participants were presented with two additional articles—one about gay rights, the other about welfare reform. The former contained the experimental treatment that I discuss here.[39]

The gay rights article was constructed from passages in actual newspaper articles.[40] The first and last paragraphs of the article remained the same across conditions, but I selectively edited the middle paragraphs to create a variety of experimental conditions. Each participant was randomly assigned to one of four conditions: (a) exposure to an article that contained no value frame (the control condition), (b) exposure to an article that contained a paragraph-long version of the pro–gay rights equality frame, (c) exposure to an article that contained a paragraph-long version of the anti–gay rights morality frame, or (d) exposure to an article that contained both frames.[41] When both frames were presented, their order of presentation was randomized. The value frames that appeared in the article were verbatim quotations or close paraphrases of real-life examples of the frames. Rather than attempting to create framing treatments that were perfectly comparable with one another, I used treatments that reflected actual media content as closely as possible.

After reading the articles, participants answered ten antonym questions taken from an SAT practice test. This task served to clear participants' short term memory before they proceeded to the posttest. Along with a variety of other questions, the posttest included two open-ended questions about gay rights. After being asked whether they favored or opposed "laws to protect homosexuals against job discrimination" participants were instructed to describe "exactly what things went through your mind as you were deciding whether you favored or opposed the policy." They were given the opportunity to type up to three lines of text in response (taking as much time as they needed). The next question asked respondents whether they favored or opposed "allowing homosexuals to serve in the United States Armed

Forces." This item, in turn, was followed by an open-ended item identical to the one described above.[42]

Evidence of Framing Effects

Virtually all of the participants offered at least some explanation of their views. The responses captured a wide range of reasons for supporting or opposing gay rights. For example, some cited the ability of gays and lesbians to contribute in the workplace or in the military. Others cited concerns about the impact of gays in the military on the morale or comfort level of heterosexual soldiers. Still others cited personal freedom as the standard on which they based their views. Though no one frame dominated, a substantial proportion of the participants (27 percent) invoked either equality or morality (one participant invoked both). Table 5.1 reports how often participants invoked equality and morality in each of the four experimental conditions. Altogether, 19 percent used some form of the word "equal" to explain what they thought about gay rights policies. Eight percent described their views in terms of "moral(s)" or "morality."

Consistent with expectations, the frequency with which participants used equality language depended on whether they had received the pro–gay rights equality frame. Of the participants who read this frame, 25 percent invoked equality in their open-ended responses, whereas only 13 percent of the participants who did not receive the frame mentioned equality. This difference of proportions was significant at $p = .01$.[43] The frequency with which participants used morality language varied across framing conditions, as well. Of those who received the anti–gay rights morality frame, 12 percent mentioned morality when they expressed their opinions about gay rights in their own words. In contrast, only 3 percent of the participants who did not receive this frame invoked morality in their answers. Again, the difference of proportions was significant at $p = .01$. In short, I found that exposure to frames invoking equality and morality led participants to explain their views in terms of these values.[44] One possible interpretation here is that participants' thought processes regarding the issue were malleable— that participants adopted other people's value words as their own words. As I show in the following section, however, the framing effects produced by the treatments were more complex than they appeared to be at first glance.

The Nature of the Effects

To gain a clearer sense of how participants used equality language to explain their views on gay rights, I coded each instance of equality language as either endorsing or challenging the pro–gay rights interpretation of equality.[45] I followed a similar procedure for each instance of morality lan-

Table 5.1. Use of Equality and Morality Language in Open-Ended Responses, by Experimental Condition (1999 Experiment)

	No Morality Frame	Morality Frame	Total
No Equality Frame	Equality language: 2 (7%) Morality language: 1 (3%) N = 30	Equality language: 11 (15%) Morality language: 7 (10%) N = 73	Equality language: 13 (13%) Morality language: 8 (8%) N = 103
Equality Frame	Equality language: 20 (30%) Morality language: 2 (4%) N = 67	Equality language: 10 (19%) Morality language: 8 (15%) N = 54	Equality language: 30 (25%) Morality language: 10 (8%) N = 121
Total	Equality language: 22 (23%) Morality language: 3 (3%) N = 97	Equality language: 21 (7%) Morality language: 15 (12%) N = 127	Equality language: 43 (19%) Morality language: 18 (8%) N = 224

guage, distinguishing between cases where participants used morality language to justify opposition to gay rights and cases where they questioned
this interpretation of morality.

I found that thirty participants invoked equality language to justify gay
rights, as in the following examples:

> The fact that, in this day and age, people can still believe that others are not
> worthy of equal rights is incredible and upsetting.
>
> It is simply a matter of equal rights for all in the United States, just as it has
> been with any minority.

Yet thirteen participants used equality language to challenge the notion of
gay rights as equal rights or the idea that gay rights policies should be
judged in terms of egalitarian principles. For example:

> Why aren't there discrimination laws for all kinds of people? Does that not go
> against equality in the truest sense?
>
> I think that we should not rely on the government to do everything for us.
> Life is not easy, and it is not up to the government to ensure that we have
> equality of outcome.

Thus, participants used equality language in two distinct ways.

Eight participants used morality language to justify opposition to gay
rights. For example:

> Being in the 90s class of "born again Christians," I feel that homosexuality is
> morally wrong; therefore it should not be sanctioned by our government.
>
> It is immoral for homosexuals to be protected in America. . . . Homosexuals
> representing our country? What does that say about our morals?

In contrast, the remaining ten respondents who invoked morality questioned
the notion that morality and gay rights clashed, as in the following examples:

> I feel that it is not moral, but I have a hard time not agreeing with such laws
> because it is not fair to not hire someone based on their homosexuality.
>
> Discrimination of any kind is morally repugnant.

As with equality language, participants used morality language in two distinct ways.

I also examined the impact of the treatments on how participants used
value language. Compared to participants who were not exposed to the
pro–gay rights equality frame, participants who received this frame were
more likely to invoke equality language in ways that justified gay rights
policies ($p = .06$) but also more likely to invoke equality language in ways

that questioned the pro–gay rights interpretation of equality ($p = .05$). Similarly, participants who were exposed to the anti–gay rights morality frame were more likely than others to invoke morality as a basis for opposing gay rights ($p = .02$) but also more likely to use morality language in ways that questioned this interpretation ($p = .07$). In short, I found evidence of two different types of framing effects: exposure to the frames encouraged participants to use value language not only in the ways endorsed by the frames but also in ways that challenged the frames. Thus, participants' thought processes were not as malleable as they initially appeared to be.[46]

Competing Frames and Framing Effects

My final analysis tested whether the frames interfered with one another's effects. As table 5.1 shows, the use of equality language was more common among participants who received the equality frame without the morality frame (30 percent) than among those who received both frames (19 percent). On the other hand, the participants who received both the morality frame and the equality frame were slightly more likely to use morality language (15 percent) than were those who received only the morality frame (10 percent). To test whether these differences across conditions were statistically significant, I estimated models of whether participants used equality language and of whether participants used morality language. The models included three independent variables: whether participants received the pro–gay rights equality frame, whether they received the anti–gay rights morality frame, and whether they received both frames. The interaction between the two frames was statistically significant ($p = .05$) in the model for equality language but did not approach significance in the model for morality language. Thus, the impact of the morality frame did not depend on whether participants also received the equality frame, but the effect of the equality frame was reduced by the presence of the morality frame.

Internal Validity and External Validity

My experimental results provide clear evidence of cause and effect in a laboratory setting. In other words, they offer internally valid evidence for framing effects. Still, there are several potential threats to the external validity, or generalizability, of these findings. One revolves around the realism of the experiment. Obviously, the simulated media exposure did not perfectly correspond to the conditions of real-life media exposure. Then again, I took steps to maximize the realism of the experiment: I chose frames that both elites and the media commonly used, and I created the experimental stimuli out of actual newspaper articles. Furthermore, previous research suggests that framing effects produced by simulated electronic newspaper articles parallel the framing effects produced by other forms of media.[47]

Another threat to the external validity of the findings stems from my relatively narrow and unrepresentative sample. In his classic article on the perils of using "college sophomores in the laboratory," David Sears warns that reliance on undergraduate student samples may produce biased experimental results.[48] On some dimensions (e.g., sex, race), my sample looked like the general public, but on other dimensions (e.g., age, prior support for gay rights) my sample was skewed.[49] Such biases in my sample may have skewed my results in certain ways. Consider, for example, the finding that participants invoked equality more often than they invoked morality. In my sample, support for equality was unusually high and support for traditional morality was unusually low. Thus, I might have found more instances of morality language and fewer instances of equality language in a more representative sample. Yet it is not necessarily the case that the framing *process* would have worked any differently within a more representative sample. As Sears himself notes, the majority view in social psychology is that most social psychological processes differ little from a student population to a more general one. Indeed, studies of framing have argued that this is the case for framing effects.[50]

FRAMING EFFECTS ON DELIBERATION ABOUT GAY RIGHTS

The results of a novel survey-experiment conducted by Vincent Price and his colleagues provide additional evidence that Americans drew on frames in public debate to make sense of gay rights.[51] Whereas my experiment tested the impact of framing on how people explained their opinions about the topic, theirs tested the impact of framing on how people engaged in collective deliberation about gay rights. The 235 participants came from a Web-based panel survey conducted by Knowledge Networks and were fairly representative of the American public. They were divided into fifty discussion groups, with participants in each group taking part in a ten to eleven minute online discussion. Half of the groups were prompted to discuss "civil unions for gay couples" and were told, "Some have characterized recognizing civil unions as a matter of extending equal rights."[52] The remaining groups were prompted to discuss "marriage for homosexuals" and were told, "Some have characterized recognizing homosexual marriages as a matter of granting special rights."[53]

Price and his colleagues found that participants frequently cited morality and equality in their collective deliberations. Some of those who received the "marriage/special rights" prompt echoed this frame, but others challenged it. Consider the following conversation (the names are pseudonyms bestowed by the researchers):

> WILL: Homosexuals are citizens of the United States, they should have the same rights as all other citizens. Legalize it and move on.
>
> JOE: We're probably moving closer to legalizing it, which is fine by me.
>
> JACK: It comes down to an issue of semantics. The term marriage is reserved for heterosexuals. People feel threatened when marriage is applied to gay relationships. Semantics aside, I think equal rights should apply to gay relationships no matter what you call it.
>
> BOB: I'm sorry that is one thing I can't agree with at all, and I don't think I'm bigoted, I just don't agree with it.[54]

Likewise, some of the participants who received the "civil unions/equal rights" frame echoed it, while others challenged it. Consider the following exchange:

> GEORGE: I really dislike the label "special rights" that so many people place on the gay attempt to simply maintain the same rights as everyone else.
>
> JAMES: These rights are not equal. My son works for United Airlines. They recognize a civil union of six months and provide benefits to such a union. If my son lived with a woman for six months they would not recognize this union and provide the same benefits.[55]

In broader terms, Price and his colleagues concluded that participants actively negotiated the meaning of frames with one another and that exposure to competing frames provided a check on the influence of framing—two conclusions that dovetail with the results of my laboratory experiment.

WHEN WORDS COLLIDE

In Lewis Carroll's *Through the Looking-Glass*, Humpty Dumpty proclaims, "When *I* use a word, it means just what I choose it to mean—neither more nor less." The framing of gay rights in public debate followed Humpty Dumpty's logic. Gay rights advocates promoted a meaning for equality that favored their stance on the issue, whereas foes promoted meanings for morality and equality that favored their position. Citizens who encountered these frames in public debate sometimes used them to explain their opinions about gay rights and to discuss the issue with one another. In this sense, political elites, like Humpty Dumpty, were "masters" of meaning: the frames they introduced into media coverage took on new lives in citizens' own words.

At the same time, active reasoning and exposure to competing frames helped ordinary Americans interpret the implications of their values in the context of gay rights. Just as Alice questions whether Humpty Dumpty can "make words mean so many different things," citizens who found value frames in public debate sometimes challenged those frames. Thus, the substance of citizens' comments about gay rights reflected critical thought as well as elite influence. Furthermore, competing frames gave citizens tools for reconciling potential conflicts between their values. For example, a person who endorsed both equality and traditional morality could have justified opposition to gay rights policies by reasoning that these policies not only undermined family values but also created special rights. Alternatively, such a person could have justified the opposite stance by reasoning that gay rights are equal rights and that (in the words of a popular bumper sticker) "hatred is not a family value." Put simply, elites were unable to frame the issue for all of the people, all of the time. Instead, both elites and citizens played roles in constructing the meaning of gay rights.

Taken as a whole, my findings suggest that political elites faced not only opportunities but also obstacles in attempting to frame gay rights in terms of values. The most basic constraint that they confronted was the need to use frames that spoke to the public's core values. As Gamson observes, some frames "have a natural advantage because their ideas and language resonate with a broader political culture."[56] In other words, not all frames are created equal. Given the prominence of egalitarianism and moral traditionalism in American political culture, it makes sense that elites on both sides of the debate invoked these values in their efforts to define gay rights.

The same logic explains why political elites on each side of the debate confronted challenges from the other side in their efforts to define the implications of these values. The public debate about gay rights was, in part, a war of words—a contest in which political elites fought framing with framing. In the battle to frame morality, gay rights opponents easily overwhelmed the other side of the debate. The virtual absence of a pro–gay rights morality frame raises the question of why some frames fail to emerge in public debate. Did this absence reflect a strategic decision on the part of gay rights supporters to deemphasize the pro–gay rights morality frame in favor of one that might resonate more strongly with the public (i.e., the pro–gay rights equality frame)? Alternatively, did it reflect a failed effort on their part to disseminate the frame through the news media? In either case, the invisibility of this frame in public debate may have been as important as the presence of the other three frames that I examined.

In the fight to frame equality, gay rights advocates held the upper hand throughout the 1990s and beyond. During the early part of this period— that is, when employment nondiscrimination and gays in the military dominated the agenda—gay rights foes presented a rival interpretation of equality through the news media. In contrast, gay rights foes seldom used the language of special rights to frame marriage and civil unions. One explanation for the pattern of findings here revolves around the possibility that anti–gay rights elites responded in strategic ways to differences across policy contexts in what frames Americans would accept. When it came to framing employment nondiscrimination and military service, gay rights opponents may have faced growing difficulty in gaining public acceptance for the anti–gay rights morality frame. Such a political environment, in turn, may have prompted their use of the anti–gay rights equality frame. When it came to framing marriage and civil unions, however, gay rights opponents may have stuck with the anti–gay rights morality frame because of its more enduring resonance among the public in these policy contexts.

NOTES

1. *Romer v. Evans*, 517 U.S. 620 (1996).

2. *Romer v. Evans*.

3. *Romer v. Evans*.

4. Donald R. Kinder and Lynn M. Sanders, *Divided By Color: Racial Politics and Democratic Ideals* (Chicago: University of Chicago Press, 1996), 164.

5. William A. Gamson and Kathryn E. Lasch, "The Political Culture of Social Welfare Policy," in *Evaluating the Welfare State*, ed. Shimon E. Spiro and Ephraim Yuchtman-Yaar (New York: Academic Press, 1983), 397–415; William A. Gamson and Andre Modigliani, "The Changing Culture of Affirmative Action," in *Research in Political Sociology*, ed. Richard D. Braungart (Greenwich, Conn.: JAI Press, 1987), 137–77; William A. Gamson and Andre Modigliani, "Media Discourse and Public Opinion on Nuclear Power: A Constructionist Approach," *American Journal of Sociology* 95 (1989): 1–37.

6. Dennis Chong, "How People Think, Reason, and Feel about Rights and Liberties," *American Journal of Political Science* 37 (1993): 867–99.

7. Dennis Chong, "Creating Common Frames of Reference on Political Issues," in *Political Persuasion and Attitude Change*, ed. Diana C. Mutz, Paul M. Sniderman, and Richard A. Brody (Ann Arbor: University of Michigan Press, 1996), 195–224.

8. George Orwell, "Politics and the English Language," in *Inside the Whale and Other Essays* (New York: Penguin, 1996), 149.

9. Gamson and Modigliani, "Changing Culture," 143. See also Robert Entman, "Framing: Toward Clarification of a Fractured Paradigm," *Journal of Communication* 43 (1993): 51–58.

10. Gamson and Modigliani, "Changing Culture"; Gamson and Modigliani, "Media Discourse."

11. William Jacoby, "Issue Framing and Public Opinion on Government Spending," *American Journal of Political Science* 44 (2003): 751.

12. Jacoby, "Issue Framing"; Kinder and Sanders, *Divided by Color*.

13. For more on citizens' use of values to form political opinions, see Stanley Feldman, "Structure and Consistency in Public Opinion: The Role of Core Beliefs and Values," *American Journal of Political Science* 32 (1988): 416–40; Jon Hurwitz and Mark Peffley, "How Are Foreign Policy Attitudes Structured? A Hierarchical Model," *American Political Science Review* 81 (1987): 1099–120; Herbert McClosky and John Zaller, *The American Ethos: Public Attitudes Toward Capitalism and Democracy* (Cambridge, Mass.: Harvard University Press, 1984); Milton Rokeach, *The Nature of Human Values* (New York: Free Press, 1973).

14. I conducted the content analysis in 1998.

15. Appendix C provides further discussion of the content analysis procedure.

16. "Supreme Court Decision Won't End Debate on Gay Rights," *National Public Radio*, 24 May 1996.

17. Linda Wheeler and Maria E. Odum, "Opponents Sitting It Out: One Group Has Permit to Protest Gay Rights March," *Washington Post*, 21 April 1993, C1.

18. Eric Schmitt, "Senate Weighs Bill on Gay Rights on the Job," *New York Times*, 7 September 1996, A12.

19. Joyce Howard Price, "Is Clinton Seeking Gay Rights Legacy? Bennett Poses Truman Comparison," *Washington Times*, 10 November 1997, A4.

20. Valerie Richardson, "Tough Challenges in Court Stymie Gay Rights Backlash," *Washington Times*, 20 December 1993, A1.

21. Ann C. Gordon, Barry L. Tadlock, and Elizabeth Popp, "Framing the Issue of Same-Sex Marriage: Traditional Values versus Equal Rights," paper presented at the annual meeting of the American Political Science Association, Chicago, September 2004. See also Seth Goldman and Paul R. Brewer, "From Gay Bashing to Gay Baiting: Public Opinion and News Media Frames for Gay Marriage," in *Defending Same-Sex Marriage, Volume III: The Freedom-to-Marry Movement: Education, Advocacy, Culture, and the Media*, ed. Martin Dupuis and William Thompson (Westport, Conn.: Praeger, 2007), 103–28; Donald P. Haider-Markel, "Media Coverage of *Lawrence v. Texas*: An Analysis of Content, Tone, and Frames in National and Local News Reporting" (New York: Gay and Lesbian Alliance Against Defamation, 2003); Donald P. Haider-Markel, Mahalley D. Allen, and Morgen Johansen, "Understanding Variations in Media Coverage of U.S. Supreme Court Decisions: Comparing Media Outlets in Their Coverage of *Lawrence v. Texas*," *Harvard International Journal of Press/Politics* 11 (2006): 64–85; Elvin T. Lim and Nicholas W. Carnes, "Whither 'Culture War?' Cultural Peace in the 2004 Same-Sex Marriage Debate," paper presented at the annual meeting of the Midwest Political Science Association, Chicago, April 2006; Vincent Price, Lilach Nir, and Joseph N. Cappella, "Framing Public Discussion of Gay Civil Unions," *Public Opinion Quarterly* 69 (2005): 179–212.

22. Stanley Feldman and John Zaller, "The Political Culture of Ambivalence: Ideological Responses to the Welfare State," *American Journal of Political Science* 36 (1992): 268–307; Jennifer Hochschild, *What's Fair?* (Princeton, N.J.: Princeton University Press, 1981).

23. Kinder and Sanders, *Divided by Color*; Jeffrey W. Koch, "Political Rhetoric and Political Persuasion: The Changing Structure of Citizens' Preferences on Health Insurance During Policy Debates," *Public Opinion Quarterly* 62 (1998): 209–29; Thomas E. Nelson, Rosalee A. Clawson, and Zoe M. Oxley, "Media Framing of a

Civil Liberties Conflict and Its Effect on Tolerance," *American Political Science Review* 91 (1997): 567–83.

24. James N. Druckman, "On the Limits of Framing Effects: Who Can Frame?" *Journal of Politics* 63 (2001): 1041–66; James N. Druckman and Kjersten R. Nelson, "Framing and Deliberation: How Citizens' Conversations Limit Elite Influence," *American Journal of Political Science* 47 (2003): 726–45; Kinder and Sanders, *Divided by Color*; Nelson, Clawson, and Oxley, "Media Framing"; Thomas E. Nelson and Zoe M. Oxley, "Issue Framing Effects on Belief Importance and Opinion," *Journal of Politics* 61 (1999): 1040–67; Thomas E. Nelson, Zoe M. Oxley, and Rosalee A. Clawson, "Toward a Psychology of Framing Effects," *Political Behavior* 19 (1997): 221–46.

25. Kinder and Sanders, *Divided by Color*, 174–78.

26. Paul R. Brewer and Kimberly Gross, "Values, Framing, and Citizens' Thoughts about Policy Issues: Effects on Content and Quantity," *Political Psychology* 26 (2005): 929–48. See also Dhavan V. Shah, David Domke, and Daniel Wackman, "'To Thine Own Self Be True': Values, Framing, and Voter Decision-Making Strategies," *Communication Research* 23 (1996): 509–60.

27. William A. Gamson, *Talking Politics* (New York: Cambridge University Press, 1992).

28. Katherine Cramer Walsh, *Talking about Politics: Informal Groups and Social Identity in America* (Chicago: University of Chicago Press, 2004).

29. Gamson, *Talking Politics*, 180 (emphasis in original).

30. See, for example, John Zaller, *The Nature and Origins of Mass Opinion* (New York: Cambridge University Press, 1992); Kinder and Sanders, *Divided by Color*.

31. Nelson, Clawson, and Oxley, "Media Framing"; Nelson and Oxley, "Issue Framing Effects"; Nelson, Oxley, and Clawson, "Psychology of Framing Effects"; Thomas E. Nelson and Elaine A. Willey, "Issue Frames That Strike a Value Balance," in *Framing Public Life*, ed. Stephen D. Reese, Oscar H. Gandy, Jr., and August E. Grant (Mahwah, N.J.: Lawrence Erlbaum, 2001), 245–66.

32. Paul R. Brewer, "Value Words and Lizard Brains: Do Citizens Deliberate about Appeals to Their Core Values?" *Political Psychology* 22 (2001): 45–64; James N. Druckman, "The Implications of Framing Effects for Citizen Competence," *Political Behavior* 23 (2001): 225–56.

33. See, for example, Brewer, "Value Words"; Druckman, "On the Limits of Framing Effects"; Druckman and Nelson, "Framing and Deliberation"; Donald P. Haider-Markel and Mark R. Joslyn, "Gun Policy, Opinion, Tragedy, and Blame Attribution," *Journal of Politics* 63 (2001): 520–43.

34. Dennis Chong and James N. Druckman, "Competitive Framing," paper presented at the annual meeting of the American Political Science Association, Washington, DC, September 2005; Paul M. Sniderman and Sean M. Theriault, "The Structure of Political Argument and the Logic of Issue Framing," in *Studies in Public Opinion: Attitudes, Nonattitudes, Measurement Error, and Change*, ed. Willem E. Saris and Paul M. Sniderman (Princeton, N.J.: Princeton University Press 2004), 133–65.

35. Gamson, *Talking Politics*.

36. Pew Research Center for the People and the Press, "Republicans Unified, Democrats Split on Same-Sex Marriage; Religious Beliefs Underpin Opposition to Homosexuality" (Washington, DC: Pew Research Center for the People and the Press, 2003).

37. For additional evidence of value framing effects on public opinion about gay rights, see Paul R. Brewer, "Values, Political Knowledge, and Public Opinion about Gay Rights: A Framing-Based Account," *Public Opinion Quarterly* 67 (2003): 173–201; Seth Goldman, "Framing Effects, Elite Competition, and the Debate over Gay Marriage: An Experimental Test," paper presented at the annual meeting of the International Communication Association, Dresden, Germany, June 2006; Gordon, Tadlock, and Popp, "Framing the Issue."

38. For more on the use of laboratory experiments in testing for media effects, see Shanto Iyengar and Donald R. Kinder, *News That Matters: Television and American Public Opinion* (Chicago: University of Chicago Press, 1987), 6–15.

39. The computer program randomized the order of the third and fourth articles so that participants had an equal chance of receiving either the gay rights or the welfare reform article first. For further discussion of the welfare reform article and its effects, see Brewer, "Value Words."

40. Appendix D presents the full text of the treatments.

41. In a further experimental manipulation, each frame was randomly attributed to either a U.S. Supreme Court opinion or an interest group spokesperson. Given that this manipulation had no effect on the dependent variables analyzed below, I collapsed conditions across source attributions.

42. Upon completion of the procedure, participants received a letter explaining the purpose of the experiment.

43. Given that my hypotheses suggested the directions of the expected effects, I used one-tailed hypothesis tests.

44. Similar findings emerged when I used logistic regression to control for the effects of the other value frame (i.e., the anti–gay rights morality frame for the use of equality language and the pro–gay rights equality frame for the use of morality language), pretest measures of participants' values, pretest attitudes toward gay rights, sex, and race.

45. A second coder replicated this procedure. The results indicated that the coding process was highly reliable: the two coders reached the same judgment for all forty-three instances of equality language and seventeen of the eighteen instances of morality language.

46. One might question whether participants' invocations of values reflected meaningful thoughts about the issue of gay rights in the first place: perhaps the open-ended responses were just empty words. To make certain that this was not the case, I examined the relationship between the use of value language and another measure of opinion toward gay rights. I used responses to the two closed-ended items described above to create a nine-point index of posttest support for gay rights. I then tested whether this index was associated with patterns in participants' use of value words. The results suggested that participants' open-ended responses were more than just noise (though they could have been either reasons behind or rationalizations for the closed-ended responses). The participants who invoked equality and used it to justify gay rights were especially likely to score high on the index of support for gay rights ($r = .20$, $p < .01$). Likewise, the participants who invoked morality as a basis for opposing gay rights were particularly likely to score low on the index ($r = -.39$; $p < .01$). Participants who invoked equality and morality in

alternative ways were neither more nor less likely to score high on the index than anyone else.

47. Nelson, Clawson, and Oxley, "Media Framing."

48. David O. Sears, "College Sophomores in the Laboratory: Influences of a Narrow Data Base on Psychology's View of Human Nature," *Journal of Personality and Social Psychology* 51 (1986): 515–30.

49. See appendix D for further details.

50. Druckman and Nelson, "Framing and Deliberation"; Nelson, Clawson, and Oxley, "Media Framing."

51. Price, Nir, and Cappella, "Framing Public Discussion."

52. Price, Nir, and Cappella, "Framing Public Discussion," 189.

53. Price, Nir, and Cappella, "Framing Public Discussion," 189.

54. Price, Nir, and Cappella, "Framing Public Discussion," 193.

55. Price, Nir, and Cappella, "Framing Public Discussion," 194.

56. Gamson, *Talking Politics*, 135.

6

The Foundations of Opinion about Gay Rights: Changes over Time, Differences across Contexts

In 1998, the *Washington Post* assembled a ten-person focus group to discuss gays and lesbians, homosexuality, and gay rights.[1] A number of participants described how their views on all three had changed over time. One man said that social contact with his wife's gay brother had altered his perspective. "I know my views have changed dramatically," he said. "I'm tolerant of [gays] now. I don't agree with [homosexuality] at all, but I'm not going to judge them. You know, who am I to judge them, right?"[2] Another participant credited gay co-workers with dispelling his fear of gay people.

These individual transformations in public opinion did not come easy, however. In describing the discussions among the focus group participants, reporters Hanna Rosin and Richard Morin present a picture of ambivalence:

> Their answers to most questions were qualified, measured, and adjusted. In each, they displayed a struggle with modern pressures to change. They were accustomed to seeing gay characters in sitcoms and movies, and they had absorbed corporate credos of tolerance at work. But many of them resisted becoming the diversity trainer's ideal image: the open-minded, multicultural American of the future.[3]

Participants also drew distinctions across circumstances in their acceptance of gay rights. For example a participant argued for "certain bounds" in employment rights: a gay person "flipping burgers" was fine, but a gay foreman of a construction crew was a different matter.[4] As for same-sex marriage, it elicited strong condemnation. "Marriage is between a man and a woman," said one participant. "You can't just open it up to whatever kind of person

109

you're living with."[5] A second participant concurred: "Homosexuality and family values just do not go together. They're in a different ballpark."[6]

The people who took part in the *Washington Post* focus group were not alone in changing their minds about some sorts of gay rights or in drawing the line at other sorts of gay rights. One striking feature of public opinion about gay rights is the sharp increase in support for the two policies that dominated the debate about gay rights in the early and mid-1990s: employment nondiscrimination laws and "gays in the military." Consider the findings of the American National Election Studies (ANES) surveys conducted in 1992, 1996, 2000, and 2004.[7] These surveys asked respondents whether they favored or opposed "laws to protect homosexuals against job discrimination" and whether they thought that "homosexuals should be allowed to serve in the United States Armed Forces." As table 6.1 shows, relatively small majorities (61 percent and 58 percent, respectively) favored or strongly favored these policies in 1992. In 1996, support stood at 64 percent for an employment nondiscrimination law and at 69 percent for gays in the military. By 2000, the percentages were 68 percent and 76 percent. Four years later, they had risen to 76 percent and 81 percent. Moreover, these shifts cut across the public. They took place among men and among women; among African Americans and among whites; among those under thirty and among those over sixty; among those with a college degree and among those without one; among those with incomes of less than $25,000 a year and among those with incomes greater than $75,000 a year.

Another striking feature of public opinion about gay rights is the contrast between public opinion about the "old" politics of gay rights, focused on employment nondiscrimination laws and gays in the military, and public opinion about the "new" politics of gay rights, centered on legal recognition for same-sex relationships. In 2004, an overwhelming majority of ANES respondents favored gay rights when it came to military service and protection from discrimination in employment. Only 36 percent, however, said that "same-sex couples [should] be allowed to marry," whereas 64 percent of those who offered an opinion said that same-sex couples "should not be allowed to marry" (see table 6.1).[8] Again, the pattern was clear among all demographic groups.

In this chapter, I take a closer look at both features of public opinion about gay rights. In doing so, I draw together the themes of the three preceding chapters: the influence of public opinion about, media images of, and social contact with gays and lesbians; the impact of signals from partisan, ideological, and religious elites; and the effects of frames invoking equality and traditional morality. First, I examine what lay beneath the transformation in public opinion about employment nondiscrimination laws and gays in the military. Here, I conclude that not only did shifts in

Table 6.1. Support for Gay Rights Policies and Feelings toward Gay Men and Lesbians (American National Election Studies, 1992–2004)

	1992	*1996*	*2000*	*2004*
Do you favor or oppose laws to protect homosexuals against job discrimination?				
Strongly favor	33%	40%	41%	51%
Favor not strongly	28%	24%	27%	25%
Oppose not strongly	15%	13%	14%	9%
Oppose strongly	25%	23%	19%	15%
N	2,129	1,436	1,469	1,025
Do you think homosexuals should be allowed to serve in the United States Armed Forces or do you think they should not be allowed?				
Strongly favor	32%	44%	52%	55%
Favor not strongly	26%	25%	24%	26%
Oppose not strongly	9%	7%	5%	6%
Oppose strongly	32%	25%	19%	13%
N	2,127	1,480	1,692	1,023
Do you think same-sex couples should be allowed to marry, or do you think that they should not be allowed?				
Should be allowed	—	—	—	36%
Should not be allowed	—	—	—	64%
N	—	—	—	1,105
Feelings toward gay men and lesbians				
Rating of 0	23%	20%	12%	14%
Rating of 1–49	27%	25%	21%	19%
Rating of 50	27%	31%	37%	34%
Rating of 51–99	23%	21%	25%	29%
Rating of 100	2%	3%	6%	5%
Mean	38	40	48	49
N	2,172	1,485	1,448	1,044

how Americans felt toward gays and lesbians contribute to the increase in support for these policies, but so did substantial changes in how Americans thought about the policies. Next, I consider the contrast between public opinion about employment nondiscrimination laws and gays in the military, on the one hand, and public opinion about same-sex marriage, on the other. Here, I argue that Americans thought about the old and new politics of gay rights in markedly different ways. Such variations, in turn, help to account for differences across policy contexts in support for gay rights.

THE FOUNDATIONS OF PUBLIC OPINION ABOUT GAY RIGHTS

A recurring theme of this book is that people base their opinions about specific political issues on the more general foundations provided by their belief systems. The ways in which people build on these foundations, however, can vary from topic to topic and from one point in time to another.
Donald Kinder and Lynn Sanders describe the process of opinion formation in the following way:

> Public opinion is a complex expression of various core ingredients: the mate-
> rial interests that citizens see at stake in the issue, the sympathies and resent-
> ments that citizens feel toward those social groups implicated in the dispute,
> especially those groups that the policy appears to benefit; and commitment to
> the political principles that the policy seems to honor or repudiate. At the same
> time, public opinion also reflects and follows political debate. Elites are con-
> stantly engaged in symbolic warfare over how complex issues are to be framed.
> Frames are opinion recipes: they are suggestions to citizens regarding which in-
> gredients, in what proportion, should be combined to make a good opinion.[9]

In the case of gay rights, Americans could have based their opinions on
some combination of their sympathies and resentments regarding gays and
lesbians, their partisan loyalties, their ideological orientations, their religious beliefs, and their attachments to the values of equality and traditional
morality.

An obvious place to begin is with public opinion about gays and lesbians.
As I described in chapter 3, Americans held a variety of thoughts and feelings
about this group, including emotional responses to gays, lesbians, and homosexuality; beliefs about whether homosexuality is innate and whether it
can be changed; beliefs about whether homosexuality is wrong; and beliefs
about whether acceptance of gays and lesbians is good for the country. All of
these aspects of opinion were strongly interrelated. Among them, however,
general feelings or evaluations regarding gays and lesbians stood out as ex-
erting a particularly strong and robust influence on public opinion about gay
rights policies. Thus, I expect support for such policies to have been greater
among Americans with positive feelings toward gays and lesbians than
among those with negative feelings toward gays and lesbians.[10]

Drawing on my findings in chapter 4, I also expect partisan loyalties, ideological orientations, and religious beliefs to have shaped Americans' opinions about gay rights.[11] During the 1990s and beyond, Democratic and liberal elites typically signaled more support for gay rights than did Republican
and conservative elites. In addition, evangelical Christian elites prominently
signaled their opposition to gay rights. Given that many Americans follow
signals from partisan, ideological, and religious elites, Democratic partisans,
liberals, and nonevangelicals among the public should have been more

likely than conservatives, Republican partisans, and evangelicals to favor gay rights.[12]

Furthermore, I expect Americans' beliefs about equality and traditional morality to have shaped their opinions about gay rights. In chapter 5, I described how political elites used each of these values to frame gay rights. The prominence within public debate of the pro–gay rights interpretation for equality suggests that egalitarianism should have produced support for gay rights policies among the public.[13] By the same logic, the prominence of the anti–gay rights interpretation for traditional morality implies that Americans who favored traditional moral standards should have expressed less support for gay rights than did those who favored changing moral standards.[14]

EXPLAINING SHIFTS IN PUBLIC OPINION ABOUT GAY RIGHTS

If some or all of these predispositions shaped public opinion about gay rights policies, then one possible explanation for the shift in support for employment nondiscrimination laws and gays in the military is that the predispositions themselves underwent shifts. For example, a shift toward greater favorability in the public's feelings toward gays and lesbians could have produced an increase in support for gay rights policies.[15] By the same logic, shifts in ideology, partisanship, religious beliefs, beliefs about equality, and beliefs about morality among the public could have contributed to the trend in policy opinions.

Alternatively (or additionally), the shift in public opinion about the old politics of gay rights could have reflected changes in how Americans weighed these predispositions in forming their opinions. What, then, could have produced the latter sort of changes? One possibility is that increasing awareness of and contact with gays and lesbians altered the underlying structure of public opinion about gay rights policies. As I showed in chapter 3, the percentages of Americans saying that they knew a gay co-worker, friend, or family member increased dramatically over the course of the 1990s. Likewise, the visibility of gays and lesbians in entertainment media increased substantially during the 1990s and beyond. As the *Washington Post* focus group results suggest, increased exposure to openly gay and lesbian peers and media figures tended to produce more favorable attitudes toward gays and lesbians as a group.[16] At the same time, increased social and virtual contact with gay men and lesbians could have dampened the impact of negative feelings about gays and lesbians *as a group* on public opinion about gay rights.

New information about homosexuality could have altered the ways in which Americans thought about gay rights, as well. In chapter 3, I discussed polls that revealed a widening dissemination of the belief that homosexuality is fixed at birth. Clyde Wilcox and Barbara Norrander suggest that Americans who came to accept that gays and lesbians cannot change their sexual orientation may have felt "bound to employ their equality values even if they [did] not approve of homosexuality. If sexual orientation is fixed at birth, then it is difficult to justify denying gays and lesbians jobs."[17] Similarly, Americans who came to see homosexuality as innate may have been less inclined to apply traditional moral standards to issues of workplace discrimination and military service or to base their opinions about these subjects on their feelings toward gays and lesbians.

Changes in the nature of elite signals regarding an issue can also produce changes in the structure of public opinion regarding that issue.[18] For example, if the messages about gay rights from partisan, ideological, or religious elites varied over time in direction or intensity, then this could have altered the impact of the public's partisan loyalties, ideological orientations, or religious beliefs on support for gay rights. In the early to mid-1990s, Republican, conservative, and evangelical elites prominently signaled their opposition to employment nondiscrimination laws and gays in the military, whereas Democratic, liberal, and nonevangelical elites signaled their support for these policies. As the debate about gay rights turned increasingly to same-sex marriage, however, the impact of elite signals on public opinion about the old politics of gay rights could have faded.

Yet another possibility is that changes in the balance of frames in the public debate about gay rights produced changes in how Americans thought about the subject.[19] In the early to mid-1990s, proponents' efforts to frame antidiscrimination laws and gays in the military as "equal rights" policies faced a fierce challenge in opponents' efforts to frame these measures as threats to traditional morality.[20] As the debate about gay rights evolved, however, gay rights opponents shifted their efforts toward framing same-sex marriage as a threat to moral values. Moreover, some gay rights foes may have grown increasingly reluctant to use the language of traditional morality to criticize employment nondiscrimination laws and gays in the military. For example, when Take Back Miami-Dade (the successor to Anita Bryant's "Save Our Children" campaign) promoted a 2002 effort to repeal an ordinance banning discrimination against gays and lesbians, the organization downplayed moral themes. Instead, it argued that, "The real issue is special rights and special powers that some people in our community want."[21] Such a shift in framing could have led Americans to reduce the weight that they attached to their moral beliefs in evaluating gay rights policies that dealt with employment nondiscrimination or military service.

In short, many forces at work from the early 1990s onward could have altered the structure of public opinion about the old gay rights. I use data from the 1992, 1996, 2000, and 2004 ANES surveys to test for changes in how citizens thought about employment nondiscrimination and gays in the military during this period, as well as to test for changes in underlying predispositions that shaped support for the policies.

MEASURING THE FOUNDATIONS OF PUBLIC OPINION ABOUT GAY RIGHTS

Each of the four surveys included an item designed to measure feelings toward gays and lesbians. In every case, the item was one in a series of "feeling thermometers" introduced as follows:

> I'd like to get your feelings toward some of our political leaders and other people who are in the news these days. I'll read the name of a person and I'd like you to rate that person using something we call the feeling thermometer. Ratings between 50 degrees and 100 degrees mean that you feel favorable and warm toward the person. Ratings between 0 degrees and 50 degrees mean that you don't feel favorable toward the person and that you don't care too much for that person. You would rate the person at the 50 degree mark if you don't feel particularly warm or cold toward the person.

The feeling thermometer of interest asked respondents to rate "gay men and lesbians, that is, homosexuals." The results indicate a sizable shift in the public's feelings toward gays and lesbians (see table 6.1). Whereas the typical 1992 respondent felt rather negatively toward this group (mean = 38), the average 2004 respondent was almost perfectly neutral (mean = 49).[22] There was a small shift toward warmer feelings from 1992 to 1996 (+2 degrees; significant at $p < .05$), followed by a larger shift in the same direction from 1996 to 2000 (+8 degrees, $p < .01$). The change from 2000 to 2004 (+1 degree) was not statistically significant. A closer look at the distributions of respondents' scores by year reveals that the percentage of respondents who gave gays and lesbians the lowest possible score (0 degrees) declined from 23 percent in 1992 to 14 percent in 2004, while the percentage offering a rating over 50 increased from 25 percent to 34 percent. To the extent that feelings about gays and lesbians shaped public opinion about employment nondiscrimination laws and gays in the military, the shift in feelings toward gays and lesbians would have served to push the public in the direction of greater support.

All of the ANES surveys included seven-category measures for partisanship and ideology.[23] Neither predisposition varied much from 1992 to 2004, ruling out a change in either as a potential cause of the shift in public opinion about gay rights.[24] Each survey also included a question that asked, "Which of these statements comes closest to describing your feelings about the Bible?" The three options were, "The Bible is the actual word of

God and is to be taken literally, word for word," "The Bible is the word of God but not everything in it should be taken literally, word for word," and "The Bible is a book written by men and is not the word of God." Given that evangelical elites frequently used a literalist interpretation of the Bible to justify opposition to gay rights, this item provides a useful measure of religious doctrine. As with their partisan loyalties and ideological orientations, Americans' views on the Bible changed little from 1992 to 2004.[25]

To measure egalitarianism and moral traditionalism, I constructed indices from responses to two batteries of items included on each survey. The first battery consisted of six statements about equality with which respondents could strongly agree, agree, neither agree nor disagree, disagree, or strongly disagree:

- Our society should do whatever is necessary to make sure that everyone has an equal opportunity to succeed.
- We have gone too far in pushing equal rights in this country.
- This country would be better off if we worried less about how equal people are.
- It is not really that big a problem if some people have more of a chance in life than others.
- If people were treated more equally in this country we would have many fewer problems.
- One of the big problems in this country is that we don't give everyone an equal chance.

Responses to these items were strongly correlated with one another; thus, they yielded a reliable measure of egalitarianism.[26] Support for equality did not vary consistently over time.[27]

The second battery consisted of four statements about moral values. Again, respondents could strongly agree, agree, neither agree nor disagree, disagree, or strongly disagree with each statement.

- The newer lifestyles are contributing to the breakdown of society.
- The world is changing and we should adjust our view of moral behavior to those changes.
- We should be more tolerant of people who choose to live according to their own moral standards even if they are very different from our own.
- This country would have fewer problems if there were more emphasis on traditional family ties.

Responses to the individual items were strongly correlated with one another and yielded a reliable index.[28] As with egalitarianism, moral traditionalism did not vary consistently over time. Thus, changes in support for equality and traditional morality cannot account for the increase in public support for employment nondiscrimination laws and gays in the military.[29]

CHANGES IN THE UNDERLYING STRUCTURE
OF PUBLIC OPINION

To analyze what shaped public opinion about the old politics of gay rights—as well as whether the underlying structure of opinion changed over time—I pooled the data from the four ANES surveys. Given that responses to the questions on employment nondiscrimination laws and gays in the military not only exhibited similar trends but were also strongly correlated with one another, I combined them to create an index ranging from 0 to 1 (with 1 indicating maximum support) that captured public opinion about the old politics of gay rights.[30] The mean for the index was .55 in 1992, .62 in 1996, .67 in 2000, and .73 in 2004. Each four-year increase was significant at the .01 level.

I estimated a model for this index that included my measures of feelings toward gays and lesbians, partisanship, ideology, beliefs about the Bible, egalitarianism, and moral traditionalism. In addition, the model included controls for a number of key background characteristics: attendance at religious services, sex, self-identification as African American, age, education, and income.[31] To capture whether the effects of these variables differed across time, I included dichotomous variables for year = 1996, year = 2000, and year = 2004, as well as multiplicative terms for each independent variable x each year variable. In doing so, I treated the 1992 effects for the independent variables as the baselines for comparison, with significant coefficients for the multiplicative terms indicating shifts in the underlying structure of public opinion from these baselines.[32]

With the exception of ideology, all of the key predispositions in the model had significant coefficients for 1992 (see table 6.2). Consistent with expectations, those who held positive feelings toward gays and lesbians expressed greater support for gay rights than did those who held negative feelings toward this group. Similarly, Democrats and those who rejected a literal interpretation of the Bible expressed greater support for gay rights than did Republicans and those who endorsed a literal interpretation of the Bible, respectively. Higher levels of egalitarianism were associated with higher levels of support for gay rights, whereas higher levels of moral traditionalism were associated with lower levels of support for gay rights.

In 1992, a respondents' feeling thermometer score for "gay men and lesbians" was easily the single best predictor of that respondent's opinion about employment nondiscrimination laws and gays in the military.[33] A 60 degree swing on this feeling thermometer would have produced, on average, a one-category shift in opinion about both policies (i.e., from strong opposition to weak opposition, from weak opposition to weak support, or from weak support to strong support). Given that respondents tended to

Table 6.2. Influences on Support for Anti-Discrimination Law and Gays in the Military (American National Election Studies, 1992–2004)

	1992	x 1996	x 2000	x 2004
Feelings toward gay men and lesbians	.56**	−.09*	−.10*	−.09†
	(.03)	(.04)	(.05)	(.05)
Party identification	−.11**	.000	.02	.04
	(.02)	(.03)	(.04)	(.04)
Ideology	−.04	−.13*	.02	.05
	(.04)	(.06)	(.05)	(.07)
Bible should be taken literally	−.11**	.05	.01	−.003
	(.02)	(.04)	(.04)	(.04)
Egalitarianism	.20**	.01	.004	−.02
	(.04)	(.06)	(.06)	(.07)
Moral traditionalism	−.23**	−.01	.09	.13*
	(.04)	(.06)	(.06)	(.06)
N		4,590		

Notes: Table entries are OLS coefficients. The first column presents coefficients for the independent variables in 1992. The remaining columns present coefficients for interactions between the independent variables and dichotomous variables for year = 1996, year = 2000, and year = 2004. Standard errors are in parentheses. The model also included controls for attendance at religious services, sex, self-identification as African American, age, education, and income, as well as the interactions between each of these variables and each of the year variables.
†Significant at the .10 level
*Significant at the .05 level
**Significant at the .01 level

rate gays and lesbians somewhat negatively, the aggregate impact of this relationship was to depress support for gay rights.

By 1996, however, the relationship between feelings toward gays and lesbians and public opinion about the old politics of gay rights was noticeably weaker (as captured by the negative and significant coefficient for feelings toward gay men and lesbians x 1996). More precisely, it declined to about five-sixths of its magnitude in 1992 (from .56 to .47). To be sure, feelings toward this group were still strongly related to support for employment nondiscrimination laws and gays in the military in 1996. The weakening of the relationship, however, suggests a shift in how Americans thought about these policies. In particular, it implies that Americans not only held increasingly positive (if still decidedly mixed) feelings toward gays and lesbians but also attached less weight to those feelings in forming their opinions. Moreover, the latter shift appears to have persisted through 2000 and 2004 (as evidenced by the negative, significant, and similarly-sized coefficients for the corresponding multiplicative terms).

The effects of partisanship and religious doctrine did not vary discernibly from year to year, though both variables were significantly related to support for gay rights in each year. By contrast, ideology went from having no discernible relationship with support for gay rights in 1992 to being significantly related to such support four years later. In other words, a gap between liberals and conservatives had emerged by 1996, with the former expressing greater support for gay rights than did the latter. By 2000, the relationship was no longer discernible; nor did it reappear in 2004. One potential explanation for this pattern is that the ideologically charged debate over employment nondiscrimination and gays in the military that took place from 1993 to 1996 served to polarize liberals and conservatives among the public—but only temporarily. When the flow of signals from ideological elites on these subjects subsided, so did the impact of ideology on public opinion.

For all practical purposes, the magnitude of egalitarianism's effect remained constant from 1992 to 2004: in each year, support for equality was positively associated with support for employment nondiscrimination laws and gays in the military. Given that respondents tended to endorse egalitarianism in all four years, this value consistently fostered support for gay rights among the public as a whole. As for moral traditionalism, its impact did not differ discernibly from 1992 to 1996. Put another way, the negative relationship between support for traditional morality and support for gay rights remained consistently strong over this four-year span. Given that respondents also tended to endorse moral traditionalism, beliefs about morality depressed opposition to gay rights in the aggregate. By 2004, however, the impact of moral traditionalism had declined in magnitude (as evidenced by the positive and statistically significant coefficient for its 2004 multiplicative term). In short, the relationship between moral traditionalism and public opinion about the old politics of gay rights was noticeably weaker in 2004 than it had been in 1992 (though it was still significant), suggesting that Americans attached decreasing weight to this principle in forming their views about employment nondiscrimination laws and gays in the military.

EXPLAINING CONTRASTS ACROSS POLICY CONTEXTS IN PUBLIC OPINION

Just as the structure of opinion about gay rights changed over time, so, too, may it have varied across policy contexts. Indeed, a number of factors could have led Americans to think about the new politics of gay rights in different terms than they thought about the old politics of gay rights. Such contrasts, in turn, could help to explain why public support for employment nondiscrimination laws and gays in the military was, as of 2004, much greater than public support for same-sex marriage.

To begin with, the role of feelings toward gays and lesbians in shaping opinion could have varied from one policy context to another. In particular, the subject of same-sex marriage could have engaged Americans' feelings toward this group to a greater extent than did the subjects of employment nondiscrimination laws and gays in the military. One might expect the marriage debate to have elicited stronger emotional reactions among the public because it cast gays and lesbians as potential family members—not just as soldiers or co-workers—and because it forced Americans to confront the notion of gays and lesbians as sexual beings.

Additionally, differences in the nature or intensity of elite signals across policy contexts could have produced corresponding differences in the structure of public opinion. If partisan, ideological, or religious elites diverged more clearly or vigorously in one policy context (e.g., same-sex marriage) than in another (e.g., antidiscrimination laws and gays in the military), then partisan, ideological, or religious divides among the public could have been more pronounced in one policy context than in another, as well. Such a difference in the impact of ideology seems particularly plausible given the differences across time in how this orientation influenced public opinion about the old politics of gay rights. In that context, the role of ideology in shaping opinion seemed to grow, then fade, in tandem with the rise and fall of employment discrimination laws and gays in the military on the agenda. Thus, it also seems reasonable to expect ideological divisions among the public to have been more pronounced for same-sex marriage than for these other policies after marriage came to dominate the public debate about gay rights. Likewise, it would be reasonable to expect religious doctrine to have mattered more in the context of same-sex marriage than in the context of employment nondiscrimination laws and gays in the military if evangelical Christians refocused their signaling efforts from the latter context to the former after the mid-1990s.

Furthermore, differences across policy contexts in the balance of frames invoking equality and traditional morality could have yielded differences across such contexts in the structure of public opinion about gay rights. In the debate about employment nondiscrimination laws and gays in the military, the push by opponents to frame their stance in moral terms seemed to diminish over time, leaving the pro–gay rights interpretation of equality as the dominant value-based frame for these policies. Thus, the balance of frames in the public debate provides a reasonable explanation for the steady effect of egalitarianism and the declining impact of moral traditionalism on public opinion about the old politics of gay rights. Even as the anti–gay rights interpretation of traditional morality faded in that context, however, it continued to occupy a prominent role in the debate about same-sex marriage. Here, the pro–gay rights interpretation of equality had not won out in public debate as of 2004.[34] Thus, one might expect Americans to have attached more weight to their moral beliefs in the context of same-sex marriage than in the context of nondiscrimination laws and gays in the military. Similarly, one might expect them to have attached less weight to their beliefs about equality in the former context than in the latter.

DIFFERENT POLICY CONTEXTS, DIFFERENT FOUNDATIONS OF OPINION

I used data from the 2004 ANES survey to examine how the predisposition described above (as well as background characteristics) were related to support for same-sex marriage. Doing so also allowed me to compare the structure of public opinion about this topic to the structure of public opinion about the old politics of gay rights.

Feelings toward gays and lesbians were strongly related to public opinion about same-sex marriage (see table 6.3). Holding all other independent variables at their means, respondents who rated members of this group at 100 degrees had a 75 percent probability of favoring same-sex marriage.[35] By contrast, respondents who rated gays and lesbians at 0 degrees had only a 4 percent probability of doing so. Such feelings were also related to public

Table 6.3. Influences on Support for Allowing Same-Sex Couples to Marry (American National Election Studies, 2004)

	Coefficient (Standard error)	Probability of Support at Minimum	Probability of Support at Maximum
Feelings toward gay men and lesbians	2.39** (.29)	4%	75%
Party identification	−.41† (.23)	36%	22%
Ideology	−1.02** (.40)	49%	16%
Bible should be taken literally	−1.25** (.22)	57%	14%
Egalitarianism	.01 (.38)	29%	29%
Moral traditionalism	−2.62** (.39)	81%	5%
N		790	

Notes: Table entries are probit coefficients. The second column presents the probability of support for a respondent at the minimum observed value of the independent variable in question, holding all other independent variables at their means. The third column presents the probability of support for a respondent at the maximum observed value of the independent variable in question, holding all other independent variables at their means. The model also included controls for attendance at religious services, sex, self-identification as African American, age, education, and income,
†Significant at the .10 level
*Significant at the .05 level
**Significant at the .01 level

opinion about employment nondiscrimination laws and gays in the military in 2004, but these relationships were significantly weaker than the one for same-sex marriage.[36] Thus, Americans appeared to attach more weight to their feelings about gays and lesbians in forming their views about same-sex marriage than they did in forming their views about the old politics of gay rights.

Democrats, liberals, and those who rejected a literalist reading of the Bible expressed greater support for same-sex marriage than did Republicans, conservatives, and those who endorsed a literalist reading of the Bible. None of these relationships was as strong as the one between feelings toward gays and lesbians and support for same-sex marriage (see table 6.3). Still, the finding of a significant coefficient for ideology suggests that public opinion about this policy was split along ideological lines in 2004, just as public opinion about the old politics of gay rights had been in 1996.[37] The results also suggest that, in 2004, the opinion divide along religious doctrine was more pronounced for same-sex marriage than for employment nondiscrimination laws and gays in the military.[38] These patterns may have reflected particularly sharp divisions along ideological and religious lines in the elite debate about same-sex marriage.

Another difference across policy contexts in the structure of public opinion revolved around egalitarianism. Whereas support for this value was positively, significantly, and strongly related to support for nondiscrimination laws and gays in the military, it was not significantly related to support for same-sex marriage. Put simply, Americans did not appear to connect their beliefs about equality to their opinions about same-sex marriage. Given the tendency among the public to endorse the principle of equality, the absence of any discernible role for this value in shaping opinion would help to explain why support for same-sex marriage was lower than support for employment nondiscrimination laws and gays in the military. A lack of success on the part of gay rights advocates in winning public acceptance of a pro-marriage equality frame (particularly when compared to their success in using egalitarianism to frame the debate about the old politics of gay rights) could account for the apparent absence of such a relationship.

Moral traditionalism was negatively related to support for gay rights across policy contexts. The magnitude of this relationship, however, was significantly greater for same-sex marriage than it was for employment nondiscrimination and gays in the military.[39] All else being equal, the most morally traditional respondents had only a 5 percent probability of favoring same-sex marriage. In contrast, the least morally traditional respondents had an 81 percent probability of doing so. In forming their opinions about this topic, Americans appeared to attach at least as much weight to their moral beliefs as to their feelings toward gays and lesbians—which is to say, a great amount of weight. The particularly strong connection between moral beliefs and opinion about same-sex marriage offers yet another explanation for why support for this policy fell so far short of support for employment nondiscrimination laws and gays in the military.

POLITICS AND THE STRUCTURE OF PUBLIC OPINION ABOUT GAY RIGHTS

The foundations of public opinion about the old politics of gay rights shifted in two ways between 1992 and 2004. One particularly important foundation, Americans' feelings toward gays and lesbians, underwent a transformation that produced greater support for employment nondiscrimination laws and gays in the military. At the same time, shifts in how Americans thought about the policies also contributed to the increase in support for them. One key change in the structure of public opinion about employment nondiscrimination laws and gays in the military was the shrinking weight that Americans attached to their feelings about gays and lesbians. Shifts in media messages about and social contact with gays and lesbians offer plausible explanations for this change. Another key change in the structure of public opinion about employment nondiscrimination laws and gays in the military was the shrinking weight that Americans attached to moral traditionalism. This change, in turn, may have reflected a decline in the prominence and resonance of the traditional morality frame as a justification for opposing the policies.

The structure of public opinion about employment nondiscrimination laws and gays in the military differed in several ways from the structure of opinion about same-sex marriage. Feelings toward gays and lesbians, religious doctrine, ideology, and beliefs about morality played larger roles in shaping public opinion about the latter than in shaping public opinion about the former, while the opposite was true for beliefs about equality. Such differences across policy contexts in how Americans thought about gay rights help to explain the large gap between support for employment nondiscrimination laws and gays in the military, on the one hand, and same-sex marriage, on the other. As for what explains the differences across policy contexts in the structure of public opinion, one plausible account implicates differences from one context to another in elite signals and frames in public debate. A complementary explanation revolves around the special power of the controversy regarding marriage to evoke emotional responses.

Of course, it is possible that the ways in which Americans form their opinions about same-sex marriage will undergo a transformation similar to the one in how they thought about the old politics of gay rights. After all, the structure of public opinion about same-sex marriage in 2004 had more than a little in common with the structure of public opinion about employment nondiscrimination laws and military service in 1992. Perhaps Americans will increasingly come to see dislike of gays and beliefs about traditional morality as irrelevant to the question of whether same-sex marriage should be legal, just as they did with the questions of whether gays and lesbians should be protected from job discrimination and whether they should be allowed to serve in the military. Such changes, in turn, would serve to boost support for same-sex marriage among the public as a whole.

Another point to consider is that the politics of gay rights could have responded to—in addition to producing—changes over time and differences across contexts in how Americans thought about the topic. To the extent that politicians and interest group leaders recognized shifts and variations in the structure of public opinion about gay rights, they could have tailored their messages to the public—their characterizations of gays, lesbians, and homosexuality; their signals about gay rights; their frames for equality and morality—accordingly. Put another way, the contestants in the battle over gay rights could have responded in strategic ways to the landscape of public opinion and the political opportunity structures that went along with it.[40]

Elites could have changed their own ways of thinking about gay rights, as well. More than a few politicians who opposed gay rights underwent changes of heart similar to those described by the *Washington Post* focus group participants. In 2002, for example, United States Senator Gordon Smith (R-OR) endorsed legislation to extend the federal hate crimes law to cover anti-gay violence, saying that the 1998 murder of Matthew Shepard had changed his mind on the issue.[41] Although Smith also made it clear that he was "not for gay marriage," a number of politicians altered their thinking even on that subject.[42] Former Minnesota Governor Jesse Ventura did so in typically colorful fashion. "I'm a tough guy," he proclaimed in 2004. "I chew on cigars; I live life to the fullest. But I don't like it when I see human rights violated. . . . We are not the Hetero States of America. America should be inclusive, not separating."[43] The following year, a number of Massachusetts state legislators switched their position on an amendment to ban same-sex marriage. One of them, State Senator James E. Timilty, explained that "when I would look at the children of these couples and see that they deserved all of the benefits that I had certainly growing up in a family, the principle of fairness changed my mind and I decided that a no vote was the correct vote."[44] The amendment failed in the Massachusetts legislature.

NOTES

1. Hanna Rosin and Richard Morin, "As Tolerance Grows, Acceptance Remains Elusive; In Majority's View, Still Unacceptable; For Some, an Uneasy Tolerance," *Washington Post*, 26 December 1998, A1.

2. Quoted in Rosin and Morin, "As Tolerance Grows," A1.

3. Rosin and Morin, "As Tolerance Grows," A1.

4. Rosin and Morin, "As Tolerance Grows," A1.

5. Rosin and Morin, "As Tolerance Grows," A1.

6. Rosin and Morin, "As Tolerance Grows," A1.

7. For additional evidence of this trend, see chapter 2.

8. For additional evidence of this contrast, see chapter 2.

9. Donald R. Kinder and Lynn M. Sanders, *Divided By Color: Racial Politics and Democratic Ideals* (Chicago: University of Chicago Press, 1996), 44. See also Stanley Feldman, "Structure and Consistency in Public Opinion: The Role of Core Beliefs and Values," *American Journal of Political Science* 32 (1988): 416–40; Thomas E. Nelson and Donald R. Kinder, "Issue Frames and Group-Centrism in American Public Opinion," *Journal of Politics* 58 (1996): 1055–78; Paul M. Sniderman, Richard A. Brody, and Philip E. Tetlock, *Reasoning and Choice: Explorations in Political Psychology* (New York: Cambridge University Press, 1991); John Zaller, *The Nature and Origins of Mass Opinion* (New York: Cambridge University Press, 1992).

10. See also Paul R. Brewer, "The Shifting Foundations of Public Opinion about Gay Rights," *Journal of Politics* 65 (2003): 1208–20; Stephen C. Craig, Michael D. Martinez, James G. Kane, and Jason Gainous, "Core Values, Value Conflict, and Citizens' Ambivalence about Gay Rights," *Political Research Quarterly* 58 (2005): 5–17; Douglas Alan Strand, "Civil Liberties, Civil Rights, and Stigma: Voter Attitudes and Behavior in the Politics of Homosexuality," in *Stigma and Sexual Orientation: Understanding Prejudice against Lesbians, Gay Men, and Bisexuals*, ed. Gregory M. Herek (Thousand Oaks, Calif.: Sage, 1998), 108–37; Clyde Wilcox and Robin Wolpert, "President Clinton, Public Opinion, and Gays in the Military," in *Gay Rights, Military Wrongs: Political Perspectives on Lesbians and Gays in the Military*, ed. Craig A. Rimmerman (New York: Garland Publishing, 1996), 127–45; Clyde Wilcox and Robin Wolpert, "Gay Rights in the Public Sphere: Public Opinion on Gay and Lesbian Equality," in *The Politics of Gay Rights*, ed. Craig A. Rimmerman, Kenneth D. Wald, and Clyde Wilcox (Chicago: University of Chicago Press, 2000), 409–32.

11. See also Brewer, "The Shifting Foundation"; Craig et al., "Core Values"; Steven H. Haeberle, "Gay and Lesbian Rights: Emerging Trends in Public Opinion and Voting Behavior," in *Gays and Lesbians in the Democratic Process*, ed. Ellen D. B. Riggle and Barry L. Tadlock (New York: Columbia University Press, 1999), 146–69; Gregory B. Lewis and Marc A. Rogers, "Does the Public Support Equal Employment Rights For Gays and Lesbians?" in *Gays and Lesbians in the Democratic Process*, ed. Ellen D. B. Riggle and Barry L. Tadlock (New York: Columbia University Press, 1999), 118–45; Clyde Wilcox and Barbara Norrander, "Of Moods and Morals: The Dynamics of Opinion on Abortion and Gay Rights," in *Understanding Public Opinion*, 2nd ed., ed. Barbara Norrander and Clyde Wilcox (Washington, DC: Congressional Quarterly Press, 2002), 121–48.

12. See also Samuel L. Popkin, *The Reasoning Voter* (Chicago: University of Chicago Press, 1994); Zaller, *Nature and Origins of Mass Opinion*.

13. See also Brewer, "The Shifting Foundations"; Paul R. Brewer, "Values, Political Knowledge, and Public Opinion about Gay Rights: A Framing-Based Account," *Public Opinion Quarterly* 67 (2003): 173–201; Wilcox and Wolpert, "President Clinton"; Wilcox and Wolpert "Gay Rights in the Public Sphere."

14. See also Brewer, "The Shifting Foundations"; Brewer, "Values, Political Knowledge, and Public Opinion"; Craig et al., "Core Values"; Lewis and Rogers, "Equal Employment Rights"; Wilcox and Wolpert, "President Clinton"; Wilcox and Wolpert, "Gay Rights in the Public Sphere."

15. Brewer, "The Shifting Foundations"; Wilcox and Wolpert, "President Clinton"; Wilcox and Wolpert, "Gay Rights in the Public Sphere."

16. See also Wilcox and Norrander, "Of Moods and Morals"; Wilcox and Wolpert, "Gay Rights in the Public Sphere."

17. Wilcox and Norrander, "Of Moods and Morals," 139.

18. See, for example, Zaller, *Nature and Origins of Mass Opinion*.

19. See, for example, Paul M. Kellstedt, "Media Framing and the Dynamics of Racial Policy Preferences," *American Journal of Political Science* 44 (2000): 245–60.

20. See chapter 5.

21. Quoted in Manuel Roig-Franzia, "Bryant Legacy Resurfaces in Fla.; Gay Groups Work to Defeat Bid to Repeal Rights Ordinance," *Washington Post*, 7 September 2002, A4.

22. For the analyses described below, I divided the feeling thermometer scores by one hundred.

23. See appendix E for additional details on question wording and coding.

24. The means for party identification were .45 (1992), .45 (1996), .45 (2000), and .48 (2004). The means for ideology were .53 (1992), .54 (1996), .56 (2000), and .54 (2004).

25. The means for the item were .63 (1992), .61 (1996), .60 (2000), and .61 (2004).

26. Within all four samples combined, the Cronbach's alpha for the index was .71.

27. The means for the egalitarianism index were .64 (1992), .56 (1996), .60 (2000), and .61 (2004).

28. Within all four samples combined, the Cronbach's alpha for the index was .65.

29. The means for the moral traditionalism index were .59 (1992), .62 (1996), .60 (2000), and .56 (2004).

30. Within all four samples combined, the Cronbach's alpha for the index was .65.

31. For further discussion of these background characteristics, see chapter 2.

32. I also conducted supplementary analyses to test the statistical significance of the coefficients for each independent variable in each subsequent year.

33. This conclusion was based on a comparison of standardized regression coefficients.

34. See chapter 5.

35. For more on the estimation of such probabilities, see Gary King, Michael Tomz, and Jason Wittenberg, "Making the Most of Statistical Analyses: Improving Interpretation and Presentation," *American Journal of Political Science* 44 (2000): 347–61.

36. This conclusion and subsequent comparisons regarding the magnitude of effects were based on the confidence intervals for the predicted probabilities presented in table 4 and the confidence intervals for the corresponding probabilities

derived from probit models for employment nondiscrimination laws and gays in the military. Here, the relevant contrasts were significant at $p < .05$.

37. See chapter 4 for further evidence of ideological polarization on same-sex marriage.

38. For same-sex marriage versus employment nondiscrimination, the contrast was significant at $p < .05$. For same-sex marriage versus gays in the military, the contrast approached this significance level.

39. For each comparison, the contrast was significant at $p < .05$.

40. For more on the concept of political opportunity structures, see William A. Gamson, *Strategy of Social Protest* (Homewood, Ill.: Dorsey Press, 1975); John C. Green, James L. Guth, and Kevin Hill, "Faith and Election: The Christian Right in Congressional Campaigns 1978–1988," *Journal of Politics* 55 (1993): 80–91.

41. Quoted in Tom Detzel, "Smith Argues for Expanding Hate Crimes Law to Cover Gays," *Oregonian*, 8 June 2002, A4.

42. Detzel, "Smith Argues for Expanding Hate Crimes Law to Cover Gays," A4.

43. Quoted in Raphael Lewis, "'Tough Guys' on Gay Marriage," *Boston Globe*, 23 March 2004.

44. Quoted in Raphael Lewis, "Gay Marriage Ban Expected to Fail," *Boston Globe*, 12 September 2005, B1.

7

The Meanings of Public Opinion about Gay Rights

On November 2, 2004, voters reelected President George W. Bush, giving the Republican incumbent a 50.7 to 48.3 percent victory over Democratic nominee (and Senator) John Kerry. As the election was taking place, Edison Media Research and Mitofsky International conducted the National Election Pool (NEP) exit poll, a survey of randomly chosen voters who were interviewed after they had cast their ballots. One question asked respondents what issue mattered most to them in deciding their vote for president. The questionnaire listed seven options. Of the respondents, 22 percent chose moral values, 20 percent chose economy and jobs, 19 percent chose terrorism, 15 percent chose Iraq, 8 percent chose health care, 5 percent chose taxes, and 4 percent chose education.

Much of the initial media coverage of Bush's victory focused on the percentage of voters who cited moral values. In particular, many commentators drew a connection between the outcome of the presidential election and the politics of same-sex marriage. The day after the election, Lee Cowan offered the following analysis on *CBS Evening News*:

> National exit polls showed that 22 percent of voters claimed moral values was their chief concern, more than those who list the economy or terrorism. . . . The president courted his predominantly white evangelical base, and it worked. . . . He had more help than he bargained for after the mayor of San Francisco began allowing same-sex marriages. It produced such an uproar among conservatives, eleven states put a constitutional amendment on their ballot to ban same-sex marriages. It pulled conservatives to the polls in droves, and the bans passed in all eleven states.

On CNN's *Larry King Live*, guests Gloria Borger and David Gergen echoed Cowan's comments:

> BORGER: Larry, what really surprised me was that, here we are a country in a time of war and what people were thinking about when you looked at these exit polls was moral issues. And I think this country is still very much involved in a culture war that has not run its course yet.
>
> GERGEN: We certainly did not anticipate that moral concerns, moral values would be listed as the number one concern by voters yesterday. Of course, that was mostly Republican voters, mostly Bush voters. But clearly, there is a continuing concern and perhaps including the war about right and wrong and framing issues in those terms. . . . In this case, I believe the eleven states that had these banning gay marriage ballot measures, there for voters to vote on, did serve as a catalyst for voters to come to the polls in greater numbers for the Republicans and probably also raised the issue of moral issues.

In short, these commentators saw public opinion about same-sex marriage as having clear political meaning in 2004: it played a crucial role in deciding the presidential election.

A closer look at the evidence, however, suggests a more complex story. On the one hand, the November 2004 election provides a striking demonstration of the impact that public opinion about gay rights can exert on political outcomes, as gay rights foes successfully capitalized on public opposition to same-sex marriage in their efforts to rewrite state constitutions. On the other hand, initial reports of the role that same-sex marriage—and, more generally, the "culture war"—played in shaping the presidential vote may have been somewhat exaggerated.

In this final chapter, I reconsider what public opinion about gay rights has meant—and may mean—for the course of politics, as well as what the case of gay rights tells us about public opinion and public debate in broader terms. At the simplest level, public opinion about gay rights can serve as a resource for politicians and activists to exploit or act as an obstacle to their efforts. Depending on how it tilts, it may provide a political advantage to one side of the debate or the other. Accordingly, changes over time and differences across policy contexts in public support for gay rights shape the strategic political environment in which gay rights foes and advocates compete. During the 1990s, for example, the growth of public support for laws protecting gays and lesbians from employment discrimination helped gay rights advocates defeat ballot measures designed to block or roll back such laws. By the same token, public opposition to same-sex marriage provided opportunities for gay rights foes to achieve political gains at the ballot box in 2004 and beyond.

On another level, the political meanings of public opinion about gay rights are open to interpretation by the various contestants in public debate.[1] Just as gay rights foes and advocates used competing frames to define the terms of the debate during the 1990s and beyond, they used their own readings of public opinion to bolster their positions in the debate. From one side, opponents of gay rights argued that constitutional amendments barring such rights were necessary at the state and federal levels to prevent "activist judges" from thwarting the will of the people. From the other side, gay rights advocates invoked trends over time and differences across generations in opinion as evidence that their side would ultimately triumph in the hearts and minds of the public.

Turning from the level of practical politics to the level of theory, the case of gay rights carries implications for how we understand public opinion and politics in such wider contexts as the "culture war" over social issues and the struggle for equal rights. In still broader terms, this case illustrates the ways in which public debate and public opinion can influence one another, as well as the ways in which both political elites and ordinary citizens make meaning of politics.

PUBLIC OPINION AND STATE BALLOT MEASURES ON GAY RIGHTS

From the days of Anita Bryant's "Save Our Children" campaign onward, gay rights foes have pushed a variety of anti–gay rights measures in cities and states around the country. Oregon, a state with a long history of direct democracy, has served as a key battlefield in the ballot box war over gay rights, with its voters deciding the fates of five statewide gay rights ballot measures over a sixteen-year span. The results of the votes on these measures illustrate the political implications of changes over time and differences across policy contexts in public support for gay rights. The campaigns for and against the measures also illustrate the ways in which gay rights foes and advocates have invoked and interpreted public opinion.

Oregon's series of anti–gay rights ballot measures began in 1988 with Measure 8.[2] This referendum, crafted by the Oregon Citizens' Alliance, was designed to overturn an executive order from Governor Neil Goldschmidt (D) that banned employment discrimination against gays and lesbians in state government. One critic argued that the order, which followed a legislative vote against a broader gay rights bill, flew in the face of public opinion:

> We've seen a number of changes under Governor Goldschmidt's administration, not the least of which is a tendency to look away from the will of the people. If we're not going to have representative government, why not just put in a king and let the process go?[3]

Meanwhile, some of the measure's opponents challenged the premise that the decision should rest with the will of the people. One newspaper column made the following case:

> Is the opinion of the majority, whether real or perceived, a valid factor in set-tling a rights question? I argue that it is not. . . . There is one golden thread that runs through both the Bill of Rights and our Constitution: protecting the rights of a minority against a stampeding majority. . . . This is not an issue for the vot-ers to decide.[4]

In the end, the voters approved Measure 8 by a 53 percent to 47 percent vote.

Having capitalized on public opinion once, the Oregon Citizens' Alliance sought to do so again in 1992 with Measure 9. This measure proposed to ban gay rights protections, declare homosexuality "abnormal, wrong, un-natural, and perverse," and require government and public schools to dis-courage homosexuality. Scott Lively, a spokesperson for the Alliance, cited public opinion in arguing that Measure 9 was necessary to block local ef-forts at enacting gay rights ordinances. "I suggest that these advances of the homosexual agenda in Oregon, in defiance of the will of the people revealed in 1988, [demonstrate] the power of the homosexual lobby and the enormous influence that it wields over public officials," he said.[5] This time around, however, voters did not favor the Alliance's side: the measure failed by a fourteen-point margin.

Two years later, the Alliance introduced Measure 13, which echoed Mea-sure 9 but conceded to public opinion by toning down its predecessor's condemnation of homosexuality. As before, spokesperson Lively cast the Al-liance's ballot box strategy as a way to implement the will of the public. "When these things pass," he said, "people realize we aren't a fringe; we are the majority."[6] Dismissing a judicial ruling against a similar measure that Colorado voters had approved in 1992 (Amendment 2), he added, "The court can't take away the knowledge that the people have spoken." Measure 13 lost by thirteen points, almost exactly the same margin by which Mea-sure 9 had lost. The twin defeats of these measures dovetailed with the broader trend toward greater public support for gay rights in areas such as employment nondiscrimination. They also provided gay rights advocates with opportunities to claim their own mandates from public opinion. For example, Oregon governor Barbara Roberts (D) cast the defeat of Measure 13 as proof that the Alliance's "narrow definition of values does not appeal to most Americans."[7] She added that "[p]oll after poll has shown that most Americans support equal rights for gay and lesbian people."

In 2000, the Alliance tried yet again with a new Measure 9 that threatened to cut funding for schools that "promoted," "sanctioned," or "encouraged" homosexuality. In doing so, the organization shifted its focus from the broader context of employment nondiscrimination to the narrower—and potentially more hospitable—context of the public school system. Contemporaneous poll results suggested that many Americans who were comfortable with gays and homosexuality in some settings were more uneasy when it came to a school setting. Consider the results of a 1999 Gallup poll that focused on the hiring of "homosexuals" for a range of jobs. Of the respondents, 36 percent said that gays should not be hired as high school teachers, and 42 percent said that they should not be hired as elementary school teachers. In contrast, the percentages opposed to the hiring of gays for the armed forces, for the president's cabinet, as doctors, and as salespeople were only 26 percent, 23 percent, 21 percent, and 8 percent, respectively. Even so, the new Measure 9 lost in a 53 percent to 47 percent vote. Shifting the context to the schools may have helped the Alliance draw more supporters, but it was not enough to produce a victory.

A subsequent shift to the context to marriage paid bigger dividends for Oregon's anti–gay rights movement. In 2004, the Defense of Marriage Coalition campaigned for Measure 36, a proposal to amend the state constitution to ban same-sex marriage. The push came half a year after Massachusetts began legally recognizing same-sex marriages and several local governments—including that of Multnomah County, Oregon—started issuing marriage licenses (albeit temporarily) to same-sex couples.[8] It also coincided with drives for similar bans in a dozen other states. National and state polls suggested that the amendments' supporters had the upper hand in the arena of public opinion. A pro–Measure 36 editorial in the *Oregonian* drew on this point in defending the ban as a necessary bulwark against judicial activism:

> Either the people of Oregon are going to reaffirm the traditional definition of marriage through Measure 36 or a handful of judges *á la* Massachusetts are going to redefine marriage for all of us. . . . Is everyone who favors traditional marriage and rejects same-sex marriage now a mean-spirited bigot? Is President Bush? The great bulk of the public?[9]

The same editorial noted that the path through the ballot box was open to same-sex marriage advocates as well as opponents:

> Gay marriage supporters can put a constitutional amendment on the ballot with an initiative petition. Measure 36 supporters showed how quickly that can be done. If public attitudes come to reflect support for same-sex marriage in the future, a constitutional amendment overturning Measure 36 would easily pass. Nothing's locked into Oregon's Constitution under our wide-open initiative system. In addition, this kind of constitutional right to gay marriage would have the added benefit of being based on widespread public support.[10]

In short, same-sex marriage foes not only sought to exploit their advantage in the court of public opinion; they also invoked this advantage as a justification for Measure 36 and its ilk.

Opponents of Measure 36 pointed to the trajectory of public opinion rather than its balance at the moment. Consider the following editorial, which also appeared in the *Oregonian*:

> It's the nature of progress that we don't always know where it will take us. Over the past decade, public opinion has evolved rapidly on gay rights. Already, young Americans are far more supportive than older ones are. Measure 36 wouldn't just lock down the debate as of this moment. It's an attempt to lock it down for years, and even generations.[11]

At the same time, state and national gay rights organizations held out hope for 2004. In light of the gay rights movement's previous wins in Oregon, as well as poll results that seemed to place their side within striking distance of victory, they saw the state as the most favorable battleground available for defeating a same-sex marriage ban.[12] The National Gay and Lesbian Task Force and the Human Rights Campaign poured money into the No on Constitutional Amendment 36 campaign, but their efforts were in vain; the ban passed in a 57 percent to 43 percent vote.[13] One of the amendment's supporters trumpeted the victory in a letter to the editor that concluded, "The people have spoken, overwhelmingly, so get over it!"[14]

It was a season of triumph for the architects of bans on same-sex marriage, as such bans passed by even wider margins in Missouri (where the vote took place in August 2004), Louisiana (where a ban passed in September 2004), and the other ten states that voted on them in November 2004: Arkansas, Georgia, Kentucky, Michigan, Mississippi, Montana, North Dakota, Ohio, Oklahoma, and Utah. Having won such a sweeping victory at the ballot box, same-sex marriage foes pressed their advantage by placing two more state bans on the ballot in 2005 (in Kansas and Texas) and nine more in 2006 (in Alabama, Arizona, Colorado, Idaho, South Carolina, South Dakota, Tennessee, Virginia, and Wisconsin). As before, they cast the bans as safeguards for the rule of majority opinion. For example, an advocate of the Virginia ban wrote that amending the state's constitution would "simply be protecting what is already law in Virginia from the actions of activist judges. Too many times the will of the people, expressed by the legislature, has been undermined by the courts."[15]

Gay rights advocates used a mix of strategies to fight the bans in a climate of opinion marked by majority opposition to same-sex marriage. In some instances, opponents of the bans essentially conceded to public opinion by emphasizing how existing state laws already precluded same-sex marriage. In states where the proposed amendment banned (or could be interpreted as banning) civil unions along with same-sex marriage, gay rights advocates also worked to highlight the former effect. For example, a letter to the editor in the *Milwaukee Journal Sentinel* argued that the newspaper's "coverage of the proposed ban on same-sex marriage reproduces the same misleading rhetoric so often used by legislators who support the ban. . . . Calling this amendment a ban on same-sex marriage only hides its real intent: to outlaw civil unions and domestic partnerships. Call this amendment what it is: a civil union ban."[16] In this way, gay rights advocates attempted to shift the emphasis from same-sex marriage, which majority opinion opposed, to civil unions, on which public opinion was more evenly divided.

Furthermore, opponents of the bans sought to broaden the scope of public debate by arguing that the amendments would affect people other than gays and lesbians. As a case in point, one opponent of the Virginia ban said that it "would open a Pandora's box of unintended consequences by . . . endangering current safeguards offered to unmarried victims of domestic violence."[17] In a similar vein, opponents of the Arizona and Wisconsin bans argued that the amendments, as written, would threaten health care and pension benefits for senior citizens.[18] In making these sorts of arguments, the bans' foes tacitly recognized that public opinion toward gays and lesbians was less favorable than public opinion toward other groups that might be affected by the amendments. By emphasizing the potential effects on groups that were more popular with voters, such as the elderly and victims of domestic violence, they sought to dilute the impact of anti-gay sentiments on voters' decisions.

Yet another way in which the bans' opponents appealed to public opinion was by casting the amendments as part of a strategy to manipulate voters. For example, an opponent of the Wisconsin ban called it a "phony issue" and a "cheap political ploy by Republicans to get out the vote on the day when their party tries to win back the governor's office."[19] In using this rhetorical approach, foes of the bans may have sought to sway public opinion by tapping into a widespread distrust of politicians and the political process. As experimental research has shown, exposure to "strategy" or "game" framing of politics can activate political cynicism among recipients and thereby shape public opinion.[20]

The winning streak for bans on same-sex marriage continued through 2005 (in Kansas and Texas) and June 2006 (in Alabama). In November 2006, the architects of such bans achieved seven additional victories.[21] They also suffered their first defeat at the ballot box, as Arizona voters rejected a ban on same-sex marriage in a close vote (51 to 49 percent). In commenting on the results, same-sex marriage opponents highlighted their winning percentage and downplayed the Arizona outcome as an anomaly. "Look at the rest of these states," said Robert Knight, director of the Culture and Media Institute. "The gays threw everything but the kitchen sink in the battle, but they couldn't win even in liberal Wisconsin. So Arizona is out on its own."[22] Maggie Gallagher, president of the Institute for Marriage and Public Policy, acknowledged that the "good news for gay marriage advocates is that they finally defeated a state marriage amendment" but also argued that "the bad news [for them] is that the vote had almost nothing to do with increasing public support for gay marriage."[23]

For their part, same-sex marriage supporters emphasized both the outcome in Arizona and the increasingly narrow margins of victory for bans on same-sex marriage in other states. Matt Foreman, the executive director of the National Gay and Lesbian Task Force, argued that "without a doubt, public opinion on marriage and partner rights is moving rapidly. What may be true today will not be true two or three years from now."[24] Shortly after the November 2006 election, his organization released a study conducted by political scientists Patrick Egan and Kenneth Sherrill. In their report, the scholars observe that the average vote for same-sex marriage bans was 71 percent in 2004 but 64 percent in 2006.[25] Drawing on a statistical model, they also conclude that "same-sex marriage [bans] would fail in most of New England, as well as in New Jersey and New York and . . . would barely pass in most of the Midwestern and Mid-Atlantic states that have yet to hold such referenda."[26] If their analysis is correct, then the opportunities for same-sex marriage foes to achieve political gains through the ballot box may be drawing to a close. Moreover, any future shift toward greater support for same-sex marriage would make it even more difficult for its opponents to win policy victories through direct democracy.

PUBLIC OPINION AND THE FEDERAL MARRIAGE AMENDMENT

As the battle over same-sex marriage played out in the states, it also played out in the clash over a proposed Federal Marriage Amendment. In May 2003, United States Representative Marilyn Musgrave (R-CO) introduced the following version of the amendment:

> Marriage in the United States shall consist only of the union of a man and a woman. Neither this constitution nor the constitution of any state, nor state or federal law, shall be construed to require that marital status or the legal incidents thereof be conferred upon unmarried couples or groups.

In explaining the rationale behind the amendment, she invoked the by-now-familiar claim that it was necessary to defend the will of the public from activist judges. "My bill," she said, "ensures the question of homosexual marriage is stricken from unelected judges and placed in the hands of the American people and their elected representatives."[27]

Not long after Musgrave introduced the amendment, a series of events triggered a backlash in public opinion against gay rights and a rise in public attention to same-sex marriage.[28] Perceiving that the climate of public opinion might be shifting in their direction, same-sex marriage foes launched a major push for the amendment. They received a political boost when President George W. Bush endorsed a constitutional ban on same-sex marriage. In part, the push for the amendment reflected an attempt by Republican politicians, including Bush, to advance their own political fortunes by capitalizing on public opposition to same-sex marriage. One former Bush adviser called same-sex marriage a "great wedge issue," adding that the president's opposition to it would "guarantee intensity on the religious right so that Gary Bauer and Jerry Falwell will be praising President Bush to the skies."[29]

At the same time, the push for the Federal Marriage Amendment also reflected an attempt by same-sex marriage foes to use their advantage in the court of public opinion to shape public policy in a way that would produce a lasting political impact. Once passed, amendments to the United States Constitution are difficult to overturn given that it takes another constitutional amendment to do so and that the amendment process is, by design, a cumbersome process.[30] For an amendment to become part of the Constitution, it must follow one of two paths. One path, which begins with a Constitutional Convention called by two-thirds of the state legislatures, has never been successfully used. The other path—the one that the backers of the Federal Marriage Amendment started down—requires the amendment to pass both chambers of Congress by a two-thirds vote and then win ratification in three-fourths of the states. Thus, the passage of a Federal Marriage Amendment would not only have handed same-sex marriage foes a victory in the present; it also would have placed them in an excellent position to block any efforts to undo that victory.

The amendment's backers faced a clear political incentive to act in the moment at hand. The short-term trends in public opinion may have been favorable to their side, but the longer-term trends looked grimmer from their perspective. In particular, the generation gap on public opinion about same-sex marriage seemed to forecast a future in which support might approach or even eclipse opposition.[31] A 2004 policy brief, written by Maggie Gallagher and Joshua Baker for the anti-same-sex marriage Institute for Marriage and Public Policy, went so far as to ask, "Has the next generation made up its mind in favor of gay marriage?"[32] The brief argued that this was not necessarily the case, but same-sex marriage foes were clearly aware of the political challenge that they would face if public opinion shifted toward greater support. After all, they had witnessed public support for other sorts of gay rights—including employment nondiscrimination and gays in the military—grow steadily over the course of the 1990s and beyond. The

Federal Marriage Amendment offered them an instrument for using their strength in the arena of public opinion to create a safeguard against potential future weakness in the same arena. It also offered them a hope for reinforcing their current advantage—and, perhaps, arresting future growth in public support for same-sex marriage—by stamping their position with the legitimacy of the Constitution.

As appealing as it was to same-sex marriage foes, however, the Federal Marriage Amendment faced formidable political obstacles. Most obviously, it had to follow the same difficult path described above to become part of the Constitution—a path that could be blocked by a one-third minority in either chamber of Congress or by a fourth of the states. It also faced a subtler barrier in the form of public opinion. A majority of the public may have opposed same-sex marriage, but public opinion about amending the Constitution to ban same-sex marriage was more evenly divided.[33] Furthermore, support for doing so fell short of the "supermajority" level typical of successful constitutional amendments.[34] Instead, levels of public support for an amendment banning same-sex marriage bore closer resemblance to the levels of support for failed constitutional amendments that would have banned flag burning or allowed school prayer.[35]

Given the nature of the amendment process and the state of public opinion, it is not surprising that the Federal Marriage Amendment suffered the same fate as these other amendments. In July 2004, a filibuster halted its progress in the Senate, and a September 2004 vote in the House fell well short of the necessary two-thirds needed to advance it. Two months after he won reelection, Bush stated in an interview that "nothing would happen" with the amendment until the Senate changed its mind.[36] By the end of 2006, it had failed again in both chambers of Congress and appeared to be doomed for the foreseeable future.

PUBLIC OPINION, SAME-SEX MARRIAGE, AND ELECTIONS FOR PUBLIC OFFICE

Although same-sex marriage foes suffered defeat in their efforts to push through the Federal Marriage Amendment, they cast Bush's reelection in November 2004 as a victory for their cause. For example, the Culture and Family Institute's Robert Knight described "the marriage issue" as "the great iceberg in this election. Most people saw only the tip and didn't realize the great mass was affecting races all over the country, right up to the presidential contest."[37] In broader terms, same-sex marriage foes presented Bush's victory—as well as the Republican gains in both chambers of Congress—as a mandate for their side of the "culture war" and warned that ignoring such a mandate would carry grave consequences. "Now that values voters have delivered for George Bush," said broadcast evangelist D. James Kennedy, "he must deliver for their values."[38]

In arguing that same-sex marriage helped to decide the presidential election, news commentators and same-sex marriage foes alike cited the plurality of NEP exit poll respondents who chose moral values as the issue that was most important to them.[39] Even in the initial aftermath of the election, however, a number of gay rights activists, journalists, and scholars challenged this reading of the exit polls. Specifically, they noted that the moral values option was a "grab bag" category that differed from the other six response options in its breadth; that the questionnaire did not explain what moral values meant; that the phrase was a loaded one that carried positive connotations; that the percentage choosing moral values (22 percent) did not differ significantly from the percentages choosing economy/jobs (20 percent) and terrorism (19 percent); and that the percentage choosing the "national security" issues of Iraq and terrorism (34 percent) substantially exceeded the percentage choosing moral values.[40]

A post-election survey by the Pew Research Center for the People and the Press provides additional grounds for questioning whether moral values in general and same-sex marriage in particular played such a crucial role in the 2004 presidential election.[41] To begin with, the percentage of respondents who cited moral values as the most important issue depended on the wording of the question. For the Pew survey, respondents were randomly divided into two conditions, each with its own question wording. One condition replicated the NEP exit poll's question and its seven response options. In this condition, as in the NEP exit poll, a plurality of the respondents (27 percent) chose moral values as the issue that mattered most to them. The second condition presented an open-ended prompt instead of a list of options, thereby allowing respondents to answer in their own words. In this condition, only 9 percent of the respondents mentioned "moral values," "morals," or "values" and only 3 percent mentioned specific social issues (including, but not limited to, same-sex marriage).

Furthermore, voters interpreted moral values in a variety of ways. The Pew respondents who received the close-ended version of the question were asked an open-ended follow-up question: "What comes to mind when you think about 'moral values?'" Among those who selected moral values as the most important issue, 44 percent defined it in terms of social issues, and 29 percent defined it specifically in terms of homosexuality or gay marriage. As the Pew Research Center's report notes, however, "Nearly a quarter of respondents (23 percent) who cited moral values as important explained their thinking in terms of the personal characteristics of the candidates, including honesty and integrity."[42] The report goes on to observe that for the respondents who did not choose moral values as the most important issue, the "pattern of responses was quite different. . . . Fewer mentioned a specific issue, candidate quality, or general religious theme; more answered in general terms, and 12 percent explicitly protested the imposition of others' values on them, said the idea was being used as a 'wedge' against Democrats, or otherwise expressed a negative reaction to the phrase."[43] Taken as a whole, the Pew findings challenge the notion of a monolithic moral values voting bloc motivated primarily by opposition to same-sex marriage.

This is not to say that public opinion about same-sex marriage played no role in shaping how voters made up their minds about the presidential race—merely that its role in doing so was relatively modest. Looking at *Los Angeles Times* exit poll data, Gregory Lewis finds that respondents who opposed same-sex marriage were more likely than those who supported it to vote for Bush, even after controlling for a wide range of other factors.[44] Still, he also finds that opinion about same-sex marriage was "far from the most important" influence on vote choice.[45] Likewise, D. Sunshine Hillygus and Todd Shields conclude from their analysis of Knowledge Networks postelection survey data that respondents' opinions about same-sex marriage were related to their voting decisions but that their opinions about the war in Iraq, the economy, and terrorism had larger effects on those decisions.[46]

Studies of state-level vote totals, in turn, cast doubt on the notion that same-sex marriage ballot measures handed Bush the 2004 presidential election.[47] Barry Burden finds that the presence of a same-sex marriage ban on a state's ballot had no impact on Bush's share of the vote.[48] Similarly, Alan Abramowitz concludes that the presence of a ban on a state's ballot failed to boost turnout.[49] Burden also observes that the wave of same-sex marriage ballots evidently did little to change the overall electoral map given that only three states changed hands from 2000 to 2004 (Bush gained Iowa and New Mexico but lost New Hampshire).[50]

The 2004 presidential election illustrates a broader point: in campaigns for public office, controversies over gay rights policies must typically compete with a host of other issues that could influence voters' choices. Looking backward, public opinion about gay rights played relatively minor roles in the three presidential elections that preceded the 2004 election. In 1992, the year that Pat Buchanan described the fight over gay rights as part of a "cultural" and "religious" war and Democratic nominee Bill Clinton promised to lift the ban on gays in the military, public opinion about the economy exerted a greater impact on the presidential vote than did public opinion about gay rights (or any other issue, for that matter).[51] By 1996, the controversy over gays in the military had faded, and Clinton's decision to sign the Defense of Marriage Act temporarily defused same-sex marriage as a campaign issue. In the 2000 presidential campaign, the most significant discussion of gay rights was relegated to the vice presidential debate. Moving forward to the 2006 midterm elections, the presence of same-sex marriage bans on the ballot in eight states did not prevent the Democrats from capturing both chambers of Congress on the strength of public opinion about the war in Iraq and corruption in government.[52]

Nevertheless, the debate about gay rights seems likely to occupy a visible role in political campaigns, including presidential campaigns, for the foreseeable future. It inspires passionate activism on both sides, and it touches on some of the public's most fundamental beliefs. Moreover, the clash over gay rights is far from being settled in either the policy arena or the court of public opinion, particularly when it comes to the question of legal recognition for same-sex couples. As a consequence, the state of public opinion should continue to provide political candidates with strategic incentives to take certain positions on gay rights and avoid others. For example, a stance for same-sex marriage would, as of 2006, have gone against majority opinion and, thus, been politically unappealing to candidates (at least those who cared about winning). By the same logic, a stance against same-sex marriage would have been politically attractive to candidates. In keeping with this, all of the leadings contenders for the 2008 presidential nominations— including Senators Hillary Clinton (NY), former Senator John Edwards (NC), and Barack Obama (IL) on the Democratic side, as well as former New York City Mayor Rudy Giuliani, Senator John McCain (AZ), and former Governor Mitt Romney (MA) on the Republican side—had, as of 2006, come out against or at least chosen not to endorse same-sex marriage.

The complex and shifting nature of public opinion, however, can create a hazardous political terrain for candidates from both parties. Consider the question of civil unions, where a stance on either side would have gone against the position of around half of the public in 2006. Here, there was no "safe" majority position, leaving candidates with two options: taking the risk of choosing a side or engaging in the sort of strategic ambiguity on civil unions that Bush used in the 2004 presidential campaign.[53] Even a politically safe stance against same-sex marriage could one day become a liability if public opinion shifts from majority opposition to majority support.

To complicate matters further, candidates must often win primary elections by appealing to party loyalists—who differ from the general public in their opinions about gay rights—and then win a general election by appealing to a broader audience. Accordingly, a position on gay rights that might produce a political wash in a general election campaign could be advantageous in one party's primary campaign and disadvantageous in the other party's primary campaign. As a case in point, a stance in favor of civil unions could have been a political asset to a candidate for the 2008 Democratic presidential nomination but a political liability to a candidate for the 2008 Republican presidential nomination. Indeed, two of the candidates for the latter nomination had, by the end of 2006, faced political challenges in dealing with previous statements on gay rights that would have been unremarkable—or even obligatory—for a contender in the Democratic race. One was Giuliani, who had taken a number of pro–gay rights stances, including a position in favor of civil unions.[54] The other was Romney, who had pledged in a 1994 United States Senate campaign to "provide more effective leadership" in fighting for "full equality for America's gay and lesbian citizens" than his then-opponent, incumbent Ted Kennedy (D-MA).[55]

THE BROADER IMPLICATIONS OF PUBLIC OPINION ABOUT GAY RIGHTS

Like all controversies over public policy, the one over gay rights has its own issue culture—that is, its own unique set of images, signals, and frames. At the same time, the case of gay rights helps to illuminate patterns in public opinion and politics that may apply to other issues. Politicians, activists, and observers alike have cast the debate about gay rights as both a central front in a culture war and a key component in a long-running struggle for equal rights. Thus, the wider clashes in American politics over social issues and civil rights provide natural starting points for considering the theoretical implications of my findings regarding the nature, origins, and trajectory of public opinion about gay rights.

Public Opinion about Gay Rights and the Culture War

In part, both public debate and the public itself have treated gay rights as a moral issue. During the 1990s and beyond, the contestants in the debate strove to frame gay rights policies in moral terms, with gay rights foes achieving particular success in casting such policies as threats to traditional morality. For their part, Americans used their moral beliefs to form their opinions about gay rights policies. Likewise, they used the language of morality to explain their opinions and to discuss the subject with one another. Considered in this light, the case of gay rights yields lessons to guide our understanding of other "culture war" issues on the political agenda.

One such lesson is that morality can mean different things to different people. This point not only stands out from the results of the 2004 Pew survey that asked voters what moral values meant to them; it also emerges from Americans' responses to the public debate about gay rights. Gay rights foes may have won the fight to frame morality in the media, but ordinary citizens sometimes challenged the dominant interpretation of morality within public debate when given the chance to describe their views on gay rights in their own words.

A second lesson provided by the case of gay rights is that the impact of moral beliefs on public opinion can change over time and differ across policy contexts. An illustration of the former point comes from public opinion about the "old" politics of gay rights, which revolved around employment nondiscrimination laws and gays in the military. From the early 1990s to 2004, Americans attached decreasing weight to their moral beliefs in forming their opinions about these policies. An illustration of the latter point comes from a comparison of public opinion about the "old" and "new" politics of gay rights. As of 2004, Americans attached greater weight to their moral beliefs in forming their opinions about same-sex marriage than they did in forming their opinions about employment nondiscrimination laws and gays in the military.

A logical extension of the second lesson is that public opinion about one "culture war" issue will not always behave like public opinion about another such issue. From the 1970s to 2000 and beyond, the trends in public opinion about gay rights stood in sharp contrast to the trends in public opinion about abortion: support for the former grew substantially, whereas support for the latter hardly changed at all. To the extent that there is a culture war going on in the United States, it revolves around issues that can differ from one another in important ways. A victory on one front in this war does not necessarily foretell victories on other fronts.

Public Opinion about Gay Rights and the Drive for Equal Rights

If the controversy over gay rights can be considered as an issue of morality, then it can also be considered as an issue of equal rights. In particular, the case of gay rights bears a number of similarities to the case of civil rights for African Americans. Just as public support for the latter grew substantially over time, so did public support for the former. In both cases, the rise in support took place in some contexts (such as employment) before it emerged in other contexts (such as marriage). Images of a target group—African Americans or gays and lesbians—loomed large in the public debate about each sort of rights, and public sentiments regarding each target group played important roles in shaping public opinion about policy measures. Advocates of gay rights invoked the same principle of equality that advocates of civil rights for African Americans invoked, and Americans' beliefs about equality shaped public opinion in both domains.

As with morality, however, equality is a complex value. In the public debate about gay rights policies—as in the public debate about race-based affirmative action—it took on competing and even mutually contradictory meanings, with advocates framing such policies as tools to protect equal rights and foes framing them as vehicles for special rights. Ordinary Americans helped to construct the meaning of equality, as well. Some challenged the pro–gay rights interpretation of equality when given the chance to talk about the issue in their own words, whereas others took the opportunity to challenge its anti–gay rights counterframe. In short, the implications of equality for gay rights were open to debate—just as they may be in debates about other "equal rights" issues.

Like morality, equality may also matter more in some policy contexts than in others. When Americans formed their opinions about employment nondiscrimination laws and gays in the military, they attached considerable weight to their beliefs about equality. In contrast, they attached relatively little weight to such beliefs in forming their opinions about same-sex marriage. Even when the public accepts one aspect of a policy dispute as an "equal rights" issue, it will not necessarily see other aspects of the dispute in the same way.

Nor will public opinion and public debate about one "equal rights" issue always mirror public opinion and public debate about another such issue. Although the cases of civil rights for African Americans and gay rights resemble one another in many ways, they also differ from one another in important respects. For example, the transformation in public opinion about the former was underway long before the transformation in public opinion about the latter took place. Similarly, civil rights for African Americans became an "equal rights" issue in the mainstream debate well before gay rights did. Thus, two issues that follow the same political path may occupy different points on that trajectory at any given point in time.

Public Opinion and Public Debate Revisited

Looking beyond both the culture war and the push for equal rights, my findings illustrate broader points about the interplay between public opinion and public debate. In part, the evidence presented in this book attests to how public debate can mold public opinion in multiple ways. Media images of gays and lesbians not only influenced Americans' beliefs and feelings about members of this group; they also influenced public opinion about gay rights policies. Signals about gay rights sent by political and religious elites guided the opinions of their followers among the public, as did cues from the pulpits of local clergy. Frames that invoked some of the public's most cherished values influenced the ways in which Americans understood the politics of gay rights.

Then again, my account also highlights the power of public opinion to constrain the words and actions of political elites. Politicians and political activists who violated an emerging norm against "gay bashing" in public debate learned to their chagrin that public opinion about gays, lesbians, and homosexuality had shifted. Those who were better attuned to the climate of public opinion sent signals that did not place their own political fortunes at risk and invoked frames that were likely to resonate with the public.

Last, but by no means least, my findings illustrate the power of ordinary citizens to resist or reinterpret the messages that they find in public debate. According to popular mythology, Abraham Lincoln once told the story of a boy who was asked, "How many legs would your calf have if you called its tail a leg?"[56] "Five," the boy replied, and was swiftly corrected: calling a tail a leg, he was told, did not make it one. Lincoln told the story with a point in mind: just because he told the public that something was so, he argued, that would not make it so—and, more importantly, that would not necessarily make the public think it was so, either. The moral of Lincoln's story is also a key point of this book: People do not always accept the definitions that public debate gives them, whether those definitions revolve around the tail of a calf or a major political controversy of the day.

NOTES

1. For analyses of how elites have invoked public opinion in other contexts, see Fay Lomax Cook, Jason Barabas, and Benjamin I. Page, "Invoking Public Opinion: Policy Elites and Social Security," *Public Opinion Quarterly* 66 (2002): 235–64; Catherine Paden and Benjamin I. Page, "Congress Invokes Public Opinion on Welfare," *American Politics Research* 31 (2003): 670–79.

2. For a more detailed history of Measures 8, 9 (1992), and 13, see John Gallagher and Chris Bull, *Perfect Enemies: The Battle between the Religious Right and the Gay Movement*, updated ed. (New York: Madison Books, 2001), 39–62.

3. Quoted in Jeff Mapes, "GOP Working to Counteract Goldschmidt's Popularity," *Oregonian*, 17 January 1988, B3.

4. Kenneth W. Armstrong, "Majority Opinion Not Key to Gay Rights; Constitution Designed to Protect Minorities from Popular Prejudice in My Opinion," *Oregonian*, 1 January 1998, D11.

5. Quoted in Phil Manzano, "OCA's Lively, Attorney Hinkle Battle over Measure 9," *Oregonian*, 26 September 1992, E1.

6. Quoted in Sura Rubenstein and Tom Bates, "Measure 13 Unscathed by Colorado Court Ruling," *Oregonian*, 12 October 1994, A1.

7. Barbara Roberts, "Oregonians Refused to Be Swayed by Negativity and Homophobia," *Oregonian*, 13 November 1994, C4.

8. Bill Graves, "Election 2004 Ballot Measures: Same-Sex Marriage; Oregon Group Already Mobilized When County Began Issuing Licenses," *Oregonian*, 8 October 2004, A6.

9. David Reinhard, "Measure 36 Foes' Upside-Down World," *Oregonian*, 3 October 2004, F4.

10. Reinhard, "Measure 36 Foes' Upside-Down World," F4.

11. "Don't Scar Oregon Constitution," *Oregonian*, 30 September 2004, D10.

12. Bill Graves, "National Gay-Rights Groups Fight Measure," *Oregonian*, 1 September 2004, C10.

13. Graves, "National Gay-Rights Groups Fight Measure," C10.

14. Ray Young, "Laws Discriminate, Period," *Oregonian*, 7 November 2004, F5.

15. Victoria Cobb, "Vote Yes for the Sake of Marriage; Don't Trust Judges to Define the Word," *Washington Post*, 22 October 2006, B8.

16. Anne DeSellier, "A New Legal Twist for Couples," *Milwaukee Journal Sentinel*, 5 March 2006, J5.

17. Quoted in Chris L. Jenkins, "Virginia Voters to Decide on Gay Unions; Proposal's Opponents Warn of Problems," *Washington Post*, 2 November 2006, T7.

18. Kim Cobb, "Retirees Help Defeat Gay Marriage Ban; In Arizona, the Campaign against the Proposal Focused on Elderly Heterosexuals," *Houston Chronicle*, 13 November 2006, A6; Stacy Forster, "Same-Sex Ban, Different Interpretations; Some Dispute Impact of Marriage Amendment on Civil Unions, Benefits," *Milwaukee Journal Sentinel*, 30 July 2006, B1.

19. Jim Stingl, "Let's Keep Wisconsin Tolerant in 2006," *Milwaukee Journal Sentinel*, 4 January 2006, B1.

20. Joseph N. Cappella and Kathleen Hall Jamieson, *Spiral of Cynicism: The Press and the Public Good* (New York: Oxford University Press, 1997).

21. They also defeated a Colorado initiative that would have created domestic partnerships for same-sex couples.

22. Quoted in Elizabeth Mehren, "Gay-Marriage Votes Get Diverse Spins from Activists; Arizona Defeats a Ban on the Unions, but Seven States Pass Them. Supporters on Both Sides See Progress," *Los Angeles Times*, 9 November 2006, A21. The extent to which Wisconsin was truly a "liberal" state is open to question given that the Democratic presidential nominees carried the state by only slender margins in 2000 (0.5 percent) and 2004 (0.4 percent).

23. Quoted in Mehren, "Gay-Marriage Votes," A21.

24. Quoted in Kevin Simpson, "Marriage, Gay Rights: Amend. 43 Supporters Revel in Double Victory," *Denver Post*, 9 November 2006, B6.

25. Patrick J. Egan and Kenneth Sherrill, "Same-Sex Marriage Initiatives and Lesbian, Gay, and Bisexual Voters in the 2006 Elections" (Washington, DC: National Gay and Lesbian Task Force, 2006), 3.

26. Egan and Sherrill, "Same-Sex Marriage Initiatives," 5.

27. Quoted in DeNeen L. Brown, "Hundreds of Couples Make Their Way to Ontario to Say 'I Do'," *Washington Post*, 22 June 2003, A15.

28. See chapters 3 and 4 for details.

29. Quoted in Carolyn Lochhead, "Vatican, President Intensify Assault on Gay Marriage," *San Francisco Chronicle*, 1 August 2003, A1.

30. To date, the 18th Amendment (which enacted Prohibition) has been the only one to be overturned by a subsequent amendment (the 21st Amendment).

31. See chapter 2.

32. Maggie Gallagher and Joshua K. Baker, "Same-Sex Marriage: What Does the Next Generation Think?" (Washington, DC: Institute for Marriage and Public Policy, 2004).

33. See chapter 2.

34. Frank Newport, "Constitutional Amendment Defining Marriage Lacks 'Supermajority' Support; Almost Two-Thirds Oppose Same-Sex Marriage, but Only 51% Favor Constitutional Amendment" (Washington, DC: Gallup Organization, 2004).

35. Pew Research Center for the People and the Press, "Reading the Polls on Gay Marriage and the Constitution" (Washington, DC: Pew Research Center for the People and the Press, 2004).

36. Jim VandeHei and Michael A. Fletcher, "Bush Says Election Ratified Iraq Policy; No U.S. Troop Withdrawal Date Is Set," *Washington Post*, 16 January 2005, A1.

37. Quoted in Alan Cooperman, "Same-Sex Bans Fuel Conservative Agenda," *Washington Post*, 4 November 2004, A39.

38. Quoted in James Rosen, "Bush Feeling Heat from Evangelicals; They Backed Him—But His Priorities May Not Be Theirs," *Sacramento Bee*, 14 November 2004, A1.

39. Another national exit poll sponsored by the *Los Angeles Times* allowed respondents to select up to two issues from a longer list of options. Of the respondents in this poll, 40 percent chose "moral/ethical values," while 15 percent chose "social issues such as abortion and gay marriage." Given that the NEP exit poll was sponsored by a consortium of major media organizations (ABC, the Associated Press, CBS, CNN, Fox News Channel, and NBC), however, it received more media coverage than did the *Los Angeles Times* exit poll.

40. See, for example, Barry Burden, "An Alternative Account of the 2004 Presidential Election," *The Forum* 2 (2004): www.bepress.com/forum/vol2/iss4/art2/; D. Sunshine Hillygus and Todd G. Shields, "Moral Issues and Voter Decision Making in the 2004 Presidential Election," *PS: Political Science & Politics* 38 (2005): 201–9; Scott Keeter, "Evangelicals and Moral Values in the Election of 2004," paper presented at the Religion and the 2004 Election Conference, South Bend, Ind., December 2005; Gary Langer, "A Question of Values," *New York Times*, 6 November 2004, A19; Gary Langer and Jon Cohen, "Voters and Values in the 2004 Election," *Public Opinion Quarterly* 69 (2005): 744–59.

41. Pew Research Center for the People and the Press, "Voters Liked Campaign 2004, But Too Much 'Mud-Slinging'; Moral Values: How Important?" (Washington, DC: Pew Research Center for the People and the Press, 2004).

42. Pew Research Center for the People and the Press, "Voters Liked Campaign 2004."

43. Pew Research Center for the People and the Press, "Voters Liked Campaign 2004."

44. Gregory B. Lewis, "Same-Sex Marriage and the 2004 Presidential Election," *PS: Political Science & Politics* 38 (2005): 195–99.

45. Lewis, "Same-Sex Marriage and the 2004 Presidential Election," 195.

46. Hillygus and Shields, "Moral Issues," 204.

47. For a county-level analysis of the vote in Michigan and Ohio, see Daniel Smith, Matthew DeSantis, and Jason Kessel, "Same-Sex Marriage Ballot Measures and the 2004 Presidential Election," *State and Local Government Review* 38 (2006): 78–91.

48. Burden, "Alternative Account." For other analyses that draw the same conclusion, see Alan Abramowitz, "Terrorism, Gay Marriage, and Incumbency: Explaining

the Republican Victory in the 2004 Presidential Election," *The Forum* 2 (2004): www
.bepress.com/forum/vol2/iss4/art3/; Egan and Sherrill, "Same-Sex Marriage Initiatives."

49. Abramowitz, "Terrorism, Gay Marriage, and Incumbency." It may be, however, that the presence of a same-sex marriage ban on the ballot boosted turnout in
nonbattleground states; see Michael P. McDonald, "Up, Up, and Away! Voter Participation in the 2004 Presidential Election," *The Forum* 2 (2004): www.bepress
.com/forum/vol2/iss4/art4/.

50. Two studies, however, conclude that the presence of same-sex marriage bans
on the ballots in eleven states may have shaped how some voters in those states
made decisions regarding the presidential election. Drawing on a Pew preelection
survey, Todd Donavan and his colleagues find that residents of states with a ban on
the ballot were particularly likely to see same-sex marriage as an important issue.
Furthermore, those who did so were especially likely to support Bush. Along similar lines, David Campbell and J. Quin Monson use data from the 2004 Election
Panel Study to show that the presence of a same-sex marriage ban on the ballot mobilized support for Bush among white, evangelical Protestants while also depressing
turnout for him among secular respondents. Both studies conclude that Bush was
the net beneficiary of the individual-level effects that the ballot measures produced.
See David E. Campbell and J. Quin Monson, "The Religion Card: Gay Marriage and
the 2004 Presidential Election," paper presented at the annual meeting of the American Political Science Association, Washington, DC, September 2005; Todd Donavan, Caroline Tolbert, Daniel A. Smith, and Janine Parry, "Did Gay Marriage Elect
George W. Bush?" paper presented at the State Politics Conference, East Lansing,
Mich., May 2005.

51. See, for example, R. Michael Alvarez and Jonathan Nagler, "Economics, Issues, and the Perot Candidacy: Voter Choice in the 1992 Presidential Election,"
American Journal of Political Science 39 (1995): 714–44.

52. Indeed, 2006 Republican Senate candidates appeared to do no better in states
with bans on the ballot than in states without bans on the ballot. See Egan and Sherrill, "Same-Sex Marriage Initiatives."

53. See chapter 4.

54. Sewell Chan, "Giuliani Building a Network of Donors, a Backer Says," *New
York Times,* 17 November 2006, A3; Patrick Healy, "Giuliani Says Nation Lacks Energy Policy," *New York Times,* 14 June 2006, B1.

55. George F. Will, "GOP Contenders on a Tightrope," *Washington Post,* 12 December 2006, B7.

56. In this case, the myth may be true: see Paul M. Zall, ed., *Abe Lincoln Laughing:
Humorous Anecdotes from Original Sources by and about Abraham Lincoln* (Berkeley:
University of California Press, 1982).

Appendix

APPENDIX A: THE POOLED 2003–2004 PEW RESEARCH CENTER SURVEYS

The pooled Pew Research Center surveys discussed in chapters 2 and 4 included the following:

- June 24—July 8, 2003 ($N = 1,001$): Same-sex marriage only.
- Oct. 15—Oct. 19, 2003 ($N = 1,515$): Same-sex marriage and civil unions.
- Nov. 19—Dec. 1, 2003 ($N = 1,443$): Same-sex marriage only.
- Feb. 11—Feb. 16, 2004 ($N = 1,500$): Same-sex marriage only.
- Mar. 17—Mar. 21, 2004 ($N = 1,703$): Same-sex marriage and civil unions.
- July 8—July 18, 2004 ($N = 2,009$): Same-sex marriage and civil unions.
- Aug. 5—Aug. 10, 2004 ($N = 1,512$): Same-sex marriage and civil unions.

Question wording and coding for the analyses presented in table 4.1 were as follows:

- Favor same-sex marriage (see text for wording): I coded "strongly oppose" as 0, "oppose" as 1/3, "favor" as 2/3, and "strongly favor" as 1.
- Favor civil unions (see text for wording): Same as for same-sex marriage.

- Ideology: "In general, would you describe your political views as very conservative (1), conservative (.75), moderate (.5), liberal (.25), or very liberal (0)?"
- Party identification: "In politics today, do you consider yourself a Republican (1), Democrat (0) or independent?" If independent or other: "As of today do you lean more to the Republican Party (.75) or more to the Democratic Party (.25)?" I coded all others as .5.
- Presidential approval: "Do you approve (1) or disapprove (0) of the way George W. Bush is handling his job as president?"
- Evangelical: "Would you describe yourself as a 'born again' or evangelical Christian (1), or not (0)?"

The analyses presented in table 4.2 were based on the October 2003 survey. Additional question wording and coding were as follows:

- Clergy support for homosexuality (see text for wording): I coded "discouraged" as 0, "accepted" as 1, and all others as .5.
- Disagreement with "traditional family" frame (see text for wording): I coded "completely agree" as 0, "somewhat agree" as 1/3, "somewhat disagree" as 2/3, and "completely disagree" as 1.

APPENDIX B: THE 1993 ANES PILOT STUDY AND THE 2003 OCTOBER PEW SURVEY

Question wording and coding for the analyses presented in table 3.2 were as follows:

- Support for an employment nondiscrimination law and gays in the military (see text for wording): I coded "strongly oppose" as 0, "oppose" as 1/3, "favor" as 2/3, and "strongly favor" as 1.
- Comfortable with homosexuality (see table 3.1 for wording): I coded "disgusted, strongly" as 0, "disgusted, not strongly" as 1/3, "uncomfortable but not disgusted" as 2/3, and "not uncomfortable" as 1.
- Feelings toward gay men and lesbians (see chapter 6 for question wording): I divided the feeling thermometer score by 100.
- Beliefs that homosexuality is natural and cannot be changed (see table 3.1 for wording): For the first item, I coded "homosexuality is unnatural, believe strongly" as 0, "homosexuality is unnatural, believe not strongly" as 1/3, "homosexuality is their natural sexuality, believe not strongly" as 2/3, and "homosexuality is their natural sexuality, believe strongly" as 1. For the second item, I coded "choose to be, believe strongly" as 0, "choose to be, believe not strongly" as 1/3, "cannot change, believe not

strongly" as 2/3, and "cannot change, believe strongly" as 1. I then summed the scores for the two items and divided by 2 (Cronbach's alpha = .78).

- Belief that homosexual behavior is not against the will of God (see table 3.1 for wording): I coded "homosexuality is against the will of God, believe strongly" as 0, "homosexuality is against the will of God, believe not strongly" as .5, and "homosexuality can be acceptable to God" or "homosexuality should have nothing to do with God or religion" as 1.
- Belief that homosexuals do not try to seduce people who are not homosexuals (see table 3.1 for wording): I coded "willing to seduce people who are not homosexuals, believe strongly" as 0, "willing to seduce people who are not homosexuals, believe not strongly" as 1/3, "don't make sexual advances on people who are not interested, believe not strongly" as 2/3, and "don't make sexual advances on people who are not interested, believe strongly" as 1.
- Confident that working with a homosexual poses no special danger of disease (see table 3.1 for wording): I coded "worry a lot" as 0, "worry a little" as 1/3, "somewhat confident" as 2/3, and "very confident" as 1.

Question wording and coding for the analyses presented in table 3.4 were as follows:

- Support for same-sex marriage and civil unions (see text for wording): I coded "strongly oppose" as 0, "oppose" as 1/3, "favor" as 2/3, and "strongly favor" as 1.
- Comfortable around gays and lesbians (see table 3.3 for wording): I coded "it makes me uncomfortable to be around homosexuals" as 0 and "it doesn't bother me to be around homosexuals" as 1.
- Favorable opinions about gays and lesbians (see table 3.3 for wording): For each item, I coded "very unfavorable" as 0, "mostly unfavorable" as 1/3, "mostly favorable" as 2/3, and "very favorable" as 1. I then summed across the two items and divided by 2 (Cronbach's alpha = .95).
- Beliefs that homosexuality is something people are born with and cannot be changed (see table 3.3 for wording): For the first item, I coded "something that develops because of the way that people are brought up" or "just the way that some people prefer to live" as 0 and "something that people are born with" as 1. For the second item, I coded "can be changed" as 0 and "cannot be changed" as 1. I then summed across the two items and divided by 2 (Cronbach's alpha = .65).
- Belief that homosexual behavior is not a sin (see table 3.3 for wording): I coded "is a sin" as 0 and "is not a sin" as 1.

- Belief that gays and lesbians are just as likely to have stable relationships (see table 3.3 for wording): I coded "less likely to have stable, long term relationships" as 0 and "don't think so" as 1.
- Belief that acceptance of gays and lesbians would be good for the country (see table 3.3 for wording): I coded "bad for the country" as 0," "wouldn't make much difference" as .5, and "good for the country" as 1.

APPENDIX C: CONTENT ANALYSIS PROCEDURE

To be included in the sample for the content analysis, an item had to contain at least one explicit mention of (1) a law, bill, ordinance, court ruling, constitutional amendment, charter amendment, or referendum regarding gay rights, or (2) a policy regarding gay rights set by a government agency, institution, or office. I excluded items that did not contain enough information to allow for the coding procedure to be applied (i.e., abstracts, items that were incomplete or missing because of errors in the database, and items that contained only a brief announcement of a publication for sale or the time of an event). If these items had been included in the analysis, few would have been judged to contain any of the frames of interest. I also excluded citations that included multiple texts (e.g., multiple opinion pieces, multiple letters to the editor, or multiple unrelated "bullet" articles) to avoid the possibility of counting two items as one (which might have rendered the sample size misleading). Finally, I excluded items that focused on politics in another nation or at the international level and items from sources classified in the 1997 LexisNexis database as "Non-U.S. Sources." Both the primary coder and the secondary coder used the following coding scheme—which lists summaries and exemplars—to identify value frames:

Anti–gay rights morality frame: Uses traditional notions of morality and "family values" to justify opposition to gay rights. Homosexuality is immoral; gay rights is a moral issue. One can have genuine moral objections to gay rights policies/homosexuality. Gay rights policies go against traditional morals or mores; moral beliefs, precedents, standards, or edicts; morality; traditional values; family values; and/or community values. Anti–gay rights policies protect/promote traditional morals or mores; moral beliefs, precedents, standards, or edicts; morality; traditional values; family values; and/or community values.

Pro–gay rights morality frame: Consists of an explicit rejection or rebuttal of the anti–gay rights morality frame. Homosexuality is not immoral; gay rights is not a moral issue. Moral objections to homosexuality cannot justify opposition to gay rights. Gay rights policies are not a threat to traditional morals or mores; moral beliefs, precedents, standards, or edicts; morality; traditional values; family values; and/or community values. Anti–gay rights policies do not protect/promote traditional morals or mores; moral beliefs, precedents, standards, or edicts; morality; traditional values; family values; and/or community values.

Pro–gay rights equality frame: Uses egalitarian principles to justify support for gay rights. Gay rights policies are about equal rights, equality, an equal voice, equal participation, equal protection, equal opportunity, and/or equal treatment for gays and lesbians. Gays and lesbians should have the same rights as/should be treated like all Americans/everybody else/people who are not gay or lesbian. Anti–gay rights policies deny gays and lesbians equal rights, equal treatment, or equal protection under the law; such policies make gays and lesbians unequal to everyone else. Gay rights policies are not about special rights, special privileges, special treatment, extra rights, preferential treatment, and/or preferred status for gays and lesbians. Such policies will not give gays and lesbians any rights or privileges that other people do not have.

Anti–gay rights equality frame: Uses egalitarian principles to justify opposition to gay rights. Gay rights policies are about special rights, special privileges, special treatment, extra rights, preferential treatment, and/or preferred status for gays and lesbians. Such policies give gays and lesbians rights or privileges that other people do not have. Gay rights policies are not about equal rights, equality, an equal voice, equal participation, equal protection, equal opportunity, and/or equal treatment for gays and lesbians. Gays and lesbians should not have the same rights as all Americans/everybody else/people who are not gay or lesbian; they are not entitled to equal protection under the law. Opposition to gay rights is support for equal rights.

The Scott's pi intercoder reliability coefficient for the anti–gay rights morality frame was .79; for the pro–gay rights equality frame it was .89; and for the anti–gay rights equality frame it was .96. The fourth frame has a relatively low reliability score: when the coders judged the presence or absence of the pro–gay rights morality frame, the intercoder reliability score dropped to .48. This was not a grave concern, however: the frame was noteworthy only for its rarity, and both coders agreed that it was absent from 94 of the 100 items.

APPENDIX D: THE 1999 EXPERIMENT

Experimental Participants

The median age for participants was 20. Of the participants, 10 percent were African American, and 54 percent were women. In response to the close-ended question about an antidiscrimination law, 17 percent of the participants opposed or strongly opposed such a law, 19 percent were neutral, and 64 percent favored or strongly favored such a law. In response to the close-ended question about military service, 19 percent opposed or strongly opposed gays in the military, 34 percent were neutral, and 47 percent favored or strongly favored gays in the military. The mean level of egalitarianism was .75, and the mean level of moral traditionalism was .48 (see chapter 6 for details about the measurement of egalitarianism and moral traditionalism).

Treatment Article

Introductory paragraph

GAY RIGHTS FINDS ITS WAY ONTO BALLOTS ACROSS THE NATION
From the Tampa Tribune, *Oct. 4, 1998*

The political cauldron of gay rights continues to boil. And as many Americans are discovering, this highly charged, divisive issue just won't go away. The question of whether homosexuals should be protected from discrimination keeps popping up on the ballot across the nation. So far, eight states and about 130 cities and counties have adopted laws protecting gays and lesbians from discrimination. Opponents of gay rights are responding with a two-pronged strategy. On the one hand, they attempt to repeal ordinances through local ballot initiatives. On the other, they push amendments that not only repeal local ordinances but prohibit government entities from ever passing new ones.

Equal rights frame

Advocates of gay rights ordinances justify such laws by arguing that all citizens, including gays and lesbians, are entitled to equal treatment. *[They point to a recent United States Supreme Court opinion which concluded/Douglass Hattaway, who leads an organization that campaigns for gay rights, recently told an audience]* that anti–gay rights amendments violate the equal protection clause of the U.S. Constitution by making gays and lesbians "unequal to everyone else." *[The court/Hattaway]* went on to argue that "in order for there to be equal rights, gays and lesbians must be protected from discrimination."

Moral values frame

Critics of gay rights ordinances base their opposition on the argument that such laws undermine moral values. *[They point to a recent United States Supreme Court opinion which concluded/Lou Sheldon, who leads an organization which campaigns against gay rights, recently told an audience]* that anti–gay rights laws are nothing more than "reasonable attempts to preserve traditional American moral values against the efforts of a politically powerful minority group." *[The court/Sheldon]* furthermore criticized gay rights laws as "endorsements of immoral behavior."

Concluding paragraph

Amid the furor, one thing is clear. The debate over gay rights will continue, as both sides battle to win the hearts and minds of legislators and voters.

Notes: The headings were not presented to experimental participants. In a further experimental manipulation, each frame was randomly attributed to either a U.S. Supreme Court opinion or an interest group spokesperson. The first paragraph of the treatment was based on a March 13, 1995 Tampa Tribune article by Booth Gunter titled, "Gay Rights Divides Communities; The Issue Stirs Emotions as It Finds Its Way onto Ballots across the Nation."

APPENDIX E: THE 1992, 1996, 2000, AND 2004 AMERICAN NATIONAL ELECTION STUDIES

Question wording and coding for the analyses presented in tables 6.1, 6.2, and 6.3 were as follows:

- Public opinion about employment nondiscrimination and gays in the military (see table 6.1 for wording): For each item, I coded "strongly oppose" as 0, "oppose" as 1/3, "favor" as 2/3, and "strongly favor" as 1. I then averaged the two values to create an index ranging from 0 (minimum support) to 1 (maximum support).
- Public opinion about same-sex marriage (see table 6.1 for wording): I coded "should not be allowed" as 0 and "should be allowed" as 1.
- Feelings toward gay men and lesbians (see text for wording): I divided the feeling thermometer score by 100.
- Party identification: I constructed this measure from the traditional ANES branching question, which categorized each respondent as a strong Democrat (0), weak Democrat (1/6), Democratic leaner (2/6), independent (3/6), Republican leaner (4/6), weak Republican (5/6), or strong Republican (1).
- Ideology: I constructed this measure from questions categorizing each respondent as extremely liberal (0), liberal (1/6), slightly liberal (2/6), moderate or middle of the road/haven't thought much about it (3/6), slightly conservative (4/6), conservative (5/6), or extremely conservative (1).
- Bible should be taken literally (see text for wording): I coded "The Bible is a book written by men and is not the word of God" as 0, "The Bible is the word of God but not everything in it should be taken literally, word for word" as .5, and "The Bible is the actual word of God and is to be taken literally, word for word" as 1.

- Egalitarianism (see text for wording): For the first, fifth, and sixth items, I coded strongly disagree as 0, disagree as .25, neither agree nor disagree as .5, agree as .75, and strongly agree as 1. I reverse-coded the second, third, and fourth items. I then averaged across items to create an index ranging from 0 (minimum egalitarianism) to 1 (maximum egalitarianism).
- Moral traditionalism (see text for wording): For the first and fourth items, I coded strongly disagree as 0, disagree as .25, neither agree nor disagree as .5, agree as .75, and strongly agree as 1. I reverse-coded the second and third items. I then averaged across the items to create an index ranging from 0 (minimum moral traditionalism) to 1 (maximum moral traditionalism).

Bibliography

Abramowitz, Alan. "Terrorism, Gay Marriage, and Incumbency: Explaining the Republican Victory in the 2004 Presidential Election." *The Forum* 2 (2004): www .bepress.com/forum/vol2/iss4/art3/.

Allport, Gordon W. *The Nature of Prejudice.* New York: Doubleday, 1954.

Alvarez, R. Michael, and Edward J. McCaffery. "Are There Sex Gaps in Fiscal Policy Preferences?" *Political Research Quarterly* 56 (2003): 5–17.

Alvarez, R. Michael, and Jonathan Nagler. "Economics, Issues, and the Perot Candidacy: Voter Choice in the 1992 Presidential Election." *American Journal of Political Science* 39 (1995): 714–44.

Alwood, Edward. *Straight News: Gays, Lesbians, and the News Media.* New York: Columbia University Press, 1996.

Bailey, Michel, Lee Sigelman, and Clyde Wilcox. "Presidential Persuasion on Social Issues: A Two-way Street?" *Political Research Quarterly* 56 (2004): 49–58.

Bartels, Larry. "What's the Matter with *What's the Matter with Kansas?*" *Quarterly Journal of Political Science* 1 (2006): 201–26.

Becker, Ron. *Gay TV and Straight America.* New Brunswick, N.J.: Rutgers University Press, 2006.

Berelson, Bernard, Paul Lazarsfeld, and William McPhee. *Voting: A Study of Opinion Formation in a Presidential Campaign.* Chicago: University of Chicago Press, 1954.

Bianco, David Ari. "Echoes of Prejudice: The Debates over Race and Sexuality in the Armed Forces." In *Gay Rights, Military Wrongs: Political Perspectives on Lesbians and Gays in the Military,* edited by Craig A. Rimmerman, 127–46. New York: Garland Publishing, 1996.

Bowman, Karlyn. "Attitudes about Homosexuality and Gay Marriage." Washington, DC: American Enterprise Institute, 2006.

Brewer, Paul R. "Value Words and Lizard Brains: Do Citizens Deliberate about Appeals to Their Core Values?" *Political Psychology* 22 (2001): 45–64.

———. "Framing, Value Words, and Citizens' Explanations of Their Issue Opinions." *Political Communication* 19 (2002): 303–16.

———. "The Shifting Foundations of Public Opinion about Gay Rights." *Journal of Politics* 65 (2003a): 1208–20.

———. "Values, Political Knowledge, and Public Opinion about Gay Rights: A Framing-Based Account." *Public Opinion Quarterly* 67 (2003b): 173–201.

Brewer, Paul R., and Kimberly Gross. "Values, Framing, and Citizens' Thoughts about Policy Issues: Effects on Content and Quantity." *Political Psychology* 26 (2005): 929–48.

Brewer, Paul R., and Clyde Wilcox. "Trends: Same-Sex Marriage and Civil Unions." *Public Opinion Quarterly* 69 (2005): 599–616.

Burden, Barry. "An Alternative Account of the 2004 Presidential Election." *The Forum* 2 (2004): www.bepress.com/forum/vol2/iss4/art2/.

Campbell, Angus, Philip E. Converse, Warren E. Miller, and Donald E. Stokes. *The American Voter*. Chicago: University of Chicago Press, 1960.

Campbell, David E., and J. Quin Monson. "The Religion Card: Gay Marriage and the 2004 Presidential Election." Paper presented at the annual meeting of the American Political Science Association, Washington, DC, September 2005.

Cappella, Joseph N., and Kathleen Hall Jamieson. *Spiral of Cynicism: The Press and the Public Good*. New York: Oxford University Press, 1997.

Chong, Dennis. "How People Think, Reason, and Feel about Rights and Liberties." *American Journal of Political Science* 37 (1993): 867–99.

———. "Creating Common Frames of Reference on Political Issues." In *Political Persuasion and Attitude Change*, edited by Diana C. Mutz, Paul M. Sniderman, and Richard A. Brody, 195–224. Ann Arbor: University of Michigan Press, 1996.

Chong, Dennis, and James N. Druckman. "Competitive Framing." Paper presented at the annual meeting of the American Political Science Association, Washington DC, September 2005.

Converse, Philip E. "The Nature of Belief Systems in Mass Publics." In *Ideology and Discontent*, edited by David E. Apter, 206–61. New York: Free Press, 1964.

Cook, Fay Lomax, Jason Barabas, and Benjamin I. Page. "Invoking Public Opinion: Policy Elites and Social Security." *Public Opinion Quarterly* 66 (2002): 235–64.

Craig, Stephen C., Michael D. Martinez, James G. Kane, and Jason Gainous. "Core Values, Value Conflict, and Citizens' Ambivalence about Gay Rights." *Political Research Quarterly* 58 (2005): 5–17.

Delli Carpini, Michael X., and Scott Keeter. *What Americans Know About Politics and Why It Matters*. New Haven, Conn.: Yale University Press, 1996.

Donavan, Todd, Caroline Tolbert, Daniel A. Smith, and Janine Parry. "Did Gay Marriage Elect George W. Bush?" Paper presented at the State Politics Conference, East Lansing, Mich., May 2005.

Donavan, Todd, Jim Wenzel, and Shaun Bowler. "Direct Democracy and Gay Rights Initiatives after *Romer*." In *The Politics of Gay Rights*, edited by Craig A. Rimmerman, Kenneth D. Wald, and Clyde Wilcox, 161–90. Chicago: Chicago University Press, 2000.

Downs, Anthony. *An Economic Theory of Democracy*. New York: HarperCollins, 1975.

Druckman, James N. "The Implications of Framing Effects for Citizen Competence." *Political Behavior* 23 (2001a): 225–56.

——. "On the Limits of Framing Effects: Who Can Frame?" *Journal of Politics* 63 (2001b): 1041–66.

Druckman, James N., and Kjersten R. Nelson. "Framing and Deliberation: How Citizens' Conversations Limit Elite Influence." *American Journal of Political Science* 47 (2003): 726–45.

Egan, Patrick J. "Lesbian and Gay Voters in the 1990s." Paper presented at the annual meeting of the American Political Science Association, Chicago, September 2004.

Egan, Patrick J., and Kenneth Sherrill. "Marriage and the Shifting Priorities of a New Generation of Lesbians and Gays." *PS: Political Science & Politics* 38 (2005): 229–32.

——. "Same-Sex Marriage Initiatives and Lesbian, Gay, and Bisexual Voters in the 2006 Elections." Washington, DC: National Gay and Lesbian Task Force, 2006.

Entman, Robert. "Framing: Toward Clarification of a Fractured Paradigm." *Journal of Communication* 43 (1993): 51–58.

Feldman, Stanley. "Structure and Consistency in Public Opinion: The Role of Core Beliefs and Values." *American Journal of Political Science* 32 (1988): 416–40.

Feldman, Stanley, and John Zaller. "The Political Culture of Ambivalence: Ideological Responses to the Welfare State." *American Journal of Political Science* 36 (1992): 268–307.

Fishkin, James S. *The Voice of the People: Public Opinion in a Democracy*. New Haven, Conn.: Yale University Press, 1997.

Frank, Thomas. *What's the Matter with Kansas? How Conservatives Won the Heart of America*. New York: Metropolitan Books, 2004.

Gallagher, John, and Chris Bull. *Perfect Enemies: The Religious Right, the Gay Movement, and the Politics of the 1990s*. New York: Crown, 1996.

Gallagher, Maggie, and Joshua K. Baker. "Same-Sex Marriage: What Does the Next Generation Think?" Washington, DC: Institute for Marriage and Public Policy, 2004.

Gamson, William A. *Strategy of Social Protest*. Homewood, Ill.: Dorsey Press, 1975.

——. 1992. *Talking Politics*. New York: Cambridge University Press.

Gamson, William A., and Kathryn E. Lasch. "The Political Culture of Social Welfare Policy." In *Evaluating the Welfare State*, edited by Shimon E. Spiro and Ephraim Yuchtman-Yaar, 397–415. New York: Academic Press, 1983.

Gamson, William A., and Andre Modigliani. "The Changing Culture of Affirmative Action." In *Research in Political Sociology*, vol. 3, edited by Richard D. Braungart, 137–77. Greenwich, Conn.: JAI Press, 1987.

——. "Media Discourse and Public Opinion on Nuclear Power: A Constructionist Approach." *American Journal of Sociology* 95 (1989): 1–37.

Gilligan, Carol. *Understanding the Gender Gap: An Economic History of American Women*. Cambridge, Mass.: Harvard University Press, 1990.

Goldman, Seth. "Framing Effects, Elite Competition, and the Debate over Gay Marriage: An Experimental Test." Paper presented at the annual meeting of the International Communication Association, Dresden, Germany, June 2006.

Goldman, Seth, and Paul R. Brewer. "From Gay Bashing to Gay Baiting: Public Opinion and News Media Frames for Gay Marriage." In *Defending Same-Sex Marriage, Volume III: The Freedom-to-Marry Movement: Education, Advocacy, Culture, and the*

Media, edited by Martin Dupuis and William Thompson, 102–28. Westport, Conn.: Praeger, 2007.

Gordon, C. Ann, Barry L. Tadlock, and Elizabeth Popp. "Framing the Issue of Same-Sex Marriage: Traditional Values versus Equal Rights." Paper presented at the annual meeting of the American Political Science Association, Chicago, September 2004.

Green, John C., James L. Guth, and Kevin Hill. "Faith and Election: The Christian Right in Congressional Campaigns 1978–1988." *Journal of Politics* 55 (1993): 80–91.

Gross, Larry. *Up from Invisibility: Lesbians, Gay Men, and the Media in America*. New York: Columbia University Press, 2001.

Habermas, Jürgen. *The Structural Transformation of the Public Sphere: An Inquiry into a Category of Bourgeois Society*. Cambridge, Mass.: MIT Press, 1989.

Haeberle, Steven H. "Gay and Lesbian Rights: Emerging Trends in Public Opinion and Voting Behavior." In *Gays and Lesbians in the Democratic Process*, edited by Ellen D. B. Riggle and Barry L. Tadlock, 146–69. New York: Columbia University Press, 1999.

Haider-Markel, Donald P. "Media Coverage of *Lawrence v. Texas*: An Analysis of Content, Tone, and Frames in National and Local News Reporting." New York: Gay and Lesbian Alliance Against Defamation, 2003.

Haider-Markel, Donald P., Mahalley D. Allen, and Morgen Johansen. "Understanding Variations in Media Coverage of U.S. Supreme Court Decisions: Comparing Media Outlets in Their Coverage of *Lawrence v. Texas*." *Harvard International Journal of Press/Politics* 11 (2006): 64–85.

Haider-Markel, Donald P., and Mark R. Joslyn. "Gun Policy, Opinion, Tragedy, and Blame Attribution." *Journal of Politics* 63 (2001): 520–43.

———. "Attributions and the Regulation of Marriage: Considering the Parallels Between Race and Homosexuality." *PS: Political Science & Politics* 38 (2005): 233–39.

Herek, Gregory M. "Stigma, Prejudice, and Violence against Lesbians and Gay Men." In *Homosexuality: Research Implications for Public Policy*, edited by John C. Gonsiorek and James D. Weinrich, 60–80. Newbury Park, Calif.: Sage, 1991.

———. "Gender Gaps in Public Opinion about Lesbians and Gay Men." *Public Opinion Quarterly* 66 (2002): 40–66.

Herek, Gregory M., and John P. Capitanio. "'Some of My Best Friends': Intergroup Contact, Concealable Stigma, and Heterosexuals' Attitudes toward Gay Men and Lesbians." *Personality and Social Psychology Bulletin* 22 (1996): 414–24.

Hertzog, Mark. *The Lavender Vote: Lesbians, Gay Men, and Bisexuals in American Politics*. New York: New York University Press, 1996.

Hillygus, D. Sunshine, and Todd G. Shields. "Moral Issues and Voter Decision Making in the 2004 Presidential Election." *PS: Political Science & Politics* 38 (2005): 201–9.

Hochschild, Jennifer. *What's Fair?* Princeton, N.J.: Princeton University Press, 1981.

Hurwitz, Jon, and Mark Peffley. "How Are Foreign Policy Attitudes Structured? A Hierarchical Model." *American Political Science Review* 81 (1987): 1099–120.

Iyengar, Shanto, and Donald R. Kinder. *News That Matters: Television and American Public Opinion*. Chicago: University of Chicago Press, 1987.

Jacoby, William G. "Issue Framing and Public Opinion on Government Spending." *American Journal of Political Science* 44 (2000): 750–67.

Katz, Elihu, and Paul Lazarsfeld. *Personal Influence: The Part Played by People in the Flow of Mass Communications.* New York: Free Press, 1964.

Kaufmann, Karen M., and John R. Petrocik. "The Changing Politics of American Men: Understanding the Sources of the Gender Gap." *American Journal of Political Science* 43 (1999): 864–87.

Keeter, Scott. "Evangelicals and Moral Values in the Election of 2004." Paper presented at the Religion and the 2004 Election Conference, South Bend, Ind., December 2005.

Kellstedt, Paul M. "Media Framing and the Dynamics of Racial Policy Preferences." *American Journal of Political Science* 44 (2000): 245–60.

Kinder, Donald R., and Lynn M. Sanders. *Divided By Color: Racial Politics and Democratic Ideals.* Chicago: University of Chicago Press, 1996.

Kinder, Donald R., and Nicholas Winter. "Exploring the Racial Divide: Blacks, Whites, and Opinion on National Policy." *American Journal of Political Science* 45 (2001): 439–53.

King, Gary, Michael Tomz, and Jason Wittenberg. "Making the Most of Statistical Analyses: Improving Interpretation and Presentation." *American Journal of Political Science* 44 (2000): 347–61.

Koch, Jeffrey W. "Political Rhetoric and Political Persuasion: The Changing Structure of Citizens' Preferences on Health Insurance during Policy Debates." *Public Opinion Quarterly* 62 (1998): 209–29.

———. "The Changing Black and White Divide on Americans' Attitudes toward Gays." Paper presented at the annual meeting of the American Political Science Association, Chicago, September 2004.

Langer, Gary, and Jon Cohen. "Voters and Values in the 2004 Election." *Public Opinion Quarterly* 69 (2005): 744–59.

Lazarsfeld, Paul, Bernard Berelson, and Hazel Gaudet. *The People's Choice: How the Voter Makes Up His Mind in a Presidential Campaign.* New York: Columbia University Press, 1948.

Lewis, Gregory B. "Black-White Differences in Attitudes toward Homosexuality and Gay Rights." *Public Opinion Quarterly* 67 (2003): 59–78.

———. "Same-Sex Marriage and the 2004 Presidential Election." *PS: Political Science & Politics* 38 (2005): 195–99.

Lewis, Gregory B., and Marc A. Rogers. "Does the Public Support Equal Employment Rights For Gays and Lesbians?" In *Gays and Lesbians in the Democratic Process,* edited by Ellen D. B. Riggle and Barry L. Tadlock, 118–45. New York: Columbia University Press, 1999.

Lim, Elvin T., and Nicholas W. Carnes. "Whither 'Culture War?' Cultural Peace in the 2004 Same-Sex Marriage Debate." Paper presented at the annual meeting of the Midwest Political Science Association, Chicago, April 2006.

Lippmann, Walter. *The Phantom Public.* New York: Macmillan, 1925.

———. *Public Opinion.* New York: Macmillan, [1922] 1965.

McClosky, Herbert, and John Zaller. *The American Ethos: Public Attitudes Toward Capitalism and Democracy.* Cambridge, Mass.: Harvard University Press, 1984.

McDonald, Michael P. "Up, Up, and Away! Voter Participation in the 2004 Presidential Election." *The Forum* 2 (2004): www.bepress.com/forum/vol2/iss4/art4/.

Mill, John Stuart. *On Liberty*. Arlington Heights, Ill.: AHM Publishing, [1859] 1947.

Moore, David W., and Joseph Carroll. "Support for Gay Marriage/Civil Unions Edges Upward; Public Remains Divided on Constitutional Amendment to Ban Gay Marriage." Washington, DC: Gallup Organization, 2003.

Nelson, Thomas E., Rosalee A. Clawson, and Zoe M. Oxley. "Media Framing of a Civil Liberties Conflict and Its Effect on Tolerance." *American Political Science Review* 91 (1997): 567–83.

Nelson, Thomas E., and Donald R. Kinder. "Issue Frames and Group-Centrism in American Public Opinion." *Journal of Politics* 58 (1996): 1055–78.

Nelson, Thomas E., and Zoe M. Oxley. "Issue Framing Effects on Belief Importance and Opinion." *Journal of Politics* 61 (1999): 1040–67.

Nelson, Thomas E., Zoe M. Oxley, and Rosalee A. Clawson. "Toward a Psychology of Framing Effects." *Political Behavior* 19 (1997): 221–46.

Nelson, Thomas E., and Elaine A. Willey. "Issue Frames That Strike a Value Balance." In *Framing Public Life*, edited by Stephen D. Reese, Oscar H. Gandy, Jr., and August E. Grant, 245–66. Mahwah, N.J.: Lawrence Erlbaum, 2001.

Newport, Frank. "Constitutional Amendment Defining Marriage Lacks 'Supermajority' Support; Almost Two-Thirds Oppose Same-Sex Marriage, but Only 51% Favor Constitutional Amendment." Washington, DC: Gallup Organization, 2004.

Norrander, Barbara. "The Evolution of the Gender Gap." *Public Opinion Quarterly* 63 (1999): 566–76.

Olson, Laura R., Wendy Cadge, and James T. Harrison. "Religion and Public Opinion about Same-Sex Marriage." *Social Science Quarterly* 87 (2006): 340–60.

Paden, Catherine, and Benjamin I. Page. "Congress Invokes Public Opinion on Welfare." *American Politics Research* 31 (2003): 670–79.

Page, Benjamin I. "The Theory of Political Ambiguity." *American Political Science Review* 70 (1976): 742–52.

Page, Benjamin I., and Robert Y. Shapiro. *The Rational Public: Fifty Years of Trends in American Policy Preferences*. Chicago: University of Chicago Press, 1992.

Pew Research Center for the People and the Press. "Republicans Unified, Democrats Split on Same-Sex Marriage; Religious Beliefs Underpin Opposition to Homosexuality." Washington, DC: Pew Research Center for the People and the Press, 2003.

———. "Reading the Polls on Gay Marriage and the Constitution." Washington, DC: Pew Research Center for the People and the Press, 2004a.

———. "Voters Liked Campaign 2004, But Too Much 'Mud-Slinging'; Moral Values: How Important?" Washington, DC: Pew Research Center for the People and the Press, 2004b.

———. "Less Opposition to Gay Marriage, Adoption, and Military Service; Only 34% Favor South Dakota Abortion Law." Washington, DC: Pew Research Center for the People and the Press, 2006.

———. "Trends in Political Values and Core Attitudes: 1987–2007; Political Landscape More Favorable to Democrats." Washington, DC: Pew Research Center for the People and the Press, 2007.

Popkin, Samuel L. *The Reasoning Voter*. Chicago: University of Chicago Press, 1994.

Price, Vincent, Lilach Nir, and Joseph N. Cappella. "Framing Public Discussion of Gay Civil Unions." *Public Opinion Quarterly* 69 (2005): 179–212.

Riggle, Ellen D. B., Jerry D. Thomas, and Sharon S. Rostosky. "The Marriage Debate and Minority Stress." *PS: Political Science & Politics* 38 (2005): 221–24.

Rimmerman, Craig A. *From Identity to Politics: The Lesbian and Gay Movement in the United States.* Philadelphia: Temple University Press, 2002.

Rokeach, Milton. *The Nature of Human Values.* New York: Free Press, 1973.

Sabato, Larry J. *Feeding Frenzy: How Attack Journalism Has Transformed American Politics.* New York: Free Press, 1991.

Schaffner, Brian, and Nenad Senic. "Rights or Benefits? Explaining the Sexual Identity Gap in American Political Behavior." *Political Research Quarterly* 59 (2006): 123–32.

Schiappa, Edward, Peter B. Gregg, and Dean A. Hewes. "Can One TV Show Make a Difference? *Will & Grace* and the Parasocial Contact Hypothesis." *Journal of Homosexuality* 51 (2006): 15–37.

Schuman, Howard, Charlotte Steeh, Lawrence Bobo, and Maria Krysan. *Racial Attitudes in America: Trends and Interpretations*, rev. ed. Cambridge, Mass.: Harvard University Press, 1997.

Sears, David O. "College Sophomores in the Laboratory: Influences of a Narrow Data Base on Psychology's View of Human Nature." *Journal of Personality and Social Psychology* 51 (1986): 515–30.

Shah, Dhavan V., David Domke, and Daniel Wackman. "'To Thine Own Self Be True': Values, Framing, and Voter Decision-Making Strategies." *Communication Research* 23 (1996): 509–60.

Smidt, Corwin E, ed. *Pulpit and Politics: Clergy in American Politics at the Advent of the Millennium.* Waco, Tex.: Baylor University Press, 2004.

Smith, Daniel, Matthew DeSantis, and Jason Kessel. "Same-Sex Marriage Ballot Measures and the 2004 Presidential Election." *State and Local Government Review* 38 (2006): 78–91.

Sniderman, Paul. M., Richard A. Brody, and Philip E. Tetlock. *Reasoning and Choice: Explorations in Political Psychology.* New York: Cambridge University Press, 1991.

Sniderman, Paul M., and Sean M. Theriault. "The Structure of Political Argument and the Logic of Issue Framing." In *Studies in Public Opinion: Attitudes, Nonattitudes, Measurement Error, and Change*, edited by Willem E. Saris and Paul M. Sniderman, 133–65. Princeton, N.J.: Princeton University Press, 2004.

Strand, Douglas Alan. "Civil Liberties, Civil Rights, and Stigma: Voter Attitudes and Behavior in the Politics of Homosexuality." In *Stigma and Sexual Orientation: Understanding Prejudice against Lesbians, Gay Men, and Bisexuals*, edited by Gregory M. Herek, 108–37. Thousand Oaks, Calif.: Sage, 1998.

Torres-Reyna, Oscar, and Robert Y. Shapiro. "Trends: Women and Sexual Orientation in the Military." *Public Opinion Quarterly* 66 (2002): 618–32.

Vaid, Urvashi. *Virtual Equality.* New York: Anchor Books, 1995.

Walsh, Katherine Cramer. *Talking about Politics: Informal Groups and Social Identity in America.* Chicago: University of Chicago Press, 2003.

Walters, Suzanna Danuta. *All the Rage: The Story of Gay Visibility in America.* Chicago: University of Chicago Press, 2001.

Watts, Mark D., David Domke, Dhavan V. Shah, and David P. Fan. "Elite Cues and Media Bias in Presidential Campaigns: Explaining Public Perceptions of a Liberal Press." *Communication Research* 26 (1999): 144–75.

Whitley, Bernard E. "The Relationship of Heterosexuals' Attributions for the Causes of Homosexuality to Attitudes toward Gay and Lesbian Men." *Personality and Social Psychology Bulletin* 16 (1990): 369–97.

Wilcox, Clyde, and Barbara Norrander. "Of Moods and Morals: The Dynamics of Opinion on Abortion and Gay Rights." In *Understanding Public Opinion*, 2nd ed., edited by Barbara Norrander and Clyde Wilcox, 121–48. Washington, DC: Congressional Quarterly Press, 2002.

Wilcox, Clyde, and Robin Wolpert. "President Clinton, Public Opinion, and Gays in the Military." In *Gay Rights, Military Wrongs: Political Perspectives on Lesbians and Gays in the Military*, edited by Craig A. Rimmerman, 127–45. New York: Garland Publishing, 1996.

———. "Gay Rights in the Public Sphere: Public Opinion on Gay and Lesbian Equality." In *The Politics of Gay Rights*, edited by Craig A. Rimmerman, Kenneth D. Wald, and Clyde Wilcox, 409–32. Chicago: University of Chicago Press, 2000.

Wood, Peter B., and John P. Bartkowski. "Attribution Style and Public Policy Attitudes Toward Gay Rights." *Social Science Quarterly* 85 (2004): 58–74.

Yang, Alan S. "Trends: Attitudes toward Homosexuality." *Public Opinion Quarterly* 61 (1997): 477–507.

Zaller, John. *The Nature and Origins of Mass Opinion*. New York: Cambridge University Press, 1992.

Index

700 Club, 60

Abnormal Behaviors Initiative. *See*
    Measure 9
Abramowitz, Alan, 140
adoption by gay parents, 7; public
    opinion about, 21, *22*, 23–24, 27,
    29, 31–33, 35; *See also* Bryant,
    Anita
ambiguity, strategic, 13, 83
American Civil Liberties Union, 72
African-Americans: civil rights
    compared to gay rights, 7–8, 12, 21,
    31, 33–37, 134; opinions about gay
    rights, 28–29, 36, 74, 110
AIDS, 3, 4, 47, 60; fear of, 50, *51*; race
    and, 29
Alabama, 134–35
Alliance for Marriage, 72
amendment 2. *See* Colorado
American Psychiatric Association, 30
Anglican Communion, 4
Anheuser-Busch, 59
Arizona, 11, 134–35
Arkansas, 134
Arlington Group, 72
Armey, Dick, 13, 60

Baehr v. Lewin, 25
Bailey, Michael, 70
Baker, Joshua, 137
Bartels, Larry, 7
Bauer, Gary, 72, 137
Bennett, William, 72
Bible, 59, 93; family values as defined
    by, 68; literal interpretation as
    predictor of opinion, 33, 115–17,
    118, 121, 122
born-again Christians. *See* evangelical
    Christianity
Borger, Gloria, 130
Bowers v. Hardwick, 3, 19
Brattleboro Reformer, 49
Braun, Carol Moseley, 72, 82
Brewer, Paul, 92
Brokeback Mountain, 43–44, 45, 49, 58
Brown v. Board of Education of Topeka, 35
Bryant, Anita: anti-gay rhetoric, 59;
    Save Our Children campaign, 3, 6,
    21, 23–24, 114, 131
Buchanan, Pat, 1, 6, 10, 13, 140
Burden, Barry, 140
Bush, George H.W., 1
Bush, George W., 6, 72; election and
    moral values issue, 15, 129–30,

138–39; led public opinion, 74, 75, 76, 78, 137; signals about gay rights, 10, 13, 43, 60, 68, 82–83

Carroll, Lewis, 87, 101
Catholic Charities of Boston, 24
CBS Evening News, 129
Chafee, Lincoln, 68
Cheney, Dick, 6, 72; daughter Mary, 61, 65n42
Cheney, Lynn, 61
Civil Rights Act of 1964, 35
Clark, Wesley, 72
clergy, 8, 13, 68, 78–81, 79, 144
Clinton, Bill, 6, 7, 30, 72, 90; led public opinion, 70–71, 81, 82; opposed ban on gays in military, 1, 3, 22, 49, 140
Clinton, Hillary, 7, 141
Colorado, 2, 21, 87, 132, 134; Amendment 2, 2, 3, 21, 87, 132; *See also Romer v. Evans*
Colorado for Family Values, 2, 91
Columbia school, 69
Congressional Black Caucus, 36
Connecticut, 3
Connor, Ken. *See* Family Research Council
Cowan, Lee, 129–30
Culture and Family Institute, 138
culture war: declaration of, 1–2, 7, 140; gay rights and abortion in, 12, 21, 33–35, 143; gay rights as example of, 15, 131, 142; role in 2004 presidential election, 130, 138; same-sex marriage as central to, 11, 138

Daschle, Tom, 68
Daughters of Bilitis, 2
Dean, Howard, 68, 72
Defense of Marriage Act, 3, 25, 72, 140
Defense of Marriage Coalition, 133
DeGeneres, Ellen, 4, 49, 56, 59
Dobson, James. *See* Focus on the Family
Downs, Anthony, 69
Druckman, James, 81

Edwards, John , 6, 65n42, 72, 141
Egan, Patrick, 31, 136
Ellen, 4, 30, 49
Employment Non-Discrimination Act, 3
Episcopal Church, 4, 73
Equal Protection Colorado, 2
evangelical Christianity, 33, 71, 73–75, 76, 77–78, 79
Evangelical Lutheran Church of America, 73

Falwell, Jerry, 6, 13, 34, 59, 60, 73, 137
Family Research Council, 20, 68, 72
Federal Marriage Amendment, 10, 15, 25–26, 136–38
Fleischer, Ari, 68
Florida, 3, 21, 23
Focus on the Family, 6, 59, 72
Foreman, Matt. *See* National Gay (and Lesbian) Task Force
Frank, Barney, 56, 60
Free Congress Foundation, 68, 72
Freedom to Marry, 20
Frank, Thomas, 7
Frist, Bill, 68, 72

Gallagher, Maggie. *See* Institute for Marriage and Public Policy
Gallup, George, 5, 10
Gamson, William, 92–93, 102
gay-bashing, 13, 45, 59–60, 68, 144
genetic basis for homosexuality: beliefs about, 32, 44, 46–47, 50–57; research into, 4, 48
Georgia, 3, 134
Gergen, David, 130
Giuliani, Rudy, 141–42
Goldschmidt, Neil, 131
Goodridge v. Dept. of Public Health, 71, 73
See also Massachusetts
Google, 82
Gordon, Ann, 91
Graham, Franklin, 73, 82

Gross, Kimbery, 92
Grossman, Cathy Lynn, 20

Habermas, Jurgen, 5
Hamer, Dean, 4
Hanks, Tom, 49
Hawaii, 3, 25
Herek, Gregory, 27–28
Hillygus, D. Sunshine, 140
Hudson, Rock, 56
Human Rights Campaign, 6, 19, 68, 134

Idaho, 134
Institute for Marriage and Public Policy, 72, 136–37
Iowa, 140

Jackson, Jesse, 36
Jacoby, William, 88
John, Elton, 56
Judaism, 32, 79

Kansas, 134–35
Kennedy, Anthony, 19, 87
Kennedy, James D., 139
Kennedy, Ted, 142
Kentucky, 134
Kerry, John, 6, 15, 60, 68, 72, 129
Kinder, Donald, 9, 92, 112
King, Martin Luther Jr., 35
Knight, Robert. *See* Culture and Family Institute
Koch, Jeffrey, 28–29
Kucinich, Dennis, 72, 82

Lambda Legal Defense and Education Fund, 2, 19
Lawrence v. Texas, 19, 25, 61, 71
Lee, Ang, 43
Lewis, Gregory, 28, 140
Liberace, 56
Lieberman, Joseph, 72
Lincoln, Abraham, 141
Lippmann, Walter, 5, 10, 47
Lively, Scott. *See* Oregon Citizens' Alliance
Louisiana, 134

Massachusetts, 24, 142; allowed same-sex marriages, 4, 25, 71–73, 124, 133
Mattachine Society, 2
McCain, John, 141
Measure 8. *See* Oregon
Measure 9. *See* Oregon
Measure 13. *See* Oregon
Measure 36. *See* Oregon
Medved, Michael, 45
Michigan, 134
Milk, Harvey, 56
Mill, John Stuart, 5
Milwaukee Journal Sentinel, 135
Minnesota, 124
Mississippi, 134
Missouri, 134
Montana, 134
Morin, Richard, 109
Musgrave, Marilyn, 136–37

NAACP, 35, 90
National Gay (and Lesbian) Task Force, 2, 6, 134
New Hampshire, 23
New Jersey, 3, 136
New York, 136
New York Times, 26, 30
Norrander, Barbara, 114
North Dakota, 134
National Organization for Women, 72

O'Donnell, Rosie, 23, 56
Obama, Barack, 141
Ohio, 134
Oklahoma, 134
Oprah Winfrey Show, 4
O'Reilly, Bill, 43–44
The O'Reilly Factor, 43, 45
Oregon, 2, 3, 21, 131–34; Measure 8, 131–32; Measure 9, 2, 21, 132; Measure 13, 132; Measure 36, 133–34
Oregon Citizens' Alliance, 131–33
Oregonian, 133–34
Orwell, George, 87–88

parasocial contact. *See* virtual contact with gays and lesbians
Pelosi, Nancy, 68
Pennsylvania, 67, 82
People For the American Way, 72
personal contact. *See* social contact with gays and lesbians
Philadelphia, 49
Planned Parenthood v. Casey, 35
Pope John Paul II, 6
Popkin, Samuel, 69
Powell, Colin, 36
presidential elections: 1992 presidential election, 1–2; 1996 presidential election, 140; 2000 presidential election, 140; 2004 presidential election, 6, 15, 129–30, 138–40
Price, Vincent, 100–01
Protecting Religious Freedoms bill, 24

Queer Eye for the Straight Guy, 49

The Real World, 4
religious war. *See* culture war
Republican National Convention, 1, 7, 34
Roberts, Barbara, 132
Robertson, Pat, 60, 73
Robinson, Gene, 4
Roe v. Wade, 34
Roman Catholic Church, 4, 24, 32–33, 79
Romer v. Evans, 87, 89, 91. *See also* Colorado, Amendment 2
Romney, Mitt, 24, 141–42
Rosin, Hanna, 109

Sanders, Lynn, 9, 92, 112
Santorum, Rick, 67–68, 80–81
Save Our Children campaign. *See* Bryant, Anita
Savage, Dan, 82
Savage, Michael, 60
Scalia, Antonin, 3, 20, 87
Schiappa, Edward, 49
Schieffer, Bob, 60

Science, 4, 48
Sears, David, 100
Sharpton, Al, 72, 82
Sheldon, Lou. *See* Traditional Values Coalition
Shepard, Matthew, 4, 124
Sherrill, Kenneth, 31, 136
Shields, Todd, 140
The Simpsons, 49
Smith, David. *See* Human Rights Campaign
Smith, Gordon, 68, 124
Snowe, Olympia, 68
social contact with gays and lesbians, 4, 13, 44, 48–49, 61; related to public opinion, 56, *57*, 58, 113, 123
sodomy laws, 3, 19–20
South Carolina, 134
South Dakota, 134
Southern Baptist Convention, 73
Specter, Arlen, 68
SpongeBob Squarepants, 59
Stonewall Uprising, 2, 29
Survivor, 49

Take Back Miami-Dade, 114
Teletubbies, 59
Tennessee, 134
Texas, 19–20, 134–5
Timilty, James E., 124
Tinky Winky. *See Teletubbies*
Traditional Values Coalition, 20, 91

United Methodist Church, 73
United Church of Christ, 73
Unitarian Universalist Association, 79
Utah, 134

Ventura, Jesse, 124
Vermont, 3, 6, 25, 68
Virginia, 134–35
virtual contact with gays and lesbians, 4, 13, 44, 49; related to public opinion, 56, *57*, 58, 113
Voting Rights Act of 1965, 35

Walsh, Katherine Cramer, 92
Watts, Mark, 59
Washington Post, 26, 61, 109–10, 113, 124
Webster v. Reproductive Health Services, 35
Weyrich, Paul. *See* Free Congress Foundation
White, Reggie, 13, 60

Wilcox, Clyde, 114
Will & Grace, 49, 56
Wisconsin, 60, 134–35
Wolfson, Evan. *See* Freedom to Marry
Wyoming, 4, 43

Zaller, John, 70–71, 73–74, 81
Zamora, Pedro, 4

About the Author

Paul R. Brewer is associate professor of journalism and mass communication at the University of Wisconsin—Milwaukee. His work on public opinion, political communication, and political psychology has appeared in a range of scholarly publications, including the *American Journal of Political Science*, the *Journal of Politics*, and *Public Opinion Quarterly*.